"THE WAR CRADLE"

The untold story of "Operation Babylift"

by

Shirley Peck-Barnes

Published by

The Vintage Pressworks
999 Tejon Street
Denver, Colorado 80204

Editing/Steve LuKanic-Los Angeles, CA
Cover art/Rolf Paul Graphics-Morrison, CO
Cover layout/Ron Densmer-George Ferguson, Inc.-Denver, CO
Copy layout/John Pughes-CD Graphics-Denver, CO

JM Printing Co. Inc. Denver, CO
October 2000

Printed in the U.S.A.

ISBN 0-9706884-0-7

For the lost children of the world.
May you find love and a warm fire...
and your way home.

war cradle (wâr krā dl) n. - a place, a safekeeping during
        hostility, conflict, or war; a state of support,
        protectively and intimately during a disturbance
        where anything is nurtured during its
        early existence.

ACKNOWLEDGMENTS

This book was conceived in 1983 during a visit with Dr. Clifford A. Bennett, a good friend and former publisher with whom I was consulting regarding another manuscript. After reviewing my portfolio of photographs highlighting my experience of sheltering some 600 Vietnamese orphans in a Denver health care facility during the last days of the Vietnam War, he was deeply touched and saddened and insisted that their story be told. He felt there was a need to shout at the senseless loss of so many children, the abandonment of thousands more, and the waste of so much human potential.

I began the project shortly thereafter, during the eighties when the world continued to have many military conflicts. Terror dominated the Middle East, South America and the Orient, and it appeared that the tragedy of the Vietnamese children could erupt again somewhere soon.

In the nineties, we witnessed miracles in the diplomatic arena. Communist governments collapsed, impregnable walls crumbled...and with the new millennium, never before has the potential for lasting peace seemed so attainable. Yet peace still eludes us. Bosnia, Kosovo, Cambodia, Africa, the Middle East and Northern Ireland remain war zones. Infant genocide and starvation are tragedies we read about every day. We need no more reminders of the terrible price children pay when they are the victims of war and poverty. The plight of the Vietnamese children should have been a turning point in staving off pain for the children of the world. Sadly, the lesson was not learned.

Operation Babylift happened and here is the story. These pages do not contain all there is, and I hope others involved in this drama will write the rest. Further, this is not a textbook documentation of the event, but rather a passionate account and the author's perception of this hole in our history. I have tried to fill in that gap with countless interviews, intensive research, and with what I have experienced. Yet much more needs to be done. We have an obligation to document the injustices and to rectify the consequences of war on children. A flood of emotion is poured into these pages. It was that kind of time.

This is still that kind of time.

I've never felt ordained as *the one* to write about this particular event in history. But years have passed and an account of *how* Babylift happened and the many factors that had a bearing on its success or failure have not been forthcoming. This is my attempt to put something into the record...and more importantly, to provide some answers to those in search of them.

Getting those who were committed to the mission to talk about the search and rescue of children was not always easy. They sometimes allowed their thoughts to flow freely, then called back later to ask that their names be removed. It was their choice, but their pain and unselfish contributions to humanity need a voice so that their efforts will be remembered and the tragedy not repeated. The non-combatants who served in Vietnam were as tight-lipped about what they saw and experienced as were many of the men who went there to fight. To many of them, I am considered an "outsider" because I was never in country. Yet there were many who allowed me a window simply because I had been to that corner of the world during another war, another time.

The administrative struggles that besieged Friends of the Children of Vietnam (FCVN), along with pending litigation regarding the parenthood of some of the orphans, undoubtedly contributed to the reluctance of those involved in Operation Babylift to discuss it. They had done an honorable thing but were chastised for it. Fortunately, Cheryl Markson made boxes of documents available to me, and Sue Walters filled in with her personal experiences in Vietnam.

Cooperation from research people and agencies was phenomenal. To Gary Flanders, Western Aerospace Museum, Oakland; Dr. Young, History Office, Air Mobility Command, Scott AFB; Chris McGee, Wright Patterson AFB Museum; and many first-names at The National Archives, Library of Congress, USAID, The State Department, The Embassy Library, and Denver Public Library—thank you. A special note of appreciation to Kay Gleichman for her timely response, as well as to June Behrendt, Ed Daly's granddaughter.

Other Vietnam veterans and Operation Babylift volunteers provided hours of interviews. Dr. Theodore K. Gleichman, Ross Meador, LeSanne Buchanan, Bill Brown, Anthony Quintana, Dr. James Ralph, Mike LeClaire, Ron Dell, Mike Barter, James Fall, Dr. Ted Ning, Esther Hahn, and Minnie Smith were among the many who shared their insight and experiences.

Numerous friends provided the encouragement necessary to complete this book, and some had the instinct for applying pressure at the precise time. To Pauline and Dr. Bennett, who took me through the first step, Dorthea Evans, Adella Hericks, Jean Thompson, Terry

Newcomb, Laurie Hawkins, Antonio Marquez, Linda Anderson, Dawn Bartholomay Barnes, Wally Yachimirsky, Charlotte Zabor, Esther Polewoda, Jean and Donna Ross, my profound appreciation.

An unexpected encounter in a hospital corridor with Dr. Richard Flanagan, a Babylift contributor, was the final thrust to push on and finish this book. His words were simple: "I'm waiting."

Frederick Ramey of MacMurray & Beck, Eugene D. Wheeler of Pathfinder Publishing, and Lee Trevvett of High Ground Publishing took the time to offer suggestions and encouragement. Considering the volume of submissions they receive, editors like these are rare and a credit to their profession.

A debt of gratitude to my Continental Care Center Board of Directors, Henry Zeligman, Charles Hayhurst and David Zapiler, for providing a haven for the children of war in the use of their building and for picking up the tab.

Paul Hindman's insightful editing skills, Cindy Culkin's penchant for meeting a manuscript deadline, Rolf Paul's brilliant design, and my publisher, Carole A. Sheller, pulled it all together.

Edward J. Daly responded to my request for an interview and information regarding World Airways. Unfortunately, his health declined and pilot Ken Healy was more than accommodating to fill in the events of 1975.

I thank President Gerald R. Ford for his personal response; the Gerald R. Ford Library in Grand Rapids, Michigan, for their photographs; Gary Hart's office for arranging my meeting with the Permanent Mission of the Socialist Republic of Vietnam to the United Nations; and Tran Trong Khanh, Press Secretary, for his efforts in pursuing a Vietnam visa on my behalf in 1984. His graciousness during our interview was followed by numerous telephone visits, correspondence, and encouragement to complete this book.

Special thanks to Huyen Friedlander Brannan for providing this book with a happy ending, and to adoptees Stacy Thuy Meredith, Tuy Buckner, Jared Rehberg, Kimberly Brinker, Tuan-Rishard Schneider and Joshua Woerthwein for sharing their stories as well.

I am grateful for the talents of Steve LuKanic, who in reading every word of the manuscript, understood my inspiration for writing this book, and in turn was inspired himself.

Everyone who writes is familiar with the erratic hours and neglect to loved ones. The unconditional support of my children, Robert,

Richard, David, and Blair, was real. They are the best thing that ever happened to me.

Family, love, togetherness...they're the dreams of every child born unto this earth.

Too many kids in Vietnam missed them all. This is for them.

PROLOGUE

Not all warriors carry guns. Some fight an equally fierce battle without them. This book is about that kind of valor.

It's about silent heroes. The kind we see every day yet do not recognize since they're not the stuff of legend, art, and adventure.

War hurts, kills and orphans children. It is totally offensive to decency. So, too, thought a handful of distinguishable people who took an unpopular but morally correct stand during the Vietnam War. They left the comfort of their homes and went to Southeast Asia to reclaim discarded babies, to breathe life back into them, to love them, and to restore the dignity of children. All were at risk to their lives and each paid an emotional price.

At first, it was just a matter of providing daily necessities and medical supplies to orphanages in Saigon. Many a housewife skimped on her weekly grocery budget to fill a small shoebox of items that could keep a child alive. But as the numbers of orphans grew, so did the passion. What started as an uncomplicated mission to rescue dying, unwanted and rejected children in a war-torn country expanded into a worldwide effort to find safe havens for them in the West.

And, as if securing the basic necessities for these thousands of human discards was not obstacle enough, they milled through tons of red tape and paperwork to give those fortunate survivors a future and the right to be counted as citizens of the world.

During the last days of the Communist insurrection in South Vietnam, it appeared that thousands of youngsters fathered by American G.I.s would remain in a fallen country that already rejected them on grounds of their racial impurity. In an effort to rescue these and hundreds of other abandoned children from poverty, discrimination and death, the heroes savagely tore through all barriers and executed a mass evacuation to the West. It provided the only protection these children would have...a virtual "war cradle". Their noble deeds defied governments, a war, and skeptics who labeled it a "babyheist."

Finally, when "Operation Babylift" ended and the doors slammed shut in Southeast Asia, the heroes disbanded and reluctantly returned to the world of their own concerns. Those who were unable to release their grasp on this misery, the unfaltering tenacious, are still actively seeking out and preserving life in slums and jungles in the far corners of the earth. They are the ones who have found their vindication.

We continue to speak in soft tones of the children left behind in Vietnam—children who grew up not knowing who their fathers were and sometimes not identifying with a mother. They were abandoned in hamlets, the streets of Saigon, orphanages, trash heaps, or were pawned off to anyone who had a spark of compassion and who was afraid neither of Communists nor of peer retaliation for their involvement with a half-American child. The heroism of those few is forever.

The orphans of Vietnam are now young adults. Those who escaped to the free world share the same scars as the children who remained in Vietnam—the dark shrapnel of war is forever embedded deep in the corners of their minds. Many will spend a lifetime searching for answers, when often there are none.

As for the hundreds of Babylift volunteers, from those who went into the field to those who stayed behind to muster life-giving necessities, like the saints and sages before them, they acted on the noblest of human virtues, compassion, to save children who had no place to run, no place to hide. Valor, to any degree, is rarely understood, and often only by those who have made that journey to the top of the mountain. The rest of us can only speculate the view. Ironically, heroes commonly don't think of themselves as heroes; they go quietly in this world only to sometimes remember and cry. That we have ordinary people among us who recognize and act on such deeds has enriched the heritage of every human being.

Operation Babylift was heroic and nothing less than colossal.

In time, when this moment in history is placed in perspective, it will appear as what it was: one of the most noteworthy and humanitarian efforts in our lifetime.

Future generations, whom we hope will be beyond war, will ponder history and wonder why it had to happen at all. It already strains belief.

CHAPTER I
THE MAVERICK FLIGHT

"To be courageous, one must have two o'clock in the morning courage..."

– Napoleon, Las Cases at St. Helena, 1823

Night.

Darkness.

Gunfire.

Infinity flashes on the horizon, projecting a silhouette of a lone figure on the tarmac.

It was not unlike a Hollywood scenario...the sort of thing of which John Wayne movies were made. The man had a contemptuous disregard for rules and authority as he swashbuckled his way through the last days of a hot war.

He was brave, hard-drinking and hot-tempered. In his arrogance he often referred to women as "broads," yet he was generous to a fault and possessed a sincerity that was rarely understood. His Vietnam exploits were headlined across front pages and dramatized on television screens all over the globe. And though his cinema-like rescue attempts were received with wide-eyed wonderment and praise from a captivated audience, officials of his own government were busy scrutinizing his every move.

God, how they wished they could nail him!

But Edward J. Daly, President of World Airways, was always one step ahead of his adversaries. A ruddy, gravel-voiced man in his early fifties, he wore a .38 caliber pistol on his right hip and a Bowie knife on his left. Either hand had a way of resting on one of the weapons at all times. Daly often repelled people with his aggressive actions, particularly when he backed up his dinner arguments by dumping his pistol on the table.

He was a "thunderbolt," a human charged with electricity. And when angry, he was dangerous. Even his critics, who hinted that

1

Daly's flamboyant parlaying adventures had a self-serving ring, were in agreement that he indeed had "balls."

It was April 2, 1975, and Daly found himself pacing the tarmac at Tan Son Nhut Airport, just outside Saigon.

What he was about to do would make history.

The first mass evacuation of orphans from Saigon was about to happen. Thousands of these children were Amerasians—those fathered by American soldiers. Thousands more were nationals, abandoned by their parents as a result of the poverty and desolation that raped the beleaguered country. The growing number of abandoned children was ignored by the Vietnamese and American governments. The politicians could not or would not arrive at a resolution to the problem. The worldwide volunteer organizations, who sustained the children in the bulging facilities, were overwhelmed by the red tape, yet determined to get as many children as possible out of the country.

One man, Edward J. Daly, would force the hand of fate while those on political perches cautiously twiddled their thumbs. And today, he was on the verge of flouting the rules again to get the first planeload of orphans to safety in America where families would welcome them and offer them homes. Daly was no stranger to adversity and he instinctively sensed the stakes were higher this time. This was not his rescue mission of refugees in Danang days earlier, or the action-packed Cambodian rice lift. This time, young lives were involved. Failure was unthinkable. Daly understood the perils of the long night ahead; and, as might be expected with the war situation, an intense and visible anger made him restless, his fists tight at his side, ready at the slightest provocation.

Something had happened earlier to make Daly behave like a bull. He had tangled with U.S. Embassy officials who declared his plane unsafe to evacuate orphans. Fueled and stocked with supplies, the plane was ready for departure, but an hour before sundown, the orphanage group scheduled to leave had followed the Embassy's advice and canceled. Irate with the bureaucracy of it all, Daly found a replacement orphanage to snap up his offer.

There was nothing the World Airlines crew could do but wait.

"Hang on," Daly yelled up to the pilot, Ken Healy, who was poking his head out of the small cockpit window. Healy watched Daly's impatience as he puffed one cigarette after another and wondered if there was something he could do for the "boss." But, he knew there wasn't. Daly could hold his own in any situation.

Daly waved again. "Those kids should show up any minute...hang on, Ken. We saddle up just as soon as they get here."

As Daly stomped up and down the tarmac, he likely had second thoughts about his involvement in an evacuation this night, wondering how he ever got involved with all of this in the first place.

His only child, Charlotte Behrendt, was initially responsible. Charlotte had taken an interest in the orphans of Vietnam through a group from Colorado which had sponsored and established orphanages and halfway houses in the war-torn country as early as 1968.

Through the sponsorship of such agencies, hundreds of abandoned children had been adopted by families all over the world. Hundreds of more adoptions were still in progress, despite the war and deterioration of the South Vietnamese government. The pressure was on to unite the orphans with prospective families before the country fell to the Communists.

While political foes slugged it out to gain supremacy over the country, havoc and destruction were claiming more little lives each day. With the final Communist thrust underway and the fall of Saigon imminent, the Westerners in Vietnam came to the realization that they themselves would have to abandon their mission and evacuate.

As a consequence of abandoning the outlying facilities, supplies were cut off and swarms of Amerasian children flooded into the last refuge—Saigon. The Vietnamese nuns who remained in the rural areas to staff the orphanages prodded the Western volunteers to seek exit routes and get as many of the children out of the country as possible. Everyone was frantic knowing that because of the Vietnamese view on racial impurity, the Amerasian children faced a destiny of poverty under the Communists and a lifetime of social banishment.

"Children are irreplaceable treasures of the country," Sister Bernadette of the Vinh Long orphanage pleaded. "But we must give them up to save their lives."

Ed Daly was their hope. What touched his daughter, Charlotte, deeply concerned him as well. Theirs was a devoted father-daughter relationship, and like any loving father, Daly responded to his daughter's plea for help. Further, because of his long involvement in Vietnam, he understood the people.

The airline Daly founded had criss-crossed Southeast Asia since 1956. World Airways was a leading contract carrier under the Military

Airlift Command (MAC), the re-designated Military Air Transport Service (MATS) of World War II. In this role, World Airways pioneered important new relationships between commercial airlines and the military. Further, the company not only mushroomed and was efficient, it was a trendsetter that had a reputation for having "heart."

Shortly before Christmas, 1970, during the peak of American troop involvement, World Airways implemented a program called "HOMECOMING-USA," a travel plan that afforded the servicemen in South Vietnam the opportunity to spend 14-day furloughs at home with their families at minimal cost. The program was received so enthusiastically by U.S. servicemen that flights were booked solid.

To understand what kind of man Daly was and to grasp why he was using his personal wealth to fly orphans from war-ravaged South Vietnam, one would have to examine his role as a humanitarian. A concern for human welfare penetrated his soul, and much of what Daly did wasn't always publicized. For example, he sent 5,000 disadvantaged children to the circus each year and threw in $2 pocket money for each child for popcorn and goodies. He also gathered up 1,000 children each Christmas and sent them to the Oakland Symphony to hear the "Nutcracker Suite." And when he heard that a home for young county wards did not have swimming facilities, he built them a swimming pool. And there was the matter of checks. Daly wrote them often, in large amounts, then unobtrusively slipped them to various recipients.

Descended from Irish ancestry and a veteran of World War II, Daly was a feisty ex-boxer who was traditionally angered into action by the presence of oppression, starvation and human suffering. And on this dark April night, his eyes were on the smallest victims of the war.

Pacing the tarmac, Daly was waiting for take-off clearance along with the arrival of the children. He was also calculating the threats to his departure. He had a natural instinct for danger and his senses scanned the horizon for sounds and signs of firefight activity. Tan Son Nhut was a prime target for the Viet Cong, and Daly was mentally rehearsing his take-off procedure to avoid attack from the ground.

It had been a long, frustrating day. Early in the afternoon, the World Airways DC-8 had arrived from Cambodia with two of the company's leading pilots, Ken Healy and Bill Keating. Refueling procedures, boarding and pre-flight check would have allowed for a departure before sundown. Days earlier the arrangements, coordinated with Charlotte's friends, had been made to evacuate 400 orphans. What Daly did not anticipate was a long, drawn-out confrontation with officials regarding conformity to regulations. The very thought of the valuable wasted hours curdled his blood, and the only consolation was that the moonless night would offer some protection from Viet Cong lurking in the nearby rice paddies. Traffic in and out of Tan Son Nhut had been especially heavy all day and was slowing down with the oncoming darkness.

During the height of the Vietnam War, Tan Son Nhut was one of the busiest airports in the world. Hundreds of flights departed and arrived twenty-four hours a day; there was never a pause in the activity. The descent upon landing on a regular flight at a normal airport is a smooth drop of one thousand feet a minute. In Vietnam, a DC-8 was an inviting target at the end of the runway where the Viet Cong lay in wait, so descents occurred from six thousand feet to the runway in less than a minute. Passengers' stomachs and the plane hit the ground at the same time. Take-off was much the same in reverse; off at full throttle and climb fast.

The military air base occupied one side of the field at Tan Son Nhut; at one time it accommodated both the American and the Vietnamese Air Forces. On the other side of the military complex stood the civilian terminal, where all commercial airliners landed. Twenty-four months before, in surveying the field, one was likely to see every kind of airplane in the world...jet fighters, jet bombers, helicopters of all makes and sizes, prop jets and commercial airliners representing numerous companies and countries. With the American withdrawal in 1973, all military planes were turned over to South Vietnam. However, for various reasons, the planes now stood idle and Tan Son Nhut took on the appearance of a Western ghost town. The control tower, still in operation, communicated with pilots in three languages: Vietnamese, French, and English. The entire perimeter of the field was surrounded by a neatly-placed fence, eight feet high, topped with reams of concertina wire; it was patrolled day and night by military guards and trained attack dogs. Additionally defending the field, were watchtowers, mines and machine guns sandbagged in position around the restraints.

The Viet Cong monitored the airport around the clock, periodically lobbing mortar shells in all directions. The main gates had been blown up numerous times, as were the perimeter security restraints.

Several thousand Vietnamese worked on the base, so it presented a serious security problem. The Vietnamese Air Force had devised an ingenious solution; they hired and trusted only their own relatives to work there.

With a swashbuckling flair, Daly operated what he claimed to be the world's largest independent charter airline company. His ambition for maintaining a successful enterprise led him into the disaster areas of Indochina in the closing days of the collapse of both South Vietnam and Cambodia.

In mid-February of 1975, Phnom Penh, the capitol of Cambodia was a city besieged. Its normal population of one million was swollen by hundreds of thousands of refugees fleeing from the Communist Khmer Rouge. Insurgents had choked off the city's life line, the Mekong River, and as a result the rice reserve was dangerously low in the city. Unless relief was forthcoming, thousands of men, women and children would die of starvation in a matter of weeks. An airlift of 40,000 tons of rice stacked in Saigon warehouses was the only option. World Airways was asked to participate and responded by ferrying four to seven daily round trips between beleaguered Phnom Penh and Saigon.

The Cambodian airlift was conducted in a setting packed with military action: 107mm rockets randomly pocked the tarmac at Phnom Penh's Ponchentong Airport. As the planes landed and departed, hundreds of near-misses resembled the adventures of Terry and the Pirates, and miraculously, only one World DC-8 was actually damaged, nearly costing the lives of its crew and captain William L. Keating. The same Bill Keating that was, in the face of Communist-led troops advancing rapidly toward Saigon, sitting in the cockpit at Tan Son Nhut, committed with the other members of Daly's crew to the cause of the orphans.

The hour was getting late in Vietnam as provinces and cities fell daily to the Communists. It was projected that all escape routes from Saigon would be cut off in a matter of days. In response to this hopeless situation, Daly pulled a DC-8 stretch jet off the rice-ferrying runs to Cambodia to aid the orphans in evacuation. Although attention was directed mainly toward aiding the children of the Friends For All Children (FFAC), he was stunned and concerned with the staggering number of orphans wandering the streets of Saigon.

Street children were everywhere. Upon assessing the flow of the homeless tykes bulging the orphanages, Daly announced that World Airways would fly out 1,500 children within the next few days. They would be flown to Australia, en route to their eventual destinations in Europe and the United States.

Daly had been informed by FFAC that the children had families waiting to receive them and that their departures had been delayed for months due to the bureaucratic paperwork. Adoptive families in America had watched the children grow through pictures and letters and were anxious after months of waiting to hold the children in their arms. Daly, no stranger to red tape, was empathetic of their concerns that the children may not be given permission to leave before the fall of Saigon.

Australia was a wise choice since many of the children were desperately ill, and the longer trip to the United States would mean more delays in the mass evacuation effort.

Then the unexpected happened—the first of several disappointments in what could be appropriately termed as "the human salvage operation of the twentieth century."

Daly had received word earlier on that Wednesday that the Australian flight was canceled because its government refused to grant him landing rights. They categorically refused to admit children in transit for other countries. (U.S. policy allowed children admission, irrespective of their ultimate destinations.)

In Canberra, a Department of Foreign Affairs spokesman denied that there had been any firm plans to bring the orphans to Australia as a holding point. Rather, it was announced that a Royal Australian Air Force Hercules would be dispatched to bring out 150 orphans for whom Australian families had begun the adoption process months earlier. Prime Minister Gough Whitlam decided to cut the red tape to expedite the evacuation of the 150 children, in spite of the incomplete paperwork. Days earlier Australia allowed FFAC to evacuate fifty of the tiny babies to its shores. It was a humanitarian gesture because many would not survive the longer flight to the U.S. The babies had been permitted to enter Australia even though they had not yet been placed for adoption. Whitlam also committed the Australian government to further contribute $1.37 million for refugee aid to Indochina.

In not allowing Daly's flight landing rights, Australia's attitude toward the orphans would remain unclear for some time. It was somewhat of a dichotomy since many Australian nationals were in Vietnam representing churches sponsoring aid to the many orphanages and providing personnel as well as supplies. Aussies had been stationed in Vietnam, and Australia was among the few South East Asia Treaty Organization (SEATO) nations that sent fighting men there.

With Australia's public refusal, Daly scaled down his planned evacuation of 1,500 babies to 600, but that also fell apart in a matter of hours that April day. Before this night was through, Daly would face a dilemma and make an unexpected decision to go with a much smaller manifest.

Since the U.S. and Vietnamese governments had no policy on the orphans during the last days of Vietnam, the airlines were hesitant to become involved in the dilemma. Friends For All Children made futile attempts to charter flights for the mission. Before Daly became involved, the agency contacted two international airlines requesting assistance in the evacuation of their orphans, but both airlines gave vague replies to the request for chartered flights. The excuse the airlines used was that they needed more time to arrange for the special flights, and neither airline (with idle planes sitting in Hong Kong) would give an affirmative reply. They also required a large advance deposit.

It was during this time that World Airways was flying the rice runs to Cambodia and was caught up in that emergency when the plight of the Vietnam orphans captured Daly's attention and his offer emerged. FFAC's Field Director, Rosemary Taylor and her staff, were elated. They would indeed get their children out of the war zone. With the lack of response from the other airlines, Daly's plane seemed to be the only alternative immediately available, and the organization was so overwhelmed by his generosity that there was little thought given to the DC-8's conversion to a cargo plane and the elimination of standard passenger accommodations. Further, Daly was willing to transport these children to the United States at his own expense. The other airlines were expecting to be paid for their services, and at a later date, when they joined the evacuation, some required a large pre-departure deposit.

Without a doubt, the offer made by World Airways to transport the orphans across the ocean to freedom made Daly, for the moment, the hero in the drama unfolding in Southeast Asia.

Then, on this April day, events took an unexpected turn. Pangs of conflict and a series of misunderstandings arose. Despite the desperation of the hour, emotions got in the way along with demands that didn't fit the picture of war.

Just as the children from the FFAC orphanages were arriving in buses to board the plane for America, officials and inspectors for the United States Agency for International Development (USAID) converged on the DC-8.

It was beyond coincidence. The arrival of the inspection team had to be the result of an informant. Only Margaret Moses of FFAC, who made the arrangements with World Airways and Daly, had information regarding the departure.

A quick inspection of the cargo transport facilities immediately caught the attention of the officials, and they assessed that Daly's plane did not meet minimum standards for passenger safety or comfort. They refused authorization for the departure of the orphans.

Simultaneously, along with the arrival of USAID, television crews and world press reporters swarmed in on the drama, focusing on the plane's lack of seats and passenger comfort. Since FFAC declared they made no contact with the press and took extra precautions to avoid the media, they assumed Daly had leaked the departure to the newsmen. Daly, after all, was a man who recognized and acted upon opportunity, and he was quite at ease with the attention from reporters. He not only complied with the request for an interview but seized the moment to dramatize the unprecedented historical event. His mind was still on the Danang crisis, and in his anger he made the comparison to the charade of that evacuation, growling, "Give the bastards a chance and they'll bring out the adding machines and leave the kids behind."

He was referring to the bureaucratic red tape as well as the lack of any government assistance or relief to the refugee and orphan crisis that had been building for months.

Daly's frankness filtered through his assessment of the events of the moment. In doing so, FFAC thought him indiscreet in his expectations of an action-packed evacuation for effective television coverage. There were accusations that he had an underlying motive in wanting to help the orphans, and suspicion mounted that World Airways, through its participation in the airlift of children, had hoped to gain recognition for the additional airline routes the company was seeking around the globe. It was a preposterous supposition since such approval had to meet stringent regulations as well as necessity. What began as gratitude from FFAC slowly materialized into suspicion and mistrust.

As the afternoon wore on, the demands on the safety officials and the pressure of the media was taking its toll on FFAC as well as on Daly, and just hours before departure, FFAC turned down Daly's offer. In the months to come this would not be the only incident of disagreement in media coverage and public relations that would arise between the agencies getting children out of Vietnam and the many people offering assistance.

The desire to protect the children and shield them from exploitation was foremost on the minds of the individuals who worked relentlessly to save the young lives. It was understandable that they were viewing the press and television coverage as a disregard for the privacy of the orphans and over-exposure of their tragedy.

On the other hand, because of its unprecedented significance and its impact on American involvement in the Vietnam War, the public was eager for information concerning the orphans. It was the only hopeful factor to soften the failure in Southeast Asia. The press, along with other segments of those working to get the orphans out of the path of war, felt it was in the best interest of the orphans themselves that all information be disseminated. It was big news. Probably the most positive and heartwarming news of the Vietnam War.

The world was sitting on the edge of its chair waiting to hear details of the escape of the children, especially since many were fathered by American soldiers and abandoned by their Vietnamese mothers. It was an hour of fear and desperation.

The lack of passenger accommodations was the biggest objection the USAID inspectors had. The World Airlines DC-8 had flown directly from the Cambodian rice lift; there had not been enough time to modify the plane for passenger comfort. All the seats had been removed for the rice cargo days earlier. When the officials pointed out that the jet lacked oxygen masks and seats, (not to mention seat belts) and noted that the crew installed wall-to-wall layers of rugs, foot deep foam rubber, blankets and pillows, safety nets and webbing for bassinet tie-down on the floor of the stretch jet, they were dismayed. Collectively they inspected the craft and decided that the makeshift passenger accommodations did not meet the required safety specifications and declared the plane unsafe.

Confusion surrounded the DC-8 as people boarded and unboarded the jet. Compromise too, was lacking, along with a perspective of the time, the place, and the war.

Meanwhile, buses were staggered on the tarmac as FFAC had already transported the children from their nurseries at To Am, Newhaven, Allambie, and HyVong to the airport. While adults belabored a point of contention, tired, insecure and anxious children were becoming lethargic from sitting under the broiling sun. A United Press reporter observing the scenario later described their faces hanging out the bus windows: "There were no smiles, just expressions of bewilderment."

Daly was in disbelief of what he was hearing from the arguing officials. He knew they were not fitting their reasoning into the emergency of the moment, but they had what was needed...authority. They could shut him down.

"This is a war, damn it! Not a trip to a Sunday strawberry social," countered Daly. "The people in Danang didn't check the accommodations. Nobody cared if we met standards. In the absence of seats, refugees piled on top of each other and the guy at the bottom didn't complain. He was damn thankful to be there!"

The comparison didn't stop there. Daly remembered the lack of oxygen masks on the Danang flight. "It didn't offer a red carpet or champagne either, but what it did provide was a last chance to freedom for those refugees."

This same kind of chance was now being offered to the unwanted orphans of Vietnam.

Daly knew his plane was "war weary"...but safe. The proud silver lady was no worse for wear and tear after trips to Danang and Cambodia, and her trim lines exemplified how majestic and vital she really was. But his judges on the tarmac did not have his level of experience. They were "paper pushers," and in Daly's mind, it was the same old story of incompetents given authority beyond their scope.

"Unsafe, hell! Compared to what?" Daly demanded. "You screwed up!" he growled, referring to the U.S. Embassy and the United States Agency for International Development. The USAID inspectors gave him a cold stare, acknowledging what he meant. Daly was implying the cancellation of the orphans' flight to freedom was "sheer retaliation" because of the refugee evacuation he staged on the previous Saturday at Danang—against USAID objections and U.S.

Embassy advice.

Danang had figured prominently in Vietnam over the years. During the sixties it was a major logistic base for the U.S. buildup and home of two U.S. Marine battalions. Its big air base and port housed more American soldiers than any other Vietnamese city.

The American soldiers called it everything from Dodge City to Dogpatch. It became a garrison town, overflowing with refugees, whores, pimps, black marketers and armed soldiers. Military Police patrolling the city were charged with keeping the Americans out of serious trouble. The Buddhist uprising occurred at both Danang and Hue with more plot, revolts, riots, and demonstrations than in any other city in Vietnam. After the Americans left in 1973, the South Vietnamese Army occupied the base.

Danang possessed some exotic charm, with the French influence still in evidence in the colonial buildings and wrought iron balconies. The whitewashed stucco houses were covered with bougainvillaea and they clustered in quiet settings of narrow streets, shaded by palm and tamarind trees. Built on a peninsula, with a sandy beach harbor and picturesque mountains to the West, it was a portrait of serenity. One could easily doubt there was a war going on in another section of the country.

But early in March of 1975, the North Vietnamese units launched strong probes into the northern provinces of South Vietnam. Quang Tri quickly fell to the Communists and Hue, the historical and cultural heart of the country, the seat of the Vietnamese emperors, was also overtaken by the North Vietnamese Army.

President Thieu vacillated about what areas in the highlands must be defended, then ambiguity persisted and it was too late. He ordered the Vietnamese Marines and the Airborne Division back to Saigon, giving permission to evacuate their families as well. Without these reinforcements the northern provinces could not be defended; the civilians left along with the soldiers, and the evacuation flooded the roads south to Danang. In a matter of a few short weeks Danang was choked with refugees swarming the streets. Among them were thousands of Vietnamese soldiers lost from their units, armed, frightened and disoriented.

Before it appeared that Danang itself was threatened, the U.S. Embassy had planned to airlift refugees flowing into the city from Hue, beginning with 40,000 on chartered flights and expanding to a quarter of a million people, using jumbo jets.

It didn't happen.

A week before the complete collapse of public order in Danang, World Airways was chartered to make twenty flights to evacuate U.S. agency personnel and Vietnamese employees. But when the flights began, the priority passengers were blocked by military police at the air base gates. Not by coincidence, crudely forged copies of the priority passes were being black marketed at high prices on the streets.

Albert Francis, the consul-general, proposed to Col. Gavin McCurty, the air attaché, that U.S. military helicopters stationed in Thailand be assigned to the evacuation of his people. The request to 7th Air Force Headquarters was turned down, thus leaving the only possible air exit via the World Airways chartered flights. By the 27th of March, the city was swollen by a million refugees, tripling its normal population in a matter of days. The final chapter of the government's rout from the north was being played out with the collapse of public order. The real source of trouble was not the civilians, but 100,000 marauding South Army of the Republic of Vietnam (ARVN) soldiers who were both armed and drunk. They roamed the streets robbing and killing people, looting homes, shooting wildly, and littering the streets with burning vehicles. There appeared to be little interest on the part of the American or South Vietnamese officials to intervene or to initiate a mass evacuation effort of the refugees from Danang. It was clear...each individual was left to find his own escape route.

Viet Cong troops in civilian clothes infiltrated the city, moving on loudspeaker trucks, attempting to restore order, but the tens of thousands of panicking refugees swarmed aboard any evacuation armada they could reach. The port was jammed with boats and barges heading away from the city.

Consul-general Francis continued in his efforts to get Vietnamese officials to take control of the air base. It progressed beyond any power of restraint, and the subsequent flights by World Airways erupted in violence. One occasion found Francis and World Airways Vice President Charles Patterson wrestling refugees from the plane's stairway so that they could close the door. Francis again appealed to the 7th Air Force in Thailand for the helicopter evacuation or for a couple of C-130 transports. That request was denied as well. The reason given was that using American military forces in Vietnam was a matter of extreme sensitivity and would skirt both U.S. law and the Paris agreement.

Throughout March 28th, the crowd control around Danang airport progressively deteriorated as rioting erupted among the refugees. People were injured and trampled to death. Fearing the security problem would endanger the plane and further evacuation efforts, Daly met throughout the night (in Saigon) with every U.S. and South Vietnamese official he could reach whom he thought might assist with the crisis. They either could not or would not help.

Daly had taken the course to a decisive point. His determination to defy the authorities would ring out in his words put over the wires. "To hell with these people (Embassy officials)! They may not care about these refugees, but I do. And we're going to move them just as damn long as we can!"

Francis called a halt to World Airways flights. But Daly had other ideas.

On Saturday, March 29th, he boarded his plane to supervise the airlift personally and ordered his Boeing 728 back to Danang without clearance from the U.S. Embassy. Daly was concerned with lives, not military strategy or the effect of more refugees swarming into the Saigon area.

That day a World Airways 727 was the last plane of the free world in and out of Danang. The scene that took place was captured by television crews and flashed across the world as a daring attempt. It was a "prudens futuri" of the chaos that was to befall all of South Vietnam in the weeks ahead. Eyewitness accounts were published in newspapers throughout the world. It would not be the last humiliation of the American withdrawal.

Incensed by the hours wasted arguing with Vietnamese officials for permission to fly into the besieged Danang, Daly made his choice. It was time to fracture a few rules of the war. His extreme anger and indignation was aroused by the passiveness and lack of cooperation of the authorities. Daly had an attitude: "Forget the paperwork clearances, and to hell with the lack of concern on the part of the government." South Vietnam was a nation under siege, and the time to act was now. This was history in the making. Daly not only had the resources to help the refugees, he was willing to do it at his own expense.

On the approach to Danang, Daly and his crew could see the air base below crowded with people but were assured by the tower that the field was under control. Over a thousand people were huddled around the Quonset hut on the flight line when the 727 touched down. Their faces were ashen as the jet engines whined down, and for a moment it was as if nothing dare stir. Not the air, or a leaf, or even a flicker of an eyelash moved in the throngs of people who were statue-like on an earth that had just stopped moving.

Silence prevailed for several minutes.

Then, without warning, pandemonium broke out. The pallid faces that earlier expressed fear and anxiety now were hardened, and suddenly the refugees became a mob in action. Motors started and began to roar across the tarmac. Refugees were packed on jeeps, motorbikes, trucks, and bicycles. When nothing else was left, sheer desperation and panic pushed them onward to reach the huge bird. When Daly and a World Airways station manager, Joe Hrezo, stepped off the loading steps at the Danang tarmac, they realized it was "a goddamn mistake." The two men couldn't get back on board before Healy pulled away from the threatening mob. Together, on foot, they raced back to the control tower. Meanwhile, vehicles filled with South Vietnamese soldiers chased after the zigzagging plane, shooting at it as well as each other. The plane was halted three times before Healy finally managed to work the plane back to the control tower. He was not going to leave without Daly and Hrezo.

As Daly was standing near the bottom of the 727's tail ramp, the mob tore viciously at him as they climbed aboard, his clothing ripped from his body, along with some of his skin. Daly was bleeding from his back, chest and arms. He had to struggle for a firm grip on the spot he salvaged for himself. The small and the weak fell to the pavement as the strong and the ruthless mauled over them.

"Last plane, last plane" some chanted in broken English and Vietnamese. Women screamed and crying children became separated from their parents. Emerging from every direction, Vietnamese soldiers stomped over the refugees making their way to the plane, flinging away guns, helmets and gear. There wasn't room for everyone and they knew it. It was a fight to the death. Each creature struggled for survival and pushed to his ultimate potential to reach a space on the last exit plane. Many died trying to get aboard.

In a matter of seconds the plane was jammed, predominantly with the troops of the South Vietnam's 1st Division's most vicious unit, the

15

Hac Bao (Black Panthers). But Daly hadn't landed in Danang to pick up soldiers; he wanted to fly out women and children and other civilian employees of the consul-general.

As terror reigned, the 727 started to taxi down the runway. Crowds screamed on the flight line and continued to run after the high velocity jet. Over-crowded vehicles chaperoning it on both sides charged after as if it dared not desert them and leap into the sky. Refugees began throwing rocks, and madness gripped those who had missed their chance. Someone lobbed off a fragmentation grenade toward the wing and the explosion jammed the flaps full open and left the under-carriage in full extension. Several refugees, in desperation, grabbed on to the structure. Minutes later they would fall thousands of feet to their deaths when they could no longer maintain their grip on the cold metal.

Other Vietnamese troops, unable to cram aboard the plane, opened fire as it limped away. Pilot Ken Healy, who flew refugees out of mainland China in the late 1940's—a man who was not easily fazed—slammed the throttles full open and lurched into the air from the taxi way.

Meanwhile, Daly was fighting for a foothold on the open tail ramp of his rescue plane, now soaring into the wild blue yonder, leaving a screaming Danang mob below. He was on this precarious perch to free a soldier outside whose body was jamming the ramp open. It must have appeared to Daly that an eternity had passed before he and Hrezo hauled the injured man and themselves to safety. It was the second rescue trip up the ramp for both that day. On the ground, Daly had hauled Hrezo aboard from the midst of the angry mob.

An ARVN soldier was not as lucky. The price on panic resulted in his body being crushed when he tried to steal a ride to his freedom. His feet protruded from the wheel well of the Boeing 727 and hung there as a testimony of his desperation. The plane limped away from Danang for the flight back to Saigon, nearly crashing on landing at Tan Son Nhut Airport. Daly and his crew considered their touchdown at Saigon "a small miracle delivered that Easter weekend."

Sick and angry at the thought of the refugees left behind, the World Airways crew knew they could have carried out thousands of the people if there had been some control and cooperation at Danang. As it was, they brought out fewer than 1,200, nearly all of them soldiers.

However, instead of lauding Daly for his performance and his compassion, USAID and Embassy officials were outraged over the Danang escapade and called it an "outrageously irresponsible and harebrained act of bravado." Furthermore, USAID considered him an embarrassment. Daly's actions countermanded their decision to apparently do nothing, and worse, it drew attention to their own mistakes and empty promises. Daly and his crew firmly defended their actions as a "humanitarian act." Whichever the case, it almost cost them their lives.

It had been a week of life and death escapes, and the final chapter in the drama of World Airways' involvement in Southeast Asia was unfolding. In the cockpit of the World jet, pilot Ken Healy, who made the chaotic last flight out of Danang, would enter a new date, April 2, 1975, into his flight log.

Occasionally interrupting their pre-flight check, Healy or Keating would appear on the ramp to see if Daly needed a hand. They were concerned that under pressure, he would lose his temper.

Finally, the group on the tarmac was breaking up. The USAID people departed and the buses loaded with the FFAC children were pulling away to return to their orphanages. It had to be a disappointment for Daly, not to mention for the children. Daly would later remark that he would never forget the confused and sad looks on their faces as they pulled away that afternoon.

Alone on the tarmac, Daly swung into action. He looked at his watch. It was 7:00 p.m. He grabbed one of his aides and declared there was still time enough to save the mission.

"Get in touch with that kid who was in the office this morning...Ross Meador...the one from the other organization, the FCVN (Friends of the Children of Vietnam). Tell him if he wants to get any kids out, get them here in an hour. I'm taking off...with or without clearance!"

It was short notice, but Daly's shouting words were a command.

Thoroughly confused in his role as rescuer at this point, Daly mumbled the word "unsafe" to himself like it was stuck in his throat. This wasn't the time for comparison, or was it? Throughout history, immigrants grasped at the opportunity to migrate to a better life, scraping up cheap passage to float on a whatever taking them from the persecution of their native lands. The size of the Mayflower alone, defy-

17

ing a vast ocean, was a miraculous phenomenon in American history and left a lasting impression on every first grader. The early settlers of the American west, in uncharted territory, trusted their lives to small covered wagons that carried their families and all their possessions.. Daly was asking himself what happened in his own century. It was becoming a plastic, easy-way-out world. There was no spirit in this generation.

"Unsafe, hell!" The chips were down in Saigon and Daly assessed it would only be a couple of weeks at the most before the Communists took over. The U.S. officials would be scrounging for transportation to evacuate, and he pictured himself sitting out on the runway with a good stogie when the time came. "Sorry, can't take you...the plane's unsafe. USAID regulations!"

It was getting dark now and the shelling in the distance lit up the sky. The Viet Cong were at it again. Noise echoed across the plains of tall grass. The smell of death was in the air, as it always was in Indochina. Anyone who had been to Vietnam could testify to the foulness of the horrible smell that permeated the air. They could not describe it to anyone back home in a letter or a word...yet they would remember it for a lifetime.

Takeoff had originally been scheduled for 5:00 p.m. Saigon time, and as Daly glanced at the multi-figured luminous dial of his watch, it was after nine o'clock and pitch black on the field. Word had come that the airport was closed because of an anticipated Viet Cong attack, and all non-military personnel were ordered off the base. Tan Son Nhut Airport was on full alert.

The children of the FFAC orphanages had long departed, the television crews were gone, as were the ARVN soldiers, and Daly and his crew were left in this lonely spot. The control tower instructed the World Airways plane to "hold your position." The radio in the cockpit was receiving the message repetitiously: "Don't take off, don't take off, you have no clearance. Do you read me? Over." The men in the cockpit were unconcerned and continued to ignore the call while they were engrossed in making instrument checks and reviewing weather data.

Then, dimly at first, two small sets of lights appeared to be coming closer to the plane, weaving their way across the dark tarmac between maintenance equipment and military vehicles. At first, Daly thought they were military patrol cars. He gripped the weapon at his side. The lights didn't seem right—they were too high. Next he detected the singing of children, defying a billion dollar war, defying the Viet Cong and even USAID. Their voices raised to the hilt were half shouting, half singing, "California, here I come!..."

Daly couldn't believe his ears.

The Volkswagen buses came to a halt, the doors quickly sprung open, and Ross Meador gave the command to his charges..."Lets go!" Without words, the fifty-seven children of the FCVN Thu Duc orphanage clamored aboard the giant plane. Five and six-year-olds tugged at toddlers beside them, crying, tired, and confused, carrying dolls, toy trucks and a conglomeration of worldly belongings. Without a doubt, and without checking anything more than Daly's smile, they put their trust in World Airways. In a matter of days their orphanage north of Saigon would be abandoned, and with no place else to go, their only hope was to reach America and the families anxiously awaiting their arrival.

Perhaps it was the "two o'clock in the morning courage" Bonaparte thought was the rarest which Daly had after all. He did not waver in his confidence in the mission, for he was there to save lives, if only one.

Moments later, just as Daly was ready to depart, a patrol car of the Army of the Republic of Vietnam appeared unexpectedly at the plane. The Vietnamese soldiers insisted on checking for any adults who may have been smuggled aboard, as young men 14 and over were considered eligible for the Vietnamese Army and expected to stay and fight. Within the group of FCVN children was a family of three; the eldest boy was 15 years old. He was huddled in the rear of the plane and the crew did their best to conceal him, but he did not miss the eye of one of the soldiers who angrily pulled him from his secluded spot. Daly intervened, pulling a $100 bill from his pocket, stuffing it into the hand of the ARVN soldier.

"Let the boy alone...what does it matter now?" he asked.

Were it not for the other soldiers on board whose attention was drawn to the incident, Daly may have pulled it off. But the ARVN hurriedly dragged the boy from the plane. The militia would not waver in their decision, and if there were fewer soldiers in number, it was conceivable that Daly may have forcefully taken the boy back. But too many lives were at stake, so the youngster was turned back over to

Ross Meador, who would later return him to the orphanage. But not before Daly pulled the $100 bill from the ARVN soldier, with one to match, and stuffed them both into the boy's pocket.

Acceptance had finally overcome Ed Daly. The FFAC buses would not be returning, and he would go with the small cargo he had. The hour was up and Daly put the word out he was leaving. He climbed aboard and sealed the door. The rest was up to Healy and Keating.

Healy made one last check and revved-up the engines of the huge jet. He looked over his shoulder into the cabin and saw the faces of babies and children, ages three months to ten years. Many were black or Caucasian, obviously the offspring of American soldiers. He thought of all those other children on the buses earlier—how they'd waited patiently through all the controversy and the disappointment on their faces when they departed. He was impressed by the children now in the cargo compartment, sitting so passively and quietly.

"It's not normal," he thought. He did not conceive that instinct was playing into the drama of escape. It was strange, as if the children knew they must be on their best behavior or be forsaken once more. As if they somehow knew they were the ones with the lucky ticket. It was the break homeless children dream of...a chance at having a real family.

The kids were nestled in blankets and snuggled up to their pillows on the bare cabin floor. It looked like one great big playpen and slumber party. Healy smiled to himself. Keating, in the copilot's seat, communicated with a nod. "Let's go home."

The flashing lights on the horizon indicated mortar activity. Sounds of firefight activity began to drift through the night air. The Viet Cong were out stalking the countryside...the night belonged to them.

Some twenty adults, including two physicians, journalist Peter Arnett, and World Airways stewardesses, were scattered among the fifty-seven children, all ready to go on Daly's instructions. The expressions of concern for what they were doing reinforced his decision. He knew they were wondering if their plane would clear the airport without further delay or trouble and if the long journey ahead would be without further anxieties. Some of the children were sick. There was no guarantee they would tolerate the trip. Suddenly in the distance, sirens brayed, alerting an impending attack of the airport.

Daly, Healy and Keating had a brief conference on the flight deck and reached a conclusion: "If the Viet Cong are coming, the airport is now under attack. Let's get the hell out of here!" Healy revved the engines, pushed forward on the throttles, gunned the four jet engines, and the huge plane thundered down the unlighted runway. "California, here we come!" The air-traffic controller at Saigon's Tan Son Nhut Airport was enraged.

"No clearance, do not move! You have no clearance for takeoff! Don't take off, don't take off! Repeat...you do *not* have clearance!..."

Daly's loud response came from the cargo section where he was overseeing the children. "Is that right? Well, watch me!"

Seconds later the World Airways maverick flight was airborne. Surprisingly, as the plane climbed in altitude, there were no cries. The cabin was as quiet and somber as the inside of a church. Instead, the babies rolled on their backs, their eyes wide with wonder. Silence prevailed for a long time, until the lullaby of the jet engines rocked them to sleep.

Although it hadn't been given a name yet, an historical undertaking without precedence had begun. Unofficially, "Operation Babylift" was underway.

It would be a long flight—25 hours and 8,000 miles via Japan. Healy registered his flight plan and headed to Yokota, a big U.S. air base on Tokyo's western outskirts where the jet would refuel.

Daly, who was paying for the $70,000 journey with his own money, had loaded milk, soft drinks, baby food and diapers aboard the plane earlier. Minutes into the flight, one of the stewardesses called from the rear of the cabin..."Any Pampers? It's diaper service time." The feisty, pistol-packing Daly reported for diaper duty, something he said he hadn't done for many years.

Finally, when all was quiet and the cabin lights were dimmed, Daly, with coffee mug in hand, found a vacant spot on the cabin floor and braced his tired body against the fuselage. Eyes closed, he pondered the frustration of the earlier hours. Thank God it was all over, he thought. The hum of the engines made him drowsy, but a soft bump to his side jerked him awake. A toddler had nestled next to him. Smiling up at Daly, the boy extended his hand to him, offering a toy. It took Daly by surprise, but it was all the reward he could want. Daly put his arm around the youngster and gently slid his beret onto the boy's head.

Competing with a sense of satisfaction that they were finally airborne, he was disappointed in not having filled the plane to capacity with babies. Then he began to seriously ponder the consequences of his actions. He had not been given permission to bring the children to the United States, and the Vietnamese government had yet to grant him permission to take them out of the country. There could be a "lynching party" awaiting him at Oakland; or worse, the flight could invoke an international incident. With the long flight ahead, it was for the moment the least of his worries. The immediate concern was whether he could deliver his precious and most unusual cargo safely, before any of the ill children on board took a turn for the worse. That some of these children might not tolerate the flight was a possibility considered by all the adults on board. Each, in his own faith, turned to thoughts of prayer.

In the days to come, when Daly was questioned about his earlier flight plans to evacuate 400 of the FFAC children from Saigon, he charged that the U.S. Embassy and USAID had blocked the flight in declaring the plane "unsafe". The Embassy countered with the response that Friends for All Children made the decision on its own. Years later an FFAC volunteer offered her thoughts; "It all boiled down to a mistrust of Daly and how he used the media We were all sorry the kids didn't get out that day. More sorry that the organization didn't respond to press and P.R. It was a hectic time and everyone was not receptive to publicity at that time. Today we understand the power and benefit of the media...that it can work in a positive way."

It is often noted that those who wait are in a state of quiescence, encumbered in prayer, pain and anxiety all at the same time. The World Airways office in Oakland remained in readiness for the word of their boss. The reports out of Tan Son Nhut were confusing, and employees lingered to hear if the flight had left Saigon. The response from Southeast Asia was that it was still planned but had not yet left the ground. Following, there was only silence from Indochina. No one could conceive what was happening. Then suddenly, dispatcher Bob Nelson made the long awaited announcement: the DC-8 had taken off at 9:30 p.m. Saigon time, carrying a cargo of orphaned children. A cheer went up, not only in the home office, but all over the country. The story was on the wires and the feeling was unanimous. "Fly on, Edward Daly, fly on!"

As Bay-area residents learned of the impending arrival of the Vietnamese orphans, their hearts opened to the destitute children of war. At the San Francisco Presidio, the Army post beside the Golden Gate Bridge, phones rang constantly with offers of help. Mike Hower, University of San Francisco Professor of Sociology and President of the Bay Area Comprehensive Health Planning Council, was coordinating an effort to round up medical personnel to meet the plane. It was not difficult as doctors, nurses, translators, the Red Cross, the Army and the adoption agencies mobilized quickly to ensure a safe and happy reception for the parent-less children.

Requesting assistance by the adoption agencies had been a mere formality with the flood of offers that poured forth once the news of the orphans' incoming flight had leaked to the press. Nonetheless, protocol was observed, and the two agencies with headquarters in Denver, Friends of the Children of Vietnam (FCVN) and Friends For All Children (FFAC), united to make a formal request for assistance, working through the U.S. Agency for International Development—the same agency that gave Daly the "thumbs down" earlier that day in Saigon.

The staff at the Presidio had arranged to receive, feed and house the children in its protective environment until the children could be processed and arrangements completed to send them on their way to a new life.

Adoption procedures had been in progress for many months for all the children on this flight. Anxious families in the U.S. and Canada had been waiting for clearances for the children to leave Vietnam and had no way of knowing that they were on Daly's plane, nor the circumstances of the hasty departure. The children, too, had been waiting and were confused about when they would be going to their new homes. So paramount was the bonding and the establishment of a relationship with a family across the sea, that a wall at the Thu Duc orphanage had been designated as a special display area to exhibit pictures and letters from their prospective parents. The children were proud of the wall and could name off all the parents and repeat, almost verbatim, all that was contained in their letters.

The American public at large had no knowledge of the status of the children except that they were orphans. Offers of homes for the children, permanent and temporary, poured into both agencies. It was finally necessary to make newspaper and TV announcements to the general public asking them not to make further offers of assistance at that time, as all necessary arrangements had been made. Further, it was necessary to keep the lines of communication open to help speed the children to their new homes. Some of the parents throughout the U.S. had waited 18 months or more to see their adopted children. They had no way of knowing that an exit from Vietnam had been underway.

It wasn't a hangman's noose that Daly found when World Airways touched down in Oakland 25 hours after his unconventional dash to freedom. Instead, there were a lot of smiles and cheers to ordain him into the order of heroes.

The children tolerated the flight well. Only two orphans, both malnourished and dehydrated, were unable to complete the trip. They were left at a U.S. air base hospital at Tachikawa, just outside Tokyo, where the plane touched down for refueling.

In Oakland, there was little time to appreciate the spectacle of the moment as the precious cargo was carried from the plane into a crowd of television crews, flashbulbs, and well-wishers. It had all the trappings of a celebrity reception. It was almost midnight and the children were immediately treated to loving care by hundreds of waiting volunteers. Some of the youngsters cried when they saw the strange faces. The attention and new surroundings frightened them. But most of them were soon running around in the barracks, shouting to each other and playing games. It was a validation of the amazing resilience of children.

It was difficult for the spectators to hold back tears as the children disembarked. The scene was reminiscent of the return of the first planeload of American prisoners of war two years earlier. If tears are an indication that a healing process has begun, this was indeed the beginning of a long need for relief of pain over America's Vietnam involvement.

When the children were finally bedded down for their first night in America at the Presidio's Harmon Hall, they did the thing most children do at bedtime—cling to their worldly possessions. Many even clutched the crayons Daly had provided for the flight and the simple toys they brought with them. The mounds of teddy bears, trucks, tricycles and toys that had been donated for their arrival would wait for another day.

Exhausted, the World Airways crew also did the expected thing.

They went home to bed.

In Washington, the Federal Aviation Administration considered filing charges against World Airways, but the agency reconsidered, saying the airline would not be punished for breaking federal air regulations with its save-the-children mission.

The first Operation Babylift flight was a success. No child had been lost. Had the mission failed, Daly had much to lose. It is doubtful if the thought of failure ever entered his mind. He was too busy doing a job that needed to be done. Daly would complete three unauthorized flights which brought Vietnamese orphans (as well as adults) to the U.S. In addition to the April 2nd flight, another occurred on April 22nd and involved 104 orphans under the sponsorship of Father Crawford, a Catholic priest who had been in Indochina for 20 years. The third flight on April 26th brought 215 Montagnard (Highlander) children from Vietnam who were destined for Denmark. These flights had neither the approval of the U.S. or Vietnamese governments and were paid for by World Airways.

Ed Daly would be honored on many occasions for his deeds in Southeast Asia, and the mementos of these honors would fill the walls of his office. But those who knew the size of his heart would agree that no plaque or any formal recognition would bear the significance of a small child offering him his toy....his only possession...during that first Babylift flight.

Columnist George Will appropriately expressed the thoughts of free men everywhere: "Breathes there an American, with soul so dead, who hasn't to himself said, 'Right on, Edward Daly!'"

CHAPTER II
THE SOLDIER'S BALLAD

Bitter are the tears of a child; sweeten them

Deep are the thoughts of a child; quiet them

Sharp is the grief of a child; take it from him

Soft is the heart of a child; do not harden it...

– The Child - Lady Pamela Wyndham Glenconner

If Ed Daly had his thoughts about what he was doing rescuing babies in the middle of a hot war, he was not alone. The American soldier in Vietnam was confronted with the presence of children at every turn. War was meant for men. The involvement of children made it decisively dirtier. Yet a life and death situation involving children could occur at any time. And it did, often, under the most nebulous of circumstances.

The small Vietnamese village seemed friendly enough since it was primarily inhabited with women and children who frequently waved to the Americans passing through in trucks and jeeps. It was on a main thoroughfare and accustomed to the complexities of war. Several old men always seemed to shuffle along the road in the absence of young men who were, presumably, either in the South Vietnamese Army or with the Viet Cong.

Sgt. Bill Brown passed through the hamlet often en route to deliver supplies to outlying combat units of the U.S. Army 1st Battalion, 11th Infantry. He did not feel uncomfortable when, for some unexpected reason, his driver stopped to check their vehicle on the village outskirts.

"Something's loose back there, Bill...just be a minute," the soldier muttered as he swung himself onto the dirt road.

Bill Brown remained in position, gripping his M-16, already clipped and ready for action. He had been in Vietnam for six months, and past experience reminded him that a standing vehicle was an easy target. Although most villagers seemed indifferent and behaved like spectators to the war, there was no trusting anyone. To compound the paranoia, every Vietnamese began to look like a Viet Cong to him. His ever-alert eyes scanned the tall elephant grass on the roadside, searching for any unusual movement.

Brown began to whistle softly to himself. He was not relaxed and anticipated any unexpected intrusion. "Hurry it up, buddy, we don't have all day," he reminded the fatigue-clad figure fumbling with the ropes.

Suddenly, Brown felt a sharp sting on the side of his face, as if he had been hit by a small, silent, yet powerful missile-like object.

Though he had not yet been wounded in action, he'd heard numerous stories from guys who swore they never felt the bullet and realized they'd been hit only when they saw blood oozing from their wounds.

Brown didn't know what to expect, and the sting was real enough. Instinctively he responded with the live mechanism in his hands. Seeking out a target, his finger hit the trigger, "rat-ta-ta-ta-ta-ta-tat."

The automatic echoed through the countryside.

Brown's peripheral vision caught sight of his aggressor, an unnoticed small boy who stood by the side of the road, grinning. His hands clutched a crudely made sling shot.

The equally fast reflexes of the soldier deflected his deadly weapon, and the ammunition shattered into the soft earth, narrowly avoiding cutting the child in half.

"Kill the sonnovabitch!" Yelled the driver, who witnessed the prank.

The airborne dust floated like a maze, dividing Brown and the child. The eyes of the warrior and the boy met in silence, and the message, without a spoken word, was clear to both. The grin never left the boy's face. It was a painted mask of the oriental unrevealed emotion, yet beneath the exterior Brown was sure the child felt terror. As for himself, Brown wanted to vomit; all he could feel was a hollow pit inside his stomach. In a silent gesture, he ordered the driver to proceed, then cautiously backed himself into the comfort of the jeep. His eyes never left the boy.

"You should have shot the little bastard," the driver said as the jeep roared down the road. "Hell, Brown, you know half of these kids are VC...." The words trailed on, but Bill Brown was in a world of his own, one of reality...of what he almost did to a mischievous little boy brandishing a slingshot. Rumors ran rampant that articles handled by children were booby-trapped and beverages sold to Americans, often by children, were laced with ground glass or poison. It seemed that there was no time or place when a soldier did not feel his life was in peril.

Yet, there was that element of doubt for Brown that probably saved the boy's life. He was re-thinking the moment as they sped along to their destination, and he was thankful he was in control that morning.

"You know, Ernie..." he interrupted the monologue of his friend. "I've been here too long. This whole goddamn war has gone on too long, just too long. I gotta get out of here before I end up hating myself. When we gotta start killing kids...well...it's a fucked-up war."

The war in Vietnam *had* gone on too long. The country's 2,000 year history was rife with struggle for colonialization over the little Asian country by the Chinese, Dutch, Portuguese, Cambodians, Catholic Missionaries, English, French and thousands of drifters and pirates in between. As a result, Vietnam became a melting pot of peoples who had criss-crossed the country for centuries.

The current civil war and conflict with the Communists represented almost thirty years of uninterrupted war and left the people not only anxious and tense, but with little hope of ever extricating themselves from the poverty that held a strong octopus-like grip on the provinces.

Even the vibrant Americans finally got tired of it. They packed up and went home in the spring of 1973. The involvement in Vietnam had divided America. Not since the American Civil War had emotions run so intense. The question pondered by millions of Americans was why our nation had become involved in a conflict that was not really a direct threat to America's security and one which did not produce territorial gain. A typical combat mission involved reconnaissance patrols humping primitive trails, only to return to base camp, knowing that the Viet Cong already occupied those same hills and villages which they had fought for so vigorously earlier that day.

There was a gnawing sense of futility in the daily search-and-destroy mission with no positions to attack, no strongholds to besiege, no long-range victories to claim. Despite the advantage of sophisticated weaponry, heavy artillery, hundreds of trained troops and even control of the skies, daily encounters yielded only a small number of captured suspects and even fewer Viet Cong bodies.

Equally as menacing as guerrilla warfare were the weather and jungle terrain of the Asian country. The Americans arrived in Vietnam at a disadvantage with both conditions and found the enemy, who was born into the elements, surpassing them in endurance.

American interest in Vietnam was created during the post World War II era. The Democratic Republic of Vietnam was then recognized as a free state within the Indochinese Federation and French Union, and a Communist threat appeared imminent. In early 1950, the newly established People's Republic of Vietnam was established by Ho Chi Minh in Hanoi. Shortly thereafter, the United States announced military and economic aid to the pro-French regimes of Vietnam, Laos and Cambodia.

The step-by-step involvement of American military personnel started in mid-1950 when President Harry Truman sent a military advisory team to aid the French in North Vietnam. President Dwight D. Eisenhower dispatched 200 Air Force technicians to help the French maintain their warplanes in their effort to regain Vietnam. In addition, Eisenhower agreed to help train the South Vietnamese Army, and President John F. Kennedy was committed to increasing American assistance. In November, 1963, Lyndon Johnson became President and the U.S. had 15,000 military advisors in Vietnam. Within two years, there was a transition from advisors to combat troops numbering over 23,000. The size of the American military force in Vietnam increased to 184,000 in 1965, 385,000 in 1966, 474,000 in 1967 and rose to a peak of 543,000 in 1969.

The arrival of the American soldier in Vietnam was a wonderment to the children of the country. The GI's immediately became a new on-site benefactor. Consequently, the kids swarmed around the Americans whenever the opportunity presented itself, looking, and begging for handouts. The hunger of the Vietnamese children was something with which the Americans could not come to terms.

Anthony Quintana of Denver went to Vietnam as an 18-year-old paratrooper. Stationed at Bien Hoa, on occasion he would go to Saigon to practice on the jump tower. After one such training session he wandered over to the Vietnamese food stand and purchased a sandwich and a bottle of orange drink. As he bit into the sandwich he realized it was raw fish and threw it to the ground. Wandering back to the truck that would carry him back to camp, Quintana glanced at the children who were fighting for the remnants of the sandwich. In their urgency to get food, they crowded around the other Americans boarding the truck. It was obvious the children were hungry, and the men began looking into their packs to see what they had available to toss to the children. Some threw cigarettes, others piasters (Vietnamese coins). And when the men exhausted their resources, someone suggested opening the box of C-rations stored beneath the bench.

Quintana had been consistently drilled to evaluate what he was giving to the Vietnamese—that anything and everything could be re-used against the Americans. Films involving children in warfare were clear in their message and indoctrination to not only not trust anyone, but to refrain from any emotion or involvement with the people. Any Vietnamese could be the enemy. There were vivid warnings about the deceitfulness of the Vietnamese, regardless of age or gender.

The C-ration cookies were an inviting treat, yet Quintana paused and observed that the cans were unique and could later be booby-trapped and offered to a soldier. He was compelled to hold back the green identifiable cans, but the expressions and pleading cries of the children were disheartening. There was something so pitiful in their faces. He thought of his own childhood in Denver and the treats his mother made, and suddenly he found himself giving in despite the warnings of the films.

"What the hell, the kids are hungry." And with that, he and the other men hurriedly began opening the cans and tossing the containers full of cookies to the extending hands. The familiar squeals of delight were a heart-warming sound in any language.

A short time later, Quintana was felled by a bullet while on a search-and-destroy mission through a village. Cutting through the left side of his skull, he didn't feel the hit and remained on his feet, firing his weapon until a medic pulled him to the ground. Though he couldn't be sure he didn't imagine it, one of the last things he remembers before being hit was a child, hiding from the war, crouched down behind boxes like a frightened animal. Quintana's eyes were locked in on a North Vietnamese soldier in his gun site, his finger tense and ready to activate his weapon. Then he heard a whimper and glanced down to see a face pleading with fear and tears. The expression on the child's face penetrated his emotions to the extent he became distracted for that golden split second, allowing his opponent the opportunity to strike. As Quintana saw the NVA soldier take aim and shoot, time stood still...everything was evolving in slow motion. His own preoccupation with the child had betrayed him.

The wound would not take Quintana's life, but it would render him paralyzed on his right side, and Vietnam would remain the decisive event of his life. His wife, Valerie, would be a pillar at his side, hearing the story repeated and understanding what others failed to.

The American soldier was different; the children of Vietnam had never seen anyone like him. For one thing, he was bigger than anyone they had ever seen, yet despite the remarkable difference in size, the children were comfortable in approaching him. In addition to being kind and humorous, he was friendly and generous in responding to their needs. Always a soft touch for candy, money or cigarettes, many units "adopted" children and even cared for them in camps and barracks. At the same time, the American soldiers were totally disarmed by the independence and self-survival they witnessed in the children who had to fend for themselves in the war-torn country.

Ron Dell was a member of the 25th Infantry Division based at Pleiku. The "Tropical Lightning," as it was called, was disbanding and re-locating from the central highlands to the south near Saigon. Convoys were dispatched in small groups to make the trip that, because of primitive conditions, often took several days. As a result, the men camped out along the highway on their way to the new destination.

Dell's unit was ordered to remain in position at the edge of a forest and the men dug in to make themselves safe. Boredom during such transitions was every bit as threatening as the elements themselves. Just across the road from the encampment, Dell noticed a small green tent which blended into the landscape. The surroundings of junk piles indicated it was a Vietnamese homestead. The dweller, a small boy about ten years old, who at first had ignored the big army, was busy with chores and seeing to his own comfort. It was the home of Jojo, an orphan who had lived along the thoroughfare for about as long as he could remember. Jovial and friendly, the youngster smiled and waved to the soldiers and then exercised his diplomatic prerogative by paying a neighborly visit to the men of the "Tropical Lightning."

At first, the Americans thought Jojo was just another homeless kid; orphans were as common and as plentiful as the mosquitoes in Vietnam. Yet surprisingly, Jojo not only spoke fluent English, but he had a precocious personality that was garnished with GI lingo, including the four letter words that often "seasoned" the American language. The men found him to be a pleasant diversion and Jojo was free to circulate the campsite.

In return for his morale-building efforts, the men shared their food with him and even scrounged a baseball cap that they plunked on his head. Jojo was full of stories about life along the highway and held the distinction of being the on-site goodwill ambassador for the small boondock strip under his domain.

After about a week, the unit was ordered to continue on to their destination and the soldiers had to decide among themselves what to do with Jojo. Some wanted to adopt him as the unit mascot and take him along, while others insisted that he be taken to one of the orphanages and placed for stateside adoption. But it was Jojo himself who made the final decision, to remain in his own squatter's surroundings, and above all, to remain in his own country.

The men realized that other units would be coming along, and with Jojo's resourcefulness, he would have no trouble in soliciting the supplies he needed. He was probably as safe in his tent along the highway as any place they could conjure up for him. It was, after all, the difference in culture and circumstances. A small child in the states would not be left unsupervised for even a brief trip to the corner grocery store. Jojo, at his tender age, was already an old man when it came to taking care of himself, and he was doing it better than anyone could do it for him. It was a story to be repeated by thousands of children who were homeless, unwanted and street-wise beyond their years.

The Viet Cong realized the military value of small children and recruited them for their assaults on the enemy. Any child just above the toddler stage was an unsuspecting decoy, and they were often sent into groups of soldiers or into street bars with parcels bearing activated grenades. Explosions would take a death toll on all in range, including the innocent child.

Children were also solicited to peddle booby-trapped Coke bottles and other destructive merchandise. And as if that were not threatening enough, the Viet Cong recruited children for spying purposes. They even went so far as to have their young spies infiltrate American installations. Following a night attack, U.S. military personnel discovered the body of a young child they had befriended who had been allowed to roam the camp freely. Tucked inside his shirt they found a map of the installation accurately detailed in every respect.

Even infants were not excused from the war's involvement. Many an infant, bundled in a blanket along with a concealed live grenade, was thrust into the arms of an unsuspecting soldier.

With all this disregard for the life of a small child, was it any wonder why American servicemen returning from Vietnam could not reconcile the beliefs that propelled them through combat? Protecting children was an instinct bred into American freedoms. Acceptance of the indifference to young life, those children involved in guerrilla warfare, was beyond the comprehension of western morality.

Mike LeClair's arrival in Vietnam left him with a feeling of uncertainty. He wasn't sure what was waiting for him. A year in the war-ridden country could have a significant bearing on his future, or it could conceivably mean the end of his life.

But the Marines had trained him well. The physical preparedness was grueling, but he could handle it. The psychological training was equally as intense. What was even more impressionable was the orientation he had received before heading into the war zone emphasizing the heavy de-humanization of the Vietnamese people themselves. They were always referred to as "gooks, slopes or slant eyes." Further, they were depicted in the training films as cruel, inhuman and the type of enemy who would slit an American's throat simply because they hated Americans.

In turn, many soldiers already in-country were balanced with the Vietnamese in their hatred for each other. As buddies were killed, both sides fell prey to vengeance and atrocities. Even the children were victims of the hatred Americans had for the Viet Cong. Children standing along the roadside begging for food became a target for the truck convoys as they passed through villages. The men, in their anger and pent-up emotions, would sometimes respond to their pleas by throwing cans of food at the kids, taking careful aim to hit them.

"Hell, this is better than the ducks at Coney Island," they would joke among themselves.

War makes men do strange things, and it can sometimes be the great equalizer in inhumanity. Unfortunately, in the Vietnam War, that inhumanity overflowed into the civilian populace. The message was clear to the incoming soldiers that all Vietnamese were hostile and inferior. Pictures were shown of young Vietnamese children or women warning the soldiers that the people were "sneaky"—that they concealed weapons and grenades on their person, laid mines, built booby traps, and sniped at Americans. The attitude was "you can't trust anybody in Vietnam, and the only good gook is a dead gook." The thorough indoctrination was "heavy and to the point" and burned into the mind of every marine. The formula applied to young and old—there was no reason for exclusion.

Mike LeClaire was not prepared to see that the Vietnamese were people, too.

It happened on Hill #55, so named because it was 55 meters above sea level. There was Hill #53, 57 and so forth, located in what was called the "rocket belt," simply because it was where all the rockets would hit. In every respect it was a rugged place, 25 miles southwest of Danang.

Adjacent to the Marine compound were massive dumps, overflowing with garbage, litter and refuse, piled in one concentrated area. One man's junk was another man's treasure, and the Vietnamese thrived on going through the Americans' trash, finding food, clothing and any usable refuse. The Marines allowed the Vietnamese the resource of the dump until they discovered that some of the people were taking tin cans back to the Viet Cong, who in turn made home-made grenades out of them. The identifiable C-ration cans were familiar items to the Americans and had all the earmarks of a booby-trap. After a few incidents confirming that the C-ration cans were being used as weapons of war, the order came down that no Vietnamese civilians were allowed to pilfer the dumps. The Marines wired off the area and guards were posted to patrol and enforce the order.

The American soldiers didn't look upon the Vietnamese as civilians. To them, all nationals were Viet Cong sympathizers. They were not even called "civilians"...they were simply called "VC".

The Vietnamese civilians who claimed that they were not collaborators with the VC were angry and could not understand why they were not able to get into the dumps. It was a valuable source for survival for them, and the placement of the fence and the guards was another reason to hate the Americans.

Then the inevitable happened. A young child of four or five crawled beneath the wire fence and began scavenging the mounds of trash. There was no shout, no rock thrown to fend him off, or no gunfire warning. Instead, the Marine guard took careful aim and leveled one shot into the small body.

As Mike LeClaire walked down the dirt road, two medics came running and cut directly in front of him, carrying the child on a stretcher partially covered with a poncho. An older Vietnamese man followed them as they raced up the steps into a plywood hooch and disappeared inside.

LeClaire was drawn into the moment and found a spot in the doorway. A ray of sun passed over his shoulder and beamed down into the drama taking place inside the room.

The corpsman pulled back the poncho to reveal a gunshot wound in the child's stomach. The intestines poured out along with the blood. Working frantically, the corpsman hurriedly pushed an airway down the boy's throat and began CPR massage. Opening his bag, the other corpsman fumbled for a syringe. Both men were desperately trying to save the child's life while the older man sat close to the boy, his left leg bent flat on the floor, his right leg pulled up to his chest. He was moaning to himself, rocking his body back and forth, unable to hide his fear and anxiety.

After several minutes, the corpsman looked into the face of the older man. Their eyes met...then ever so slowly the corpsman's head moved from side to side.

There was a moment of silence.

Suddenly, pain erupted and emotional distress and grief penetrated the room. The father of the child reached up with his open hand extended, reaching to a God for mercy, a sign of compassion or kindly forbearance. All LeClaire could think was that this was happening every day, all over Vietnam. Children were dying for no apparent reason, simply because they were there.

The intense pain of the Vietnamese father over the loss of his son would be that one vivid moment that for Mike LeClaire would sum up his Vietnam experience. The raised palm could very well have been a fist; an angry voice could have spilled forth, saying in its native tongue,"This cannot happen...this is my son...what have you dared to do to my son? You are the intruder into our lives...I hate you American!"

Rather, it was a man in torment of the moment, the times...the war.

LeClaire remembered what he had once seen written, that "those who have suffered much are like those who know many languages; they have learned to understand all and to be understood by all." It was clear now that the Vietnamese father had been through this experience before; he had lost others he loved.

What LeClaire had witnessed was that the instinct for pain and compassion remained intact, even in the presence of hate and anger. It brought to light the fact that people caught between fighting forces were indeed human after all, and they were loving and caring people in their own culture. They could laugh and tell jokes in their own language and care about the same things Americans do. It was this monster called War, this sickness that divided men and had them believing the other was inhuman, that was the real "enemy." It validated that the only real difference between the Vietnamese farmer and the American businessman was, after all, opportunity, and that a predestined geographical place of birth was what would affect a man's degree of success or happiness.

Abuse and bullying were prevalent among the roaming street kids. It wasn't uncommon to see an older child ransacking the possessions of one who was weaker. Such scenes were commonplace in Vietnam, and although the American soldiers related to sibling rivalry, many a confrontation ended abruptly with an intrusion by the big man in fatigues. The American soldier would not stand for the abuse of a child, whether it was an unfair fight on the streets of Saigon, or a child terrorized in a village in the highlands. Frequently, the grunts on patrol were drawn into the moment when a child's dignity was violated.

Patrols of the countryside were an everyday routine for the men. On one occasion a Marine squad approached a village that appeared deserted. There had been a firefight just over the ravine the day before when rockets had missed their target and landed close to the small hamlet, terrifying its inhabitants. Many fled, but evidence of small fires indicated that some of the villagers were still there.

Jerry Kowalski was walking point for his unit. He slowly headed into the village ahead of his squad. Cautiously, he moved from hut to hut. As he walked past a small structure he heard a soft whimper...then the cries of a child, followed by the voice of a man laughing and speaking Vietnamese in a melodious tone. Kowalski hesitated, then walked around the hut, still alert and cautious. As he peered into the open window, he saw a young girl laying naked on a grass mat. The elderly Vietnamese was astride her small body, his penis erect and fondling her genitals. The girl could not have been more than eight or nine years old.

Kowalski froze for a second, swinging back against the outside wall. He had a kid sister back home, Jessie, who had just passed her eighth birthday. She had been a change-of-life baby for his folks, and from the beginning, Kowalski became her primary care giver, teaching and measuring every inch of her growth. He loved his little sister more then anyone on earth and always carried her picture with him. Sometimes when he was walking patrol and the heat was overbearing, along with the bugs and stench of the war, he would pretend that he was carrying Jessie on his shoulders like he did around the block back home. It made the mission easier. He even found himself talking to her, as if she were right there with him.

"Jess this is a tamarind tree. Ain't it beautiful? And you know what, Jess? When you sit in the jungle and listen to all the sounds, it isn't spooky. It's like a symphony of nature...you can hear the monkeys, and even the ugly lizards have a sound."

Then the moan of a child pulled him back to reality. He was in Vietnam. More cries came from the hut—it was the sound of human pain. Kowalski swung around quickly and stormed inside the hut in rage. He lunged at the Vietnamese rapist and pushed him outside, instantly pumping bullets into his body. As his buddies came running to see what happened, Kowalski went back into the hut and found the little girl rolled over, sobbing, streaks of blood on her thighs. He picked her up and held her close to him. He kissed her gently, wiping the tears from her eyes.

"It's okay, little sister, it's okay."

With her tightly in his arms, he started toward the villagers who were huddling in a group. But as he passed his patrol he muttered, "Cut the bastard's balls off and stuff them in his goddamn mouth."

One of the men reached to his belt for a knife.

An old woman emerged to take the child from Kowalski's arms, nodding her head as if in agreement. Kowalski almost resisted giving the little girl up; it was as if he were holding his Jessie. The patrol passed through the village silently and began the long hump back to camp. Their faces were expressionless. Kowalski continued on point; he could feel Jessie on his shoulders.

The American soldier had a natural instinct for wanting to befriend and help what he felt were the innocent victims of war. Yet the friendliness of the children was sometimes a ploy on unsuspecting soldiers who had not come to terms with children involved in guerrilla warfare.

It was always a dilemma of trust. They had a clear picture of the many orphans lying in the gutters and doorways of Saigon, harmless and helpless. An unsuspecting American with his guard down could become the victim of the war's incriminations.

Youngsters were commonly found toiling in the rice paddies along with the older Vietnamese. They were friendly to the Americans, and the soldiers would return a wave as they passed. Therefore, it was not unusual for the young marine on patrol to respond to the small boy who was smiling as he approached through the grass.

"GI numba wun." The youngster came forward muttering the "pidgin" English phrase. Though it was a Vietnamese phrase that lacked sincerity—and the soldiers knew it was said with tongue in cheek—it still flattered them to hear it.

"Hi, GI," the youngster scrambled closer toward the marine, dragging the large heavy machete used for cutting cane and clearing paths. It seemed too heavy for one so small.

"You got smoke, buddy?"

The leatherneck grinned. It was funny to watch the kids smoke. Back at the base they would offer cigarettes to the kids who hung around the compound, and some of the guys would teach them to smoke, drink beer and swear in English. It was almost a tradition carried down through wars—American GI's acting like bad boys and playful in their vices. The guys got a big kick out of hearing the kids struggle with the cuss words containing syllables difficult for them to pronounce. "Motherfucker" came out without the "R's" and upon hearing it the Americans would always laugh.

The marine reached into his pocket and handed the child a cigarette, half expecting the youngster to put it in his pocket and ask for the next handout. Instead, the boy pointed toward the paper tube in his mouth and indicated that he wanted a light. "You mean some goddamn grunt was here and taught you how to smoke it, too?" The soldier chuckled to himself as he snapped the lighter shut and watched the youngster demonstrate his experience in puffing the smoke. To further flaunt his manhood, the boy swung the heavy machete over his shoulder.

The two continued to walk side by side. As they approached the edge of the clearing, a Huey appeared overhead. The sound of the helicopter engine was similar to the chatter of a machine gun. The leatherneck looked up to wave and suddenly felt a sharp pain at the base of his left foot. As he turned to look back, he could see the blood spouting from his heel and a part of his boot and flesh lying on the ground. It had happened so fast, he didn't hear a gunshot. A second later he felt a sharp slash in his right foot and turned to see his toes oozing blood.

The youngster with the machete was running into the tree line, blood dripping from the blade over his shoulder.

Weakened by both pain and shock, the stricken marine took careful aim and eased on the trigger. A loud crack filled the air.

"You muddafudda!" the child screamed before he dropped and lay silent.

The enemy came in all sizes, and they were no strangers to courage for their cause.

Throughout the ages, men came home from wars re-thinking their actions. The memories of the spontaneous act often weighed heavily upon their conscience and, even though they were victims of circumstances, the involvement nurtured guilt. The American soldier in Vietnam had seen it all...the meaningful and the necessary destruction, as well as the useless killing.

It was the doubting and the confusion as to which was which that left an unhealed infection on the soul. The Vietnam experience was to remain an emotional conflict for thousands of men and women who served in the country.

Americans, known for their benevolence, pitched in whenever they could to help save the lives of the Vietnamese nationals. Military doctors, nurses and helicopter crews often jeopardized their own safety for the lives of others. Though they were well trained in their jobs, they were always at the risk of the Viet Cong who infiltrated the country side.

Mike Barter was a door gunner with the American Huey troops at Vinh Long in the Delta. Known as the "Outlaws," the crews were considered some of the most savage men in Vietnam. They would gather down to the jungle and rice paddies, firing at close range and taking as many hits into their rotor blades. Bullets shattered their windshields or came up through the floor. After their strafing encounters, they would land on the hot battlefield, get out and count their VC dead. They were the cowboys of the sky and behaved like wranglers heading home from a cattle rustle.

When the Outlaws were returning home from a mission, to further enhance their involvement in the war, they would monitor the radio channels. Often the guard frequency was filled with so much excited chatter and useless babble that key transmissions had to be sorted out.

Returning late from a reconnaissance mission to Cambodia, during which their chopper took direct hits and was limping back to Vinh Long, Barter's crew picked up a "mayday" from the rice fields below.

"Medevac, medevac, emergency! Please come in! Repeat. Emergency. Any Medevac unit, please come in! Do you read me? Over."

The voice cracked on the radio again. It came from a Med Cap team in the paddies below. These were teams of doctors and nurses under the Medical Civil Assistance Program who were out in the villages giving inoculations to Vietnamese civilians and monitoring disease control.

"We read you," Mike Barter's helicopter pilot responded. "What do you have? Over."

"We need a dust-off down here," the team in the paddy responded.

It was a term used for medical evacuation missions by helicopter and referred to the great amount of dust thrown up by the rotors of the medevacs as they came in to land.

"I have a little girl badly gored by water buffalo. Must evacuate immediately to hospital. Can you come in?"

The chopper crew knew that medevac flights took anywhere from three to five hours for non-military emergencies in the Delta because of minimal U.S. forces there. The haul to Cambodia had been a long one. In addition to the chopper limping along from the hits it took, the men were exhausted, out of supplies, and were keeping their fingers crossed that they would make it back to base.

"What do you say, fellas, anybody in a hurry to get back to the barn?" the pilot shouted above the rotor blades.

There were the usual loud chuckles and groans in response. Barter wanted to yell back, "It's been a rough day for everyone." But all he could do was circle his thumb and finger in the "O.K." sign.

"Let's go help the kid."

The chopper circled the VC-infested area and found the small group hovered over the unconscious, bleeding child, who was hurriedly placed aboard the Huey. They were airborne again within seconds.

What had happened was the result of the children teasing a water buffalo, an animal who was not normally hostile. The beast became irritated with the harassment and charged the helpless girl, who was unable to clear the gully. Her body was gored and bleeding profusely. The chopper headed for the nearest medical facility at Ben Tre.

Several days later the Med Cap doctor got word to the chopper crew that the little girl was alive and recovering.

For Mike Barter, that one life-saving trip balanced out his whole tour in Vietnam. It was not a war-connected incident and it was something that could have happened anywhere, anytime. The availability of their chopper saved the child's life, and that made the Outlaw crew feel that their mission was not only one of war, but more importantly, of peace in Vietnam.

The war in the Delta was different. Barter had come to terms that it was not the same when he came down from the highlands to join the Vinh Long Outlaws. The ground fighting was done largely by ARVN (the Army of the Republic of Vietnam) troops, who were supported by American Special Forces (Green Berets). The bulk of the American concentration was to the north, and the helicopter crews at Vinh Long, My Tho and other Delta cities were the life support of the ARVN troops.

It was the third trip into the landing zone that afternoon for the Outlaw chopper crew. They had painted "Vietnam Sucks" on the bottom of the Huey for all the world to see when it was airborne. It adequately expressed the sentiment of the men who were once again edging into the small, perilous LZ (landing zone) to lift out the ARVN's, the friendly Vietnamese army.

It wasn't exactly the kind of duty Barter, a door gunner, relished. Just days earlier he had been shot at by one of the ARVN's after their nine-troop carrying helicopter deposited them into the LZ. Soldiers don't get much cover jumping out of a helicopter in a hot LZ, and American troops habitually leap out of the choppers long before they hit the grass. But the ARVN's had to literally be pushed from the helicopters, and often at gun point. Upon disembarking days earlier, one of the ARVN's turned in anger and shot at the crew as it lifted off. Barter returned the fire and then was faced with the humiliation of having to jump out and pull the man back on board to be medevac'd from the area.

Now Barter's crew was back in the same hot area to evacuate the same group of ARVNs who were huddled close to the ground.

Just as the chopper edged into the LZ, mortar fire erupted. Simultaneously, the enemy opened up in a firefight from the surrounding tree line and the small group of nine ARVN scrambled aboard. But as they did, the other two groups awaiting evacuation panicked and raced for the small helicopter, all twenty-seven men struggling for a place on board. The chopper was overloaded and faltered as it attempted to lift off, whining and bouncing forward in its effort to leave the firefight. Bullets whizzed passed and mortar fire threatened closer when the bird pulled up under its heavy weight again.

"Come on, baby," Barter muttered to himself, straining his body forward as if the gravity pull would somehow help them to be airborne.

Just as they were about ten feet off the ground, one of the Vietnamese soldiers lost his grip and fell out of the chopper.

"Hey, you guys up there!" Barter called on the intercom to the pilot. "We just lost one. I can see him, he's okay."

Mike could see the fallen soldier's desperation from the grass, waving, hoping someone had seen where he had fallen...that the chopper would come back.

"I don't particularly want to go back down there," Barter added as he kept his eyes on the firefight from the tree line. Bullets were whizzing by the rotor blades.

"Neither do I," the pilot responded, "but I think we'd better...the poor sonnovabitch must be scared shitless."

"Well, that makes thirty more of us!" Barter yelled back.

With that, the helicopter circled and returned to the small LZ, the crossfire becoming more intense with their re-appearance. As they wavered past the young soldier, Barter reached down and locked his arm on the soldier and lifted him off the ground, his body dangling in mid-air as he struggled to get hold of the skids. Barter glanced down into the face of a Vietnamese boy not more than fourteen years old. The look of fear and helplessness was etched in the young soldier's face. He was bawling like a small child and at the same time trying to be a man so that Barter would not lessen his grip and let him drop again.

The crack of shots and tracers surrounded the Huey, and Barter managed to continue firing his machine gun, shooting into the tree line and at the same time keeping his hand locked on the arm of the young boy.

"He's nothing but a goddamn kid!" he yelled, sounding shocked on the intercom.

"Let's get the hell out of here," someone else shouted.

As they limped back to base, rotors whining, they discovered that the mortar fire had filled the back end of the chopper with shrapnel and they'd lost hydraulic power to the tail rotor. They were forced to make a running landing with an overload of men. Barter felt sure they were all going to "buy the farm" on impact and found himself puckering up for what was coming. The force of the landing tore the skids into shreds as the chopper hit with full force, yet all aboard survived. It took Mike Barter two hours before he could bring himself to sit down; it was a narrow escape.

For his part in rescuing the young soldier, Barter was awarded the Vietnam Cross of Gallantry with a palm leaf. The medal had little to do with his viewpoint after the experience. He could never come to terms with the realization that children were fighting a man's war.

But America had children in war, too.

Some of the 17 and 18-year-old American troops were not mature or adaptable to war either. Young draftees in Vietnam and young volunteer sailors on ships in outlying areas broke down in combat. Many at such a tender age, on the threshold of adulthood, lost their lives. Others were sent home maimed or psychologically unfit for not only duty, but life itself. Though they may not have been considered "children" in the eyes of the government, they were emotionally too young for the experience. In most states they could neither vote nor drink. But all governments pluck the very young to do in the field what the diplomats cannot achieve across the conference tables. For centuries, old men relegated the young as scapegoats of their mistakes.

Despite the cruelty of war, the GI's were the good guys to the orphans of Vietnam. In addition to the necessities of life, money and medical care, they gave them attention and love. Many orphanages were fortunate to have a few military contacts who could be called on for support, whether it was emergency measures of getting a child evacuated to a hospital or scrounging supplies and bootlegging anything from technical surgery to supplying food, clothing, and shelter for the young ones. Military doctors and nurses gave medical assistance and supplies to aid the nuns in their overpowering and never-ending effort of administering to the sick and dying children.

Americans built playgrounds, orphanages, schools and churches and were called upon to perform thousands of acts of charity. They even went so far as to protect and harbor abandoned children who had turned informants on the Viet Cong and who, as a result of the betrayal, would have a price on their heads the rest of their lives. Children with amputated limbs were provided with prostheses, and the demand for toys and candy was endless.

The friendliness and overwhelming generosity of the Americans gave the children a sense of security and, in turn, the soldiers related to them as both mother and father surrogates. The children shined boots, cleaned barracks, and took care of their American buddies. To further enhance the identification of this coveted status, the soldier even had uniforms cut down to fit the small tykes.

Even the hard-core, worldly street kids of the larger cities crowded around the GI's and could usually count on them for handouts. Their familiar chant, "Hey buddy, you got dollah?" was seldom ignored and the Americans would dip into their pockets.

The American presence in Vietnam represented mother, father, Santa Claus, and the tooth fairy all rolled into one. Then they were gone. They left behind memories and monuments of their deeds. They left behind their jackets and their pictures and their *Playboy* magazines. They also left behind children of their blood, and that was half the tragedy.

But if history is destined to be repeated, as it usually is, since the beginning of time invading armies and occupation of foreign troops have always produced changes in a country. Somehow, the American soldier was a unique kind of individual in war and occupation. Perhaps because America itself is a melting pot, there is more tolerance and sensitivity for the children of foreign lands.

Although he hadn't been officially given the coveted distinction of "American GI" (government issue), until World War II, "GI Joe" was established in spirit as far back as the days of the early American settlers. The welfare of children during war and conflict has always been a main concern of the American fighting man and can be traced back to the earliest footprints on the American continents. Rescuers of children whose parents were killed in Indian attacks leap out of history books as the early frontiersman of America frequently laid down his life in defense of children, women, and homestead.

During the Revolutionary War, even in the most desolate camps, swarms of women and children went with the army everywhere it traveled. Inasmuch as there was no system of sending allowances home, wives and children accompanied the soldier-husband-father into the field of battle. Young mothers died in childbirth and fathers were killed in combat. The orphaned children were quickly taken into another soldier's family and raised as one of their own.

The spirit of the twentieth century soldier truly emerged from the Civil War. As Sherman's troops marched deeper into the South, the Union soldiers were so sympathetic and congenial with children that the officers had to be alert to keep them from adopting the orphans they found along the way.

During one drive into Dixie, Sherman's patrols discovered two little toddler age girls in a shattered cabin, covered with dirt and wearing cotton grain bags with holes cut for arms and neck. The men thought they were children of slaves. Frightened, the girls huddled together, shivering and half-starved. The men laid aside their rifles, heated water, and bathed and fed them. Unable to get any information regarding their parents from townsfolk, they brought the girls back to camp. The soldiers pilfered clothing from the aristocracy to dress the youngsters and carried them on their backs during the long marches. At night, the girls were protected by fathers who dreamed of their own children back home. At the end of the campaign, a young lieutenant returning to the North took them home.

The Yankee GI was also both protective and forgiving. After setting fire to barns and corncribs, soldiers sometimes learned that small children were hiding inside. Disgusted, but concerned, they would plunge into the smoke to drag out frightened, blubbering children and send them on their way home.

The drummer boys of the Civil War were youngsters trained to beat out the commands of battle, the only means understood by foreign non-English speaking volunteers. Despite their youthful innocence, the young recruits were a vital part of the unit and a target for the enemy. So protective of the drummer boy were the soldiers that they kept him to the rear of the march, and the older men took great care to assure that the youngsters were fed and warm. Often, as they marched through towns, women would thrust knapsacks of food into the hands of the drummer boy, thinking of their own young sons off somewhere in battle.

As Sherman drove inland into South Carolina his troops came upon the small town of Orangeburg, where they found that the villagers had already set fire to their houses, barns and cotton crops to keep them from the hands of the Yankees. The one remaining building was the orphan asylum, where some 300 children were moved from Charleston in an attempt to keep them out of Sherman's devastating path. The hard-driving general and his soldiers surrounded the building. Aghast at what they found inside, they blinked back tears as they watched the frightened urchins in rags say their morning prayers and eat a meager breakfast of corn mush and molasses. Sherman ordered the building guarded, fearful the townspeople would burn it, then moved his army on...but not before he left ample supplies for the children.

Children also entered into the events of the Spanish-American War, the Indian Wars and World War I, when the American doughboy was known to share his rations with the children of France.

During World War II, as the Germans occupied southern France, women and children were packed into box cars and dispatched eastward to labor camps and gas chambers. In an attempt to rescue them, camps were infiltrated at night by underground agents. Parents, in the dark of night, were unexpectedly confronted with the decision to put their children in the hands of strangers. Many times they were forced to wake a child for escape and a separation that might be forever. These hunted children were smuggled out of the country or hidden with underground families all over Europe.

The eventual American occupation of Europe resulted in thousands of incidents and stories involving children of the war-ravaged continent. American volunteers flooded Europe's rescue missions and took on the momentous task of the identification and re-unification of displaced orphans with their families and relatives.

The American forces were wholeheartedly welcomed by children of North Africa. The German command, during their occupation, had shipped vast quantities of African foodstuffs out of the country and on to Germany, thus stripping the villages of vital supplies. The depletion left the children in Oran starving. When the first American troops came ashore with only canned field rations carried in their packs, they gave their own source of livelihood to the pitiful-looking Arab children. The soldiers themselves didn't get much to eat and for days lived on cigarettes and oranges as they fought their way across the land.

Second Lieutenant James Fall of Marion, Indiana, assigned to the

391st Fighter Squadron, was forced to bail out of his P-47, crippled by flack, over Rosel, France, shortly after D-Day, 1944. Fall landed on the Poret Family farm, which was by then transformed into a battle zone with the Canadian troops advancing just hundreds of yards away. Hitting the ground rendered him unconscious and broke his left leg. Upon awakening he found a group of armed Hitler Youth hovering over him, and he was convinced they would execute him on the spot.

Later, as Fall hobbled down the narrow path on his broken leg, he was greeted by the Poret children, who disregarded the turmoil around them and ran to greet the American. Fall, looking down at their pitiful faces, was reminded of his two small sisters at home who were about the same age. Instinctively, without considering the consequences of his actions, he reached down into his pockets to empty the cache of candy and gum into the hands of the children. There was silence. His captors quickly raised their guns, suspecting he was reaching for a weapon. Fall thought they would shoot—that this would be his last day. He had no way of knowing he would survive this incident and later be placed in solitary confinement in a German prison camp for the rest of the war.

At war's end, the American soldier befriended the children of the enemy. Chocolate, Coca Cola and cigarettes became the new goodwill ambassadors in Germany and Japan.

Following the end of World War II, Berlin was a city divided into American, British, French and Russian sectors. The unmet Russian demand that the Allied occupation forces vacate Berlin heated-up the Cold War. The Soviets isolated the city by roadblocking supplies into the sectors and in building the Berlin Wall. The West counteracted by implementing the "Berlin Airlift" to rescue the starving city. Located in the heart of Berlin, the airport was hampered by a hazardous approach. It was a precarious attempt each time U.S. cargo planes landed and took off, yet the Americans were cheered on by German children staggered along the runway. So taken by the pitiful-looking kids, one crew attached candy bars to their handkerchiefs and threw them out the pilot's small window. It wasn't long before the Americans contrived an ingenious parachute drop...throwing hundreds of candy-handkerchief parcels. The American Santa Clauses continued the drops throughout the duration of the crisis, by which time hundreds of children greeted them daily.

The Korean conflict inflicted a harsh fate for the children of that country as well, who were often separated from their parents by panic or death. With no place to go, they wandered in packs around the countryside, homeless and afraid. Thousands suffered from starvation, disease, and malnutrition, and many lay down on the roadside seeking ditches for shelter where they often died.

With the Communists on the move in Korea, the government officials were concerned with the mechanics of war. It was the American soldier who was sensitive to the needs of the homeless children and who was offering some relief to the thousands swarming around every military encampment for food and shelter. It was the intercession of the GI, in his voluntary contributions of money and the scrounging of supplies, that managed to keep the packs of children alive and in some degree of health until they could be sent to orphanages that were being established throughout Korea. Appropriately, the effort to save the orphans of Korea was called "Operation Kiddy Car."

The American soldier was a noble breed to the children of the world; there just wasn't anyone like him. Ernie Pyle gave his life trying to describe him. Millions of words and thousands of books were written about him. "GI Joe" was magnificent in the movies, exalted on Broadway and memorable in television series. Toys were designed to depict him and his battlefield equipment. Even a doll was created and named after him, an honor previously given only to Shirley Temple.

Children role-played him in their backyards while teenagers the world over scrambled for any GI patches and clothing in an attempt to dress like him.

The American GI *was* "number one"! He was considered the most macho of men, the best-dressed and best-equipped soldier in the entire world. And he was the richest. He was everyone's buddy. His popularity was phenomenal and assured wherever he went. His presence through time and place provided a protection—a war cradle of sorts. Was there any doubt he would be missed when he left Vietnam?

More than anything, he was very kind...and he laughed a lot. Was it any wonder then why the Vietnamese children and the American soldier understood each other? Each was just trying to get through it all. Each was resisting adulthood, even though war had thrust them into it. After all, who could blame either for behaving as they did? It was a happier place, that child land.

CHAPTER III

ORPHANAGES OF VIETNAM

"Be kind, for everyone you meet is fighting a difficult battle."

– E. C. McKenzie

In 1973, after American military troops departed Vietnam, there were more than 25,000 children in orphanages in the war-torn country, and thousands more wandered the streets alone or in gangs. With the incidence of abandoned children growing in massive numbers, many childless couples world-wide responded to the opportunity to adopt a Vietnamese child. Some even arranged transportation to Vietnam to select a child and, during their visit, came to terms with the truth of the intolerable environment and hopelessness that faced the homeless children of that country.

Imagine walking into an overcrowded orphanage and instantly being surrounded by young ones of all ages, some grabbing your legs and all of them hoping you will take them home with you. To the average American couple, a visit to a provincial orphanage was a cultural shock filled with heartbreak.

Mike and Caroline Summers would never forget the experience; for years to come, it would compound the sorrow and the pity of the Vietnam drama. Their destination was a foundling home on the outskirts of Saigon. In order to reach the compound, they had to drive slowly for several miles on a desolate muddy road. Throughout the journey, the tropical rain ruthlessly battered the windshield, making it virtually impossible to detect the shacks that dotted the landscape. Finally they came upon a compound of neglected buildings crying out for repair. Within seconds of stepping from the car, they were surrounded by curious children who paid no mind to the rain; they knew why the Americans had come. A small fragile nun on the porch dismissed them with two claps of her hands, but only to a short distance where they continued to gaze in disbelief at the presence of the strangers.

The Summers had been expected, and without words, they hurried into the building where room after room overflowed with malnourished children. For many of the orphans, this was the only home they had ever known. Little grass mats covered the porch, and it was apparent some of the children slept there because the rooms inside were filled. They were everywhere, varying in age. The American couple had to be careful as they walked. Occasionally, a small hand reached out to grab at the hem line of Caroline's dress.

The rough-hewn wooden floor had finger-width spaces between the planks, exposing the ground below. Small groups of children were crouched down, their faces pressed horizontally along the cracks, watching the insects milling about beneath the structure. One of the children would drop a spitball into the ant hill, then they would all erupt in giggles as they watched the confusion below. Occasionally, a little head from across the room would jerk up, wanting to join in the fun, but most of the other children on the cots ignored the noises; they were too weak to care.

Sometimes there were three and four to a small cot, clinging to each other. Cribs were worse. Four to six babies were symmetrically crowding the length of it. Some infants slept in unpadded cardboard cartons positioned on the floor because there were not enough cribs.

Although the surroundings reflected an atmosphere of cleanliness and neatness, the odor of urine and feces assaulted the nostrils as a child worker moved from crib to crib, performing the endless job of changing diapers. With a diaper shortage and no clothes dryer to help, the stacks of clothes looked stained and untouchable.

The provincial orphanage, one of countless others like it in South Vietnam, was overflowing with these small, discarded humans, most of whom would not make it to their first year. The mortality rate for infants was uncontrollable.

It was well into November and the monsoon season was thrashing its rain on the tin roof, which offered little protection as the water poured through the gaps. Instead, old feed bags covered the frail bodies and rubbed them raw. Babies covered with skin rashes and boils were common. There was little to offer in either treatment or medication. Malnourished, diseased, and dying, some lay so weak that they could not wince or brush the flies and insects congregated on their open sores. The dry season to come undoubtedly produced more insects, and one could only imagine the discomfort the babies suffered during the heat.

An immediate reaction to what her mind was interpreting found Caroline tightly clinging to her husband. How she wished she could pick up each and every child, brush away the flies and mosquitoes and hold them tightly.

Mike, with his arm around Caroline, followed the little French nun from room to room, unable to speak and feeling a pain inside so great that he wanted to break out and scream against the injustice. He wasn't ashamed of the tear that escaped his eye and trickled down his cheek.

Sister Mary Francine was warm and kind, yet very fragile-looking in her long white robes. She, too, walked nervously. The faint smile never dared to leave her face for fear the couple would reject the occasion of selecting a child.

She led them into the toddler room where the children spent most of their day in cribs and playpens. Because of the added cost, there was not enough staff to handle the toddlers. Many of them seemed withdrawn and passive. It was hard for Mike and Caroline to tell if they were abnormal or if they were just deprived of stimulation.

There were only a few toys scattered about, and by appearance they were well worn. With no items of stimulation in the cribs, some toddlers were entertaining themselves by chewing on the peeling rails. The most impoverished surroundings in the western culture could not compete with the gloom and desolation of this place.

The couple followed the nun to a crib in the far corner of the room. Silent for a few moments, she folded her hands over her breast as if to pray and simply said, "This is Tam."

The little girl before them was lying on her back. She had pulled her foot up to her mouth and was sucking on her big toe. From time to time she would place her hands on both feet and clap them together. Knowing she had a captivated audience, there was mischief in her eyes as she began to perform. Then, she began to gibber in her own unintelligible language. The strangers did not go away as others had before. They continued to stare at her.

The three adults remained silent. The woman kept blinking her eyes repeatedly, as though she were denying the tears that fought to flow. Caroline smiled at her husband. It was an expression of complete approval. Then she reached down to pick up the little girl.

Tam greeted Caroline's reach by pulling herself up and clinging to the side of the crib. There was no mattress and her bare feet sprang up from the wooden slats and rested on the soft warm body whose arms were now holding her tightly.

Mike tenderly kissed the child's cheek, then slipped his arm around his wife's waist. There was little doubt; they were a family.

Without speaking, the nun turned, tucking her hands into the mandarin sleeves of her robe and retraced her steps back to the entrance of the building. They could not see her face, but as she walked Sister Mary Francine was crying, her rosary briskly swinging with the flow of her body.

"Thank you, Lord. Another one saved," she mumbled.

Mike followed the nun to her small office where he affixed his signature to a paper already laid out on the desk. Sister Mary Francine carefully signed her name beside his, then folded the documents and placed them in his hands.

She smiled. "There, that is done."

Caroline Summers stood on the porch clutching the pretty child whose ash colored hair matched her own. She was unaware the rain had begun to diminish as she studied the delicate face of her new daughter. The child returned the curiosity by touching Caroline's face.

In exploring her features, Caroline thought how handsome the father must have been and that the mother, too, was surely beautiful.

Then, as if suddenly being brought back to reality, she thought of the mother who may have stood on this very porch months before, giving her child to the nuns. It was an emotional experience she had not anticipated. What a sacrifice it must have been to abandon a child so small and helpless.

Sister Mary Francine knew all their stories well. It was a familiar one in war-torn Vietnam. Tam was the child of a young Vietnamese woman and an American soldier. It was after he had been killed that the young woman discovered she was expecting his child. The soldier had a wife and a child back in the States; it would serve no purpose to make Tam's birth known to them. And, because the child had inherited her father's western features, the young mother knew it would suffer in this racially pure environment. It was this concern that led the young mother to bring the child for refuge. She heard children were being sent to America from the orphanage and she felt it was Tam's only hope for a normal life.

The Summers were from the mid-western United States. Two

years earlier they had lost an infant who would have been Tam's age had she lived. Unable to bear another child, Caroline grieved for the one she had lost and looked to adoption to fill the void. Mike Summers was an airline pilot who routinely flew to the Far East, and these assignments presented an unusual opportunity to search for the child they longed for.

The adoption scenario was not uncommon in South Vietnam in 1973. Children of the poverty-stricken war torn country were departing for homes all over the world. Several adoption agencies had become well established in Vietnam, recognizing that while there was a shortage of adoptable babies in the western world, there were thousands of Vietnamese babies in real need of families and their love.

Frequently, adoptive parents came to Vietnam to claim a child, but more often representatives of the agencies sponsoring the orphanages served as escorts for the children. Though adoptions were being processed as rapidly as possible, there was much red tape and governmental objection. Therefore, a lapse of eighteen months was not unusual before a child left the poverty of Asia for a new, healthy environment with the families who were anxious to receive them. Unfortunately, the supply of children far exceeded the demand. Not everyone who wanted a baby was open to accepting a foreign child.

The waiting period for adoptions in America was uncertain. With the new morality sweeping the country, young unmarried mothers were keeping their babies. The acceptance of illegitimate children grossly changed the climate of adoption options for childless couples.

The Summers were in their late thirties, late by most standards for parenthood, and the possibility of a toddler being available to them was almost non-existent in the United States. As a result, they turned to the American-based adoption agencies supporting orphanages in Vietnam. The couple wanted a child to love and be a part of their family. It was not an impossible dream in Vietnam.

Cooperation from a Vietnamese mother made such adoptions easier and faster. It was the abandoned children, without identification, who were enmeshed in red tape and bureaucratic delays.

Children are the future of a country, and even a devastated country like Vietnam did not want to lose them to foreign adoptions, despite their own inability to adequately provide for them. The growing number of orphans was becoming an embarrassment to the government, simply because by approving foreign adoptions, they were admitting that they could not be cared for in their country.

"We'll take good care of her, Sister," Mike assured the nun as he took her hand.

"Yes, I think that you will. I have no present to give Tam and I am sorry that I do not have a pretty dress for her to wear to America. You see, we do not have much here."

The nun smiled, lowering her dark eyes. Mike touched her shoulder, reassuring her that poverty did not require an apology.

Together, they joined the new mother and small cluster of child care workers who usually assembled for such farewells. Mike removed his coat and covered the child, then the three disappeared down the steps to the waiting car. In a minute they were gone.

There was silence as the car disappeared down the road, swallowed by both rain and jungle. The nun clapped her hands twice and the small group dispersed. She walked up the steps to return to the sound of the cries inside.

"Tomorrow, maybe someone will come from the agency for another child," Sister Mary Francine prayed to herself, looking to the sky for a sign of hope.

The "agency" that Sister Mary Francine was looking to for salvation was one of seven of the organizations functioning in Vietnam who were chiefly concerned with saving the children and who made donations and offered support to the orphanages. Representation included the U.S., Australia, Canada, Germany and England. The volunteers were often church-sponsored or were from an independent organization, as well as charitable groups that functioned in many other underdeveloped countries. Emotionally, they were intertwined in a common bond. They had a strong mutual concern for the young lives being lost from lack of facilities and the manpower to care for them.

Sister Mary Francine received one hundred dollars a month from the Ministry of Social Welfare for the children in her care. The average grant, $1.50 per month, per child, from the Vietnamese government, was far from sufficient, but every bit helped.

With orphanages and refugee camps dramatically increasing, the nuns looked to foreign groups of volunteers for further assistance. So many facilities were seeking financial help that they welcomed the few hundred dollars they received each month from chapters in the States. Since the organizations themselves were now functioning as adoption agencies, Sister Mary Francine often relinquished children for placement to homes in various countries. She argued with herself, thinking that the babies should be given financial support within Vietnam instead of being taken out of the country. On the other hand, there was no alternative for the Amerasians but to send some of them to Americans to be placed in good homes. This gesture of surrendering the children assured that the volunteers would be back with donations to help those left behind. It was a compromise to a desperate situation.

The flow of children out of Vietnam was very slow, and when a new child appeared, there didn't seem to be any room left to add one more. Yet Sister Mary Francine never turned a child away, telling herself, "I will manage. It is just one more."

The nuns who ran the orphanages were a unique group of women. Many of them had gone into convents at an early age. It was the custom of devout Catholics to offer their young children into a life of service to God and church. Vietnam had several convents that came into existence during the late 1800's. The nuns who founded one of the best known facilities, Sacred Heart Orphanage, belonged to the Order of St. Paul of Chartres, an order that existed in Vietnam since 1884. They were primarily concerned with educating Vietnamese and French students, and they survived the Japanese occupation. Located in Danang, the nuns began caring for orphans in 1947 and continued with that mission when the need became so critical during the sixties. The charity of the sisters knew no limits in their efforts to help the children; they accepted any child, in any condition, at any time.

The Good Shepherd Home in Vinh Long was another group of nuns who dedicated themselves to caring for orphans and runaway girls. It was a haven run by Irish nuns who came to Vietnam in 1958 from County Cavan. They renovated a French officer's compound and converted a two-story building to rehabilitate bar girls and prostitutes, picked up under the strict morality laws established by the late President Ngo Dinh Diem. The home had a good reputation for teaching the girls to provide for themselves, and the success rate for not returning to a life of crime was high. The war provided the opportunity for the Vinh Long shelter to open its doors to orphans as well.

Because of the political unrest in Vietnam, the religious orders in Europe were hesitant to send additional personnel to help. Therefore, many nuns from those European orders were all but abandoned and had to structure their orphanages independently.

Catholic Relief Societies provided much aid to the sisters in their missions, but what was sent was never enough to meet all the needs.

Who were these nuns in a country ravaged by terror and war? Mostly Vietnamese nationals, they grew up with conflict and knew all too well the impact of war on their country. Further, they had to be resourceful individuals and feisty to endure the demands of seeking provisions, resolving whatever problems they were enduring without the assistance of a local bishop or head mother superior.

What these nuns lacked in size (they were all small and fragile looking), they made up for in endurance and spirit. They tilled the soil, built buildings when necessary, scrubbed floors, cooked, sewed, administered to the sick, and generally rolled up their sleeves to tackle any of the hundreds of tasks required to run an orphanage with hundreds of children. And they did it without pay and in the name of humanity.

They were dedicated to writing letters to their stateside sponsors, thanking them for their donations. Fortunately, they were not shy about asking for more help, either.

Nuns were respected in Vietnam. They were rarely the victims of crime or physical violation. Friend and foe alike regarded these women as the redeemers of human suffering.

Before World War II there were few orphanages in Vietnam, but that is not to imply child abandonment did not exist. It did, and to some degree, in great proportions. Like any country ridden with destitution, children in Vietnam were rejected for a multitude of reasons: poverty, homelessness, illegitimacy, congenital defects, mixed parentage or simply self-preservation. As there were no legal or social pressures on a woman to keep her baby, abandonment was the easiest option. Since birth certificates were rarely issued, a mother could simply walk away from her baby without legal or social repercussions. Too, abandonment was a common practice by women who had already given birth to several unwanted babies; any biological bond that may have existed would submit to the even stronger instinct of self-preservation. Since little or no specialized medical care was available, infanticide was practiced, and babies who were malformed were left to die.

A cultural difference between the orient and the West, which most affects the children, is the definition of the "family." In the U.S., a child is an orphan when both parents are dead. However, in Vietnam, because of the "extended family" concept, a child is never considered an orphan as long as there is a living relative. Consequently, in

Vietnam there were very few true orphans since the parentless child was, supposedly, simply taken in by the closest relative or neighbor. In many instances a relative would take in a child and utilize them for their own purpose as a cheap way of acquiring household help or field labor. One could easily conclude that this noble social practice was wildly abused and placed the child into a lifetime of servitude and exploitation. Even during the French occupation, after World War II, orphanages were scarce. The need for establishing the care institutions by western missionaries came initially from Europeans who had their own concepts about the worth of abandoned children. The Vietnam War, which escalated in the sixties, saw the children as the undisputed victims of the war.

By 1966, there were 83 known orphanages or children's homes in South Vietnam, caring for over 11,000 children. A short eight years later in 1974, that figure more than doubled and there were 134 registered orphanages and children's homes in the Saigon area alone. In addition, there were 326 day care centers caring for over 44,000 children.

If orphanages were unheard of in the Asian country before World War II, the reverse became commonplace in the sixties and seventies. In the summer of 1974, Highway 1, the modern four-lane road between Saigon and the former American Base at Bien Hoa, was saturated with orphanages. On that twenty-mile stretch of road there were more orphanages than gas stations. Orphanages became a prosperous business in South Vietnam. The majority of these facilities were supported by funds collected from American sources.

There was never a doubt that a need existed for the institutions and organizations to establish havens for homeless, unwanted children in the war-ravaged country. Despite the loss of pride and the humiliation in seeing starving children roaming the countryside and city streets, it was difficult for the Vietnamese to grasp the magnitude of the situation. Perhaps it was because survival was becoming an individual effort even for adults, much less coping with small infants and children who had special needs. The need for outside help and concern was extensive and imperative. Yet, the Vietnamese government did not formally request help from the many available international agencies such as the Red Cross or Save the Children, although both initiated assistance on their own.

Instead of letting all these children die, missionaries and adoption agencies went to Vietnam to gather up all the rejects in orphanages. The course was charted to respond to the human need.

Although the orphanages had little more to offer, it was a good deal better than what awaited the children living in the streets and countryside. In fact, it was minimal for what was truly needed. Most unlicensed orphanages were the worst of all. Some nationals saw orphanages as a profitable enterprise. Receiving a small pittance from the government, they were nothing more than a roof over the orphans' head and a corner in which to sleep. Ill-fed, sick and dirty, the children were victimized by greedy managers who saw an opportunity to benefit financially from their misfortune.

During the war, the American soldiers were highly visible, providing support with their time and money. When they left in 1973, the orphanages lost that vital resource. Many foreign aid organizations started what they called "Foster Orphanage Plan." Under this plan, people all over the world made monthly contributions to the orphanages of their choice. It was the only source of income for many and their link to survival. Yet, with the war winding down in 1975, the demand for shelter far exceeded the availability of space.

The average individual had no realistic concept of what was involved in caring for children in orphanages. The sheer numbers alone were overwhelming, the problems unsurmountable. The children needed more than food and a home. Usually, they arrived at the orphanages in poor physical condition with undiagnosed problems. Many had ear infections, pneumonia, bronchitis, hepatitis and primary tuberculosis. Others were covered with lice, had worms, intestinal parasites, typhoid, anemia, conjunctivitis, boils, fungus infections, scabies, thrush and vaginal infections. Any child over the age of two could be expected to have extensive dental decay, and it was not unusual for damage from early polio to show up when the child began to walk. The illnesses overwhelmed the nuns, most of whom had little or no medical training.

Almost all of the children were deficient in both physical and emotional development for their age, usually due to malnutrition, vitamin deficiency, and lack of stimulation. All the children lacked love, attention and good nutrition, and when the orphanages were able to provide that, it produced dramatic results. However, many of the facilities were meager in what they did provide. Sometimes it was little more than a corner to sleep and a bowl of rice. Usually, there were no doctors and only a self-trained nurse.

Some of the children were severely handicapped by conditions such as polio, napalm burns, missing limbs, blindness, deafness, cerebral palsy, tuberculosis, congenital heart defects and cleft palate deformities. Because there was no expertise as to handle them, they were usually placed to the side in an orphanage. With the growing number of children left homeless, and with so many needing basic daily necessities, there was no time to give special attention to the comparatively few severely handicapped.

An exception was Doug Gray, an ex-British Medical Corpsman who came to visit Vietnam in the late sixties and began working with the mentally disturbed at Phu My Hospital. Single-handedly, he began to help the lost children of Vietnam, those stricken with polio, cerebral palsy, and numerous other crippling diseases, and who were the least desirable candidates for adoption.

Seeking out the forsaken children, often found tied to a bed post in a darkened back room of an orphanage, Gray brought them to his Saigon center and began the long, slow process of therapy, operations, and rehabilitation. A registered nurse, he played a role in every step of the child's healing process, from surgeon's assistant to floor scrubber. During the early days of 1974, he picked up twenty-seven disabled children from outlying facilities and within months had twenty of them walking and using their once-shriveled legs. He was not paid a salary and lived on a budget of three to four dollars a day, which included providing care and food for forty-seven patients.

Not many would consider helping the severely handicapped, but Doug Gray was challenged by it and was truly one of the unsung heroes in the drama of the children of Vietnam.

Father Oliver was another very special person.

A Redemptorist priest, he arrived in Vietnam in 1920. He had a long, white beard set off by his black robe and it reached down to the rosary he wore at his waist. He was never without the jet black, horn-rimmed glasses that protruded from his gentle face, and he topped his entire attire with a white safari helmet. At a glance he looked like something out of a French Foreign Legion movie. Though he was well into his seventies, he had the energy and vigor of a man half his age and was a familiar figure to the needy of Saigon with his involvement in many projects, all benefiting the poor and homeless.

Father Oliver had three orphanages that ministered to homeless children. All were poor and inadequate, yet he took the sickest babies, those no one wanted, and did what he could to help. In addition, he ran homes for destitute war widows and a facility for young unwed mothers.

Over the years he became involved in hundreds of charitable offerings, the largest being an institution called, "la Pension Notre Dame," (Notre Dame Boardinghouse). It was an old building in dire need of repair, but in 1974 Father Oliver had over 2,000 people under his care. No one who appeared in need was ever sent away.

Few orphanages were beautiful, well-equipped or placed in ideal settings. There were those established as convents by religious orders a century before in which young nuns were trained to run schools for children of the villages. Converted to orphanages, some had infirmaries that were staffed and equipped to handle moderate emergencies, and their playgrounds were filled with useful areas for the children.

As for most others, many came into existence out of the growing demands overrunning the country. During the American presence many were well-stocked with supplies. Money flowed in from soldiers' generosity. Medical teams from nearby bases serviced the orphanages and many children were taken to American medical facilities for needed surgery and attention. Since no funds were allotted for orphan care, the procedures were "bootlegged" by the staff. But, when the Americans departed, all support ceased and the orphanages were left to fend for themselves.

The economy of Vietnam was surviving as a direct result of the American aid that was beefed-up in the sixties. With the departure of the U.S. in 1973, thousands of Vietnamese nationals, who were dependent upon the installations for jobs, were abruptly left without work. The influence of the American dollars alone stretched across the provinces and was the life blood of not only the cities and hamlets, their hotels and restaurants, but of the street vendors and souvenir shops, and even the bar girls of Saigon. The departure of the American money distressed the adult population, leaving thousands of men and women without means of subsistence.

What of the children who were the future hope of this badly devastated country? Thousands of them were homeless, living in boxes, on streets and in alleys, scrounging for food and without any hope of being taken into Vietnamese families. As a result of the drawn-out conflict, countless children were being abandoned daily in maternities, to orphanages, on the streets—even in scrap heaps. Leaving a child in hospitals and child care institutions became a solution for mothers. Abortion clinics did not exist in Vietnam and contraception or birth control pills were unavailable to the populace. Both methods were too complicated for the peasants, and strong catholic beliefs interfered in the practice of either of these methods. No effort was extended by the missionaries or churches to fend off the growing birth rate, nor were the Buddhists active in promoting birth control.

Regardless of the surmounting birth rate, a large percentage of the new-born would die in the first year of life. In the excitement of the American withdrawal, the hundreds of infants being born and discarded daily were too insignificant for the concerns of the military strategists or Vietnam's government. They were all but forgotten. Control of the country superseded any focus on human suffering.

Perhaps it was naive of the organizations (that had labored in Vietnam over a decade) to sustain the belief that they could halt, reverse, or even attempt to gather up a minimal portion of the discarded humans that increased daily. For a time, they may have thought they were gaining, as numerous orphanages and child care centers mushroomed overnight throughout the provinces. It may have seemed for the moment that the feeble whimpers of children were being heard since nationals and foreigners alike, who found children wandering alone, took them to the sanctity of care centers.

With the American de-escalation of the war, and the rapid deterioration of the economy, survival was the primary concern of the average Vietnamese.

Homeless children were everywhere, yet no Vietnamese family could afford to feed another mouth. It was left to the western volunteer organizations, with their external support, to stand fast in protecting and saving the lives of the abandoned children.

UNICEF or CARE gave powdered milk automatically to the orphanages. Even though orphanages were poverty-stricken, the donor organizations began to monitor the use of funds sent to them. Volunteers would arrive unannounced to find the milk that was sent for the children watered down so much that it lacked any nourishment. One group fed the milk to their livestock in an attempt to fatten them up for a higher price on the market. With that money they intended to buy food for the children. There was a serious cultural gap in both communication and priorities. Nuns serving as directresses of the facilities would not budge in their philosophies or even try to understand how they could better utilize the funds. It was backward logic.

Another orphanage in Danang received a considerable monthly allowance, yet inspections repeatedly demonstrated neglect and lack of progress. It was considered one of the poorest run homes.

The offices were neat and presented themselves as a thriving home for children. Pictures of youngsters and their adopted families covered the walls. Considering the general condition of most Vietnamese orphanages, at first glance the entire compound seemed clean and neat. Yet, closer observation indicated that the facility was economically disadvantaged and presented a far different picture.

The handicapped children were confined to one corner of the courtyard in a room considerably darker than the rest. Four severely retarded boys were restrained in a seat, tied with strips of cloth. Others were lying in cribs made of wooden slats spaced about one inch apart. Sometimes a sheet covered the slats, more often not. All were malnourished and were only given attention at feeding time.

In another room, babies were crowded into cribs or even laid on the bare cement floor. The smell of urine was everywhere and the diapers were saturated.

A similar situation emerged when the directress of an orphanage, located in the Delta, was questioned about what she did with the funds she received each month from a stateside chapter, earmarked for care of the orphans. She pointed to the new wing she was constructing; she had reasoned that she would receive more funds from the Vietnamese government if she had a larger facility. The money was directed toward the new building and not distributed for the care of the orphans. The war was winding down and soon all funds would be cut off. The nun had decided to invest in her buildings, confident it would make the compound a more valuable parcel of real estate. Since the orphans would grow into adults within a few years, she was planning for future options of use for the building.

There were numerous other abuses and it was almost impossible to monitor every donation. In some instances it was clear that the managers were thinking ahead how they could benefit rather than how to meet the demands of the children at hand. It was evident that in an economic crisis, life was considered secondary.

Go Vap was the largest national orphanage in Vietnam. Conditions there were perhaps also the poorest. Catholic Relief and other agencies sent teams, and for certain periods conditions improved, but basic problems still existed. There were over 400 children confined to a small veranda and courtyard. Regimented and herded together, they were slapped into submission by emotionally disturbed residents who were their caretakers. The scene was inhuman. There was never enough food, water, or supplies to provide for the children...most were too weak to fight for their share, or emotionally too inept to fend for themselves. Others were forced to sit up against a wall for long periods of time while a monitor held a stick in hand to whack the child who dare to move. The children sat motionless and did not even cry. Older babies suffered the indignity of being plunked down, naked, into buckets. Where, in these repository playpens, their little arms and legs dangled helplessly for hours. Infants withered and died of starvation, unable to suck from the inadequately propped bottles. Soaking in their own waste, skin raw and unable to even cry for help, they would simply stop living.

Since there was an enormous geriatric population in Vietnam, there were a few orphanages that took in old people as well. Only a few designated geriatric facilities were available in Vietnam and they were over-crowded with sick, feeble or abandoned people. They, too, sometimes had a few children, and it was sad to see them sandwiched in between the aged. It was usually an abusive situation, with the older residents dominating the children, working them, becoming impatient and hitting them, and sometimes even taking their food.

Conversely, there were positive situations existing with children and the elderly. Generally orphanages were over-run with children, but often there were a few older homeless Vietnamese as residents which frequently proved advantageous. Whenever possible, the older people worked, too.

A blind lady at the Sadec orphanage could change a diaper with greater speed and loving care than most. The elderly cooked, cleaned, worked in gardens, chopped feed for the livestock and washed clothes, in addition to taking care of the babies.

In comparison to orphanages in the big cities, the rural facilities lacked equipment and supplies but were generally clean and neat. Actually, there was nothing to litter them since the children each had only one set of clothing to wear. There were no toys, and furniture consisted only of beds, cribs, or floor mats. The same dishes were re-used at meal time for all the children, and the only laundry consisted of diapers, clothing, and some bedding.

The infant rooms were, perhaps, the most depressing since they were overcrowded with cribs and boxes in which the babies slept. With the shortage of workers, the babies lay in their cribs most of the time, wet and crying, the smell of stale urine permeating the surroundings.

Since a staff worker cost $10 to $15 a month, many orphanages found them unaffordable and opted for cheaper, untrained help. Bottles that were sometimes too hot were propped on dirty pillows for infants at feeding time. There was never enough time or staff to hold the infants, even though it was vital to their life and development to be held and loved.

When babies were placed outside in large playpens, flies were the problem. An older child would be given the task of swatting the flies with an old diaper. The bottom of the playpen was warped plywood. Another playpen consisted of strips of wood spaced an inch apart with galvanized aluminum pans placed under the pen. Feces and urine would drip down into the metal containers, eliminating the need for diapers. A quick hose-down of the pen was done when the children were removed and the pans below emptied. The entire concept would have appeared utterly disgusting to the westerner, but for the Vietnamese it was a workable solution to a diaper and staff shortage.

Toddlers were served meals as they all sat on a long bench. Each nun fed approximately twenty children, using one bowl and one spoon for all. Sickness too was passed on by the use of one utensil. Afterward, they were all placed on long ten-seat toilets for an hour.

The only toys available were used for decoration, placed high out of reach. There were no books, crayons or other such items to stimulate them. Children created their own amusement with cans and sticks or anything they could find useful to their fantasies.

Often, a small infirmary was available with medicines and, sometimes, an examining table. With only these meager items it was considered somewhat "equipped." It was, however, in many instances only for "appearance's" sake since the irreplaceable supplies were rarely used.

Each child in the orphanage had his own unique history. All the stories were different, yet somehow the same. Another similarity was obvious...their sadness.

Many children were crippled and had no braces or crutches. Dental hygiene was unheard of. Many more had rotting teeth, bloated stomachs and open sores.

The staff at the nurseries and orphanages knew each child's story well. Rosemary Taylor, an Australian who joined a refugee team sponsored by the Australian Council of Churches, writes of these tribulations in her books, *Turn My Eyes Away* and *Orphans of War*. At Newhaven nursery in the Saigon area, they had a little boy who had been abandoned in a public vehicle and was malnourished to the extent that his arms and legs were emaciated. His stomach was bloated and his entire body was covered with ugly boils. The staff named him "De Profundis," (out of the depths). With devoted care and love, the little boy survived all of his medical and emotional problems and even thrived to be placed with a family in the United States.

Cuc was a little girl of seven who was found wandering about a marketplace, begging for food. From her dark skin she appeared to have been fathered by a black soldier. Or it was suspected she may have been a lost refugee from one of the dark-skinned mountain tribes, the Montagnards. Cuc could not read or write and often drifted into a corner alone. The other children shied away from her, perhaps due to her darker color or her backwardness.

The words of Rabindranath Tagore had come to life: "I am the outcast...the uninitiated. Born in the household of exile I was rejected by the respectable, out of grace with playmates, a homeless stranger to the neighborhood..."

Eventually Cuc found a friend in another mixed-blood child who was also shy. Clinging together, they would set themselves apart from the others. The act of rejection wedged its way into the lowest level of poverty.

Nguyen Van Hung was a little boy who was found abandoned on a road near An Khe by a Vietnamese soldier, who then gave the child his name. About one year old and half-black, he was bright and alert and responded vigorously to those around him. He, too, eventually found a loving family in America.

Many of the children were brought to orphanages by neighbors or strangers who found them wandering about or crying on the roadside. American soldiers were outstanding in rescuing and bringing babies and children to the foundling homes when they were found in need.

Child abuse was prevalent in Vietnam. Children were found brutally beaten by their Vietnamese parents. Billy was a child about three years old who was brought to the orphanage with his body covered with abrasions. It was the result of his mother's attempts to kill him. The intervention of a neighbor saved his life. There were many others who could not be saved.

Though it was clear that the nuns wanted to keep as many children as possible, hoping they could raise them to adulthood, many times, as a hasty after-thought, they would relinquish them when volunteers brought supplies. More often these were children who were critically ill, had seizures, or some deformity the nuns could not handle.

Vincent was such a child. He was given to the Friends For All Children volunteers because, although he was a happy and active boy, he was subject to epileptic seizures. The nuns reported that Vincent had fallen from his crib as an infant, hitting his head on the stone floor, and had developed problems as a result of the accident. Since the orphanage had limited medical means of controlling neurological disorders, and Vincent was in need of more specialized treatment, he was relinquished for adoption.

Another child about a year old weighed only nine pounds. A bruised face also revealed her teeth were smashed, and her back was covered with cigarette burn scars. One leg that had been fractured had knitted out of alignment. When found, she was a child terrified by anyone who came near her, and though she was fragile and malnourished, she began healing slowly. The miracle was that she did.

Another agency found David squirming and covered with blood after his mother was killed during a street firefight. In death she managed to shield her son beneath her body.

Each child had a story. There was much grief within the walls of the orphanages, and they could only provide a bit of sanctuary from the devastation occurring outside, every day, every minute. Each child's story was more distressing and painful than the last. All had suffered well beyond their years.

Phu My Hospital on the outskirts of Saigon had more than 1,500 patients, most of whom were impossibly ill. It was under the direction of the Sisters of St. Paul de Chartres. It was not an asylum for impossible recovery or relief from disease. It was merely a last place, a home, for the unwanted in the most pitiful human condition. Death claimed 25% of them annually. Mentally retarded children were placed among the elderly incurable patients, most of whom were paralyzed or helplessly spastic. Many had lost limbs and had terminal ill-nesses. It had an exceptionally large population of blind patients (200), some whom might benefit from a specialist if one were available. The hospital was understaffed, which is why they tied up the children or placed them on wooden toilets of sorts. Some were chairs with a hole cut in the seat and a little pan beneath, while others were long benches with a series of holes cut in them. The children were placed or tied in these chairs all day, every day. Often they would try to get up and run about, but they were restrained. A little girl who was mentally retarded was chained to a chair. She had open sores and scratches on her legs, and her joints were swollen from rickets. Vitamin deficiency resulted in many illnesses and ailments.

The large hut-type buildings had about 125 people in each room. Adults who were able wandered around the rooms while others sat on pallets for beds, clinging to their worldly possessions tied in a small bundle. Many of the beds had holes in the pallets to accommodate a pipe running down to a pot. It was a make-shift toilet for those who could not get up to relieve themselves. On extremely hot days, the stench from excrement and dying people was overpowering. Scattered among the adults were sick children lying on the ground, or in wood-en box beds. An FCVN inspection report detailed the cost of running Phu My in 1974: " A total of 1,320 pounds of rice is prepared daily on a wood burning stove. There are no appliances of any sort. Washing for 2000 is done by hand on stone slabs with cold water and bar soap. The heat in the kitchen is unbearable with 24 huge caldrons bubbling away over blazing fires. Dutch ovens bake 250 loaves of bread a day. Water is a brown liquid, drawn by hand from a well."

In his search for babies, Ross Meador, an FCVN volunteer, would often stop at Phu My. At first he found it difficult to enter the wards. When he did, he would take his camera and take pictures of the patients. Joking and laughing with them, he wanted to bring them joy. He would tell them that they were beautiful and "that they belonged in Hollywood." Often a patient refused to have his picture taken, but he would later relent and call Meador back. It was always a happy occasion for them when Ross arrived for a visit.

Phu My greatly improved over the years, primarily due to Rosemary Taylor and financial assistance from various factions. Nurseries were improved and a program set up whereas older children were assigned babies to hold and cuddle during feedings. It worked well. Older children went to school and toddlers had their own section. The adult patients, too, were motivated to become more involved with gardening, food preparation, cleaning and laundry and even some nursing duties.

It wasn't just the children living in the institutions who suffered. Everywhere there were hundreds of children needing someone or something.

Although the orphanages had little more to offer, it was a good deal better than what awaited the older children living in the streets and countryside. Separated from their families for a variety of reasons—dislocation, death, abandonment, homelessness—some were runaways from refugee centers and orphanages. They were referred to as "Bui Doi," the "dust of life," for they lived like dust...going wherever the wind takes them. They were of no value to anyone. They slept in doorways or any shelter they could find, alone or often grouped together in small bands. Saigon overflowed with thousands of them, staking out territory in the hostile, lonely streets. They lived by their wits as beggars, pickpockets, pimps and shoeshine boys, often stealing and selling their loot. Many were on drugs. With no future, they only existed from day to day.

With the war winding down, poverty and misery were everywhere. Human life was of little value. Walking the streets of Saigon, or anywhere, one was confronted on every corner by a child begging. Often times they carried an infant in a dirty sling around their necks or a toddler on their backs. Women sat against buildings with infants in their arms, desolate. Children plowed through huge garbage piles looking for morsels of food. They were on every curb, every street, and in every alley...dirty, hungry and lonely.

The children of North Vietnam were undergoing similar hardships. The government declared that they did not have an orphan problem since children were absorbed by other relatives when their parents were killed. There are no figures available to the West to indicate the number of orphans or the mortality rate of infants and children in the North. But if statistics bear out, the death rate in South Vietnam, which was not only a warmer climate but richer agriculturally and with the presence of concerned charitable organizations, was still phenomenal. We can assume that the losses in the North, where there were no similar positive commodities, were even greater than in the South.

Thousands of children wandered to the South with the mass refugee flow from the North after the Communist takeover in 1954, when Vietnam was divided. At that time, there was no open demonstration for the concern of orphans by the North Vietnamese. There was no attempt at a truce to settle the homeless children or any sign of volunteers from Communist satellite countries to intervene in a humanitarian capacity. It was a different kind of war, one fought by an enemy without mercy. The people felt it and made the desperate dash to choose the exit to the South.

During the ten years of bombing of the North (1963-1973), the Communists alleged that almost every major hospital and school in North Vietnam was destroyed. They claimed that in addition to several hundred hospitals and medical clinics that were damaged or totally destroyed, there were 5,500 schools included in this estimate that were annihilated or partially damaged.

With the signing of the Paris Peace Accords in 1973, the U.S. government pledged to help repair damage to schools and hospitals. But evidence of the alleged massive destruction was never forthcoming, and Congress refused to appropriate money to help with the reconstruction. Uncle Sam, who had been generous world-wide after both World Wars I and II, adopted the philosophy of its enemies in the past who destroyed similar institutions and never made restitution. War was, after all, war. The American taxpayer had borne the burden of financial aid to countries all over the world and, in addition to rebuilding enemy territory, had come up empty-handed too often.

Churches and volunteer agencies representing charitable groups in the U.S., Australia and Europe began working in South Vietnam to meet the needs of the children in the Saigon government-controlled areas. And although they wanted to expand their aid to all of Vietnam, they did not respond to the needs of the children of the North. The reasons for this are not clear, but one could stem from the attitude of the Communist government of North Vietnam. They claimed they were capable of taking care of their own. Refugees were not allowed to leave the country because they were needed for the labor force for reconstruction. Further, the North Vietnamese government refused to allow children from their controlled areas to be adopted by families from other countries.

Several million Vietnamese, from both the North and South, died as a result of the war. The children, the next generation, were the future hope of the country. The Vietnamese were a people of great national pride, and for them to see their children taken and raised in another country was to suggest that they were incapable of taking care of them, or that there were others who could do it better. There was another factor, a fear among Vietnamese that when peace finally came, they would not be able to relocate their families separated by the war and they would discover that their children were sent to another country. It was a fear that would have substance. After the Communist takeover of South Vietnam in 1975, many Vietnamese fled their country, only to end up in refugee camps all over the globe. Then the searching would begin to find the children they relinquished earlier to adoption agencies. They would try to find their families and loved ones, and a search for their children would lead to heartbreaking moments for Americans who adopted the "orphans."

The bottom line to the dilemma was that finding families in other countries for the abandoned babies seemed the only human solution to the problem of the orphans. To let them die, which seemed inevitable if they were to stay in Vietnam, was a total waste of human life; a total deprivation of human potential. Too, it became a blessing to the thousands of childless couples in the United States and Europe who had lost all hope of ever raising a child of their own.

After the Americans left, the following two years found the North Vietnamese pushing toward the South with a violent determination that shattered the country in every direction and accelerated the end of the conflict.

In spite of the Armageddon around them, the Western volunteers not only stayed in Vietnam, they pushed on with a new ferocity in their mission to afford support and relief to the neglected and abandoned children. Their strength and the uniqueness of their dedication may have been drawn from a strong belief in humanity.

In the last days of 1974, it became clear to everyone that time was running out and the end was coming. Key northern provinces in South Vietnam were falling without a struggle, and the highways were overflowing with refugees heading south to Saigon, the last stronghold. The madness of the war and bombing drove thousands from the rural areas to the cities. It broke up families and shifted millions of people from one place to another. Those who remained in the countryside were forced to hide in the jungles or mountain caves. There was no survival from the intensive shelling and destruction. Too, there was fear of reprisals for collaboration with the Americans. The Amerasian children were fighting a dual foe, the Communist hostile power and rejection from their own countrymen.

Many children lost their entire families. The extended family of friends and neighbors was not anxious to feed another mouth. Therefore, with the flow of homeless people, there were more homeless children discarded and wandering with the crowds, begging and crying, the victims of abuse, hunger and oppression.

Children were everywhere in the capital city, thousands of them roaming the streets. It didn't matter what time of day or night, children were moving in packs. They slept in doorways, in boxes, under any protrusion that could afford shelter. It was not unusual to notice small babies with them. They converged on garbage heaps, scooped water from puddles to drink, and loitered on every street corner, in every alley. Dirty...homeless...miserable. Yet, they were survivors.

In the early months of 1975, the war was winding down. South Vietnamese soldiers were giving up provinces without a struggle. Moral was low, supplies were depleted, and the country was exhausted from the war.

All outside help dwindled to a trickle. It was now a country alone. More alone were the millions of children, oppressed, without the warm hands of their mothers or other human beings to comfort them.

The cities were controlled by the Saigon government, though Communist infiltration was heavy. But the countryside all around them belonged to the Viet Cong. People migrated from the hamlets and villages to swell Saigon's population. With a population of only half a million in 1954, in 1974 it bulged with over two million, and more were fleeing into the city's slums and camps every day to escape the devastating effects of the war.

Fifty percent of the general population was under fifteen years of age, but in refugee camps in the Saigon-controlled territory, the under-fifteen population was over seventy percent. There were more than 575,000 children in these refugee camps, with the majority of them living in the controlled zones and having lost one or both parents.

During the last months of war, poverty gripped the country. Stealing and pilfering was rampant. Inflation soared and necessities became scarce. Money itself was scarce. With the American departure, the thousands who lost their jobs were not able to find others. Parents believed the children in orphanages looked better and were better fed and clothed than their own, though not much better. So, for the "good of the child," they abandoned them. As the agencies handling foreign adoptions strove to empty the orphanages, the children kept coming. What these parents living in horrible conditions did not understand was that growing children needed love and personal attention more than they needed an abundance of food and shelter. The orphanage was not a good substitute for the family. It was revealed that the majority of these children died before the age of six, most of them within the first year or two. A major problem was lack of love and attention and emotional stimulation.

The needs of all the people during the last days was enormous. The American government had provided over 2.5 billion American dollars in aid to Saigon after withdrawal, all of it for military purposes. Less than one percent of the funds was designated for humanitarian assistance. Corruption and graft overtook the South Vietnamese government and it was every man, every child, for himself during April, 1975.

Yet, despite the massive efforts of the western volunteer agencies to assist in the situation of the children of South Vietnam, the attempt deteriorated beyond their grasp.

The plight of the orphans of Vietnam was soon to pass into history. On the last day of the month, the doors of Southeast Asia were finally slammed shut and South Vietnam was a country alone.

When Saigon fell in 1975, the conquerors, at last, had the victory they sought. They had won the country and defeated the Americans. But victory had its inherent drawbacks...they had poverty and pain, and much misery to contend with. It was not the end...it was only the beginning.

It was the fate of the gambler at best...winner takes all.

CHAPTER IV

THE FRIENDS OF
THE CHILDREN OF VIETNAM:
THE BEGINNING

"God will not look you over for medals, degrees and diplomas, but for scars."

– Elbert Hubbard

Poverty and misery became a way of life in Indochina long before the American involvement, but the tide of human suffering that erupted during the Vietnam war years swept the homeless children into a swift current of unprecedented cruelty. For the orphans who lived in the streets, more often with a sibling at their side or an infant strapped to their back, there existed a sense of hopelessness. Vietnam had become an ugly place. The oppressed had no hope for deliverance. There was no future, and death was everywhere. Unbeknown to the forgotten children, a small crusade was merging on the horizon...a crusade that would save thousands of them. And it started with just one man.

"Bac-si-mi," Vietnamese for American doctor, is what they called him. A 49-year-old internist from Denver, Colorado, Dr. Theodore K. Gleichman was a tall, distinguished and handsome man, graying at the temples. His big love was the hours he spent at the My Tho Orphanage in the Delta, which was overcrowded with small babies and children. He was assigned to the civilian hospital in the area but found time to steal away for a few hours to help at the foundling home where conditions were also poor. Infants were abandoned by their mothers in the hope that their babies would be well cared for and safe in the big orphanage building. It seemed far more secure to them than the jungle village from which they came. The tragedy was that eighty percent of the babies died before they were six months old from lack of nutrition and medical care.

Any attempt to relieve human suffering in southeast Asia was like trying to empty the ocean with an eyedropper. Ted Gleichman was no stranger to the effort. As a young physician he had served as a battalion surgeon in the Burma-India-China Theater during World War II and was well acquainted with the disheartening attempts to change medical conditions in that part of the world. He was sure that there had been no improvements when the Vietnam War surfaced.

Gleichman's desire was not to be where the action was, but to be where the need was. A course proceeding to this point compelled him to enlist in the Volunteer Physicians for Vietnam Program (VPVN). The program was a medical mission under the auspices of the United States Agency for International Development (USAID), implemented in July of 1965. Recruiting was handled by the American Medical Association.

Dr. Gleichman's Denver practice was prosperous, his own children were grown, and he found a need within himself to respond to the call to serve the two-month tour required of each volunteer. Though only a short eight weeks, they were exhausting. Doctors worked around the clock, seven days a week, under emergency conditions with inferior equipment and a lack of supplies. Often, they worked under fire, and always with the threat of Viet Cong attack. Gleichman was not certain what impact such a short tour would have on improving health conditions in the country, and like so many other physicians, he could not leave his practice or family indefinitely. The financial compensation offered for the services that Theodore K. Gleichman, M.D., contracted for assignment to Vietnam in October, 1966, were minimal. Each physician received a round-trip ticket and $50,000 worth of government insurance. Individuals attempting to take out additional private policies were turned down by every insurance company because Vietnam was too "risky." They were not paid salaries but did receive $10-a-day living allowance. All other expenses, plus any loss incurred by their absence from the States, came out of their own pockets. It was estimated that it cost USAID approximately $2000 to have an American physician in Vietnam for two months, cheap by any standards for a medical professional and the services they provided. On the other hand, physicians individually lost in excess of $10,000 a month income from an average practice during the two-month stay in the war zone.

But the experience the volunteers acquired in medical and surgical practice helped offset the loss in finances. Unusual diseases and fungus infections that they would never encounter in their stateside practices were treated on a regular basis. The incidence of diseases and blindness was also remarkable. The older people usually suffered from injury and trachoma, and many children experienced war-related injuries.

As many as 150 patients were treated and seen by a physician daily. The surgical load (mostly war casualties) was demanding and far beyond the numbers they would encounter in any busy metropolitan hospital. The tremendous workload was the reason most volunteers stayed only for two months. Some physicians felt the strain and returned to the United States before the completion of their contracts, while others felt challenged by the circumstances and returned for repeated tours.

Despite the lack of financial compensation, physicians like Gleichman responded from all over the United States, Canal Zone and even Puerto Rico for the tours. Over one thousand physicians served tours in Vietnam over the years until the spring of 1975.

South Vietnam had only 900 Vietnamese doctors; about 600 of those were occupied with military government duties, leaving about 300 to serve the 14 million civilians. With a war in progress, USAID sought to relieve this tremendous imbalance and developed the rotation program of American doctors for the short tours. The doctors were assigned to one of the 30 civilian hospitals in the 45 provinces of South Vietnam, and the tours varied from regional facilities to small rural hospitals in the central highlands. The Delta area of South Vietnam where Gleichman was stationed utilized the greatest number of VPVNs. Most of the American military units were in areas north of Saigon. Fewer Americans were stationed in the Mekong Delta where the Vietnamese were fighting the war. American advisors provided helicopter support needed by the Vietnam Army for their operations in the area.

More than a third of the 14 million people in South Vietnam at the time were living in the Mekong Delta, having migrated there from the more densely populated regions to the north. It was considered the richest land in all of Vietnam and was the center of the South

Vietnamese economy for a long time.

The Delta was "hell-hot," like a blast from opening an oven door—the kind of searing heat that sucks the breath from your lungs. Early morning temperatures would hit 110 degrees and high noon was unbearable. In addition to the heat, it was very humid. Mildew spread like cancer and was impossible to avoid. Insects ate human flesh, and the earth actually squished as one walked upon it. The cultural shock for many of the physicians never subsided throughout their tour. The few who served in Asian countries during their military careers were acquainted with the customs, climate and the remoteness. But for those who had not served in the Southwest Pacific Theater, each day was a new experience in discomfort. Any second thought regarding their involvement as to "what am I doing here?" would soon disintegrate as many newcomers found themselves gowned and performing surgery within the hour of reaching their assigned destinations.

Hospitals overflowed with civilian casualties brought in every day from little villages where there was fighting. The Viet Cong infiltration was deep in the Delta and consequently there was much confrontation. American and South Vietnamese rescue teams shuttled little Vietnamese buses to make the daily runs with the wounded. The incoming casualties never ceased, and physicians got numb quickly just from the sheer numbers that stretched out on litters, on the floors and placed in any unoccupied spot. In attempting to keep up with the flow, Gleichman's thoughts would wander back to his ocean-eyedropper theory.

Many of the patients were Viet Cong posing as civilians. Many of those brought to the hospitals suffered from bullet wounds, but the majority were injured by mines, booby traps or mortar fire, the usual Viet Cong weapons. It was a war of amputations. The doctors considered removing a bullet minor; people with arms and legs blown off were major. Non-war casualties had to wait for treatment, sometimes as long as two or three weeks, because the staff was too busy with emergencies.

Often, peasants came out of the jungle after days of hard travel to the hospitals, their wounds open, seething with maggots, gangrenous, and the patient in irreversible shock. Travel at night in Vietnam was impossible due to Viet Cong activity. As a result, the Americans left the hospitals after sundown and there was no staff or security to monitor the facilities. When people died in the night, the survivor in the same bed would start screaming, and sometimes the body would be removed by a janitor, but usually the dead were not discovered until morning. Due to the overcrowded conditions, beds were occupied by two, sometimes three patients, and if they were children, four would share a bed.

Fortunately, none of the doctors volunteering for Project Vietnam had been injured, but they were always aware that Viet Cong guerrillas could easily infiltrate the hospital and attack them. Or worse, a patient who was a Viet Cong could easily have stuck a knife into them any time they leaned over a bed.

The My Tho Hospital was the only one in the province and was originally constructed by the French sixty years before. Since that time, the hospital had undergone remodeling and additional buildings were added to house clinics and laboratories and other support systems. The main surgical and medical building housed over 225 additional beds. More beds were located in separate buildings for communicable diseases, tuberculosis, pediatrics and maternity cases.

Located in Dinh Tuong Province, My Tho bulged with a population of 90,000 people. Gleichman was one of the two American doctors assigned there, sharing responsibility for the 750 to 1,000 patients crammed into the old 500-bed institution. Additionally, it was staffed with three Vietnamese doctors, four Filipino physicians, and two American nurses. The remainder of the staff was Vietnamese.

The time Gleichman spent at the hospital consumed all of his waking hours. Treating civilians was relegated to weekend hamlet-hopping in helicopters. On these trips into the district, the team would organize mass immunizations for cholera, smallpox, and typhoid, seeing as many as 250 people on sick call at each village. Immunization registers were unheard of and impossible to implement. Therefore, civilians were inoculated without any record of what they previously had.

It was a hectic schedule, but as someone once said, "work is love made visible." Gleichman shared that feeling, but he wanted something more, and he was to find it at the orphanage.

The My Tho orphanage was a two-story concrete structure run by eight native Catholic nuns. They took care of 250 children and babies and had an additional 200 old men and women who were sick, helpless, and had no place else to go.

Blue shutters covered the windows of the building, and the French structure projected an air of dignity. The cobblestone courtyard was dominated by a venerated shrine of the Blessed Virgin, with trees and vegetation dotting the landscape. A high concrete wall surrounded the compound and a humble sign hung over the street entrance.

The nuns were elated by the interest Gleichman took in their mission and the emotion he openly showed toward the children. A doctor becomes seasoned by the visibility of internal human organs, blood and suffering, but the needless loss of a new life reaches into the depths of him and bothers him forever. In taking off hopelessly mangled arms and legs, there is no prostheses to offer. There were so many children without legs, with improvised crutches, begging in the streets. The orphanage could not house them all. A child without arms or legs had nothing; there was no place for him. If he had no family, he starved, and since room had to be made for new casualties at the hospital, he was discharged to the boundaries of "nowhere" in the streets.

Workers at the orphanage were without adequate supplies, and food consisted of powdered milk and rice. Vitamins, medications, diapers, clothing, blankets and other daily necessities were absent. There wasn't even a medical book on the premises. Without the basic necessities and so many sick around them needing care and attention, even healthy-born babies withered and died.

Hookworms were found in practically all of the children, and twenty-five percent exhibited enlarged spleens due to malaria. Ascites and nephritis, along with poliomyelitis, were also common, as were all sorts of staph-skin infections.

About thirty percent had advanced cases of tuberculosis and cholera. Typhoid, hepatitis and meningitis were prevalent, as was almost everything found in a medical book. Yet, anybody who needed help and appeared at the orphanage door was taken in if there was still room on the floor to throw another sleeping mat.

So moved by the experience, Gleichman began to tape letters of his experiences in My Tho and send them back to Denver to be distributed among his peers and patients.

In his own words, he tried to convey what he was experiencing:

> "I will try to tell you something about the orphanage where I work in the afternoon. This is one of the most fascinating places I have seen in my life and also one of the saddest at the

same time. The orphanage houses about 450 people, including some 250 children. There are about 120 children who are orphans, anywhere from a few days old to school age, plus 60 to 70 who are deaf-mutes and who they (the staff) are attempting to teach to speak. There are also several hundred old people, mentally deficient, crippled, senile, etc. The only ones I seem to have presented to me to treat are the small children and infants. There is a wonderful Vietnamese nun who takes care of them. She has the most perfect Asian face, framed by her white nun's habit, and seems to know and really care about these poor children. I have never seen such evidence of malnutrition, disease, and neglect in my life as I see each day in the fifteen to twenty babies that she presents to me. There may be many more who need care, but I have the feeling that she will only show me a certain number for fear that I will become overburdened and not appear on the scene.

After working at the orphanage for a couple of weeks, I asked the nun what the mortality rate was, and she said 80%. I could not believe my ears and asked for the records, which she produced with some difficulty, and I am sure this figure is correct. I made some counts on it just for the year 1966, and of nineteen babies admitted in January, eighteen are already dead. Of twenty-eight admitted in February, twenty-three are already dead, three were adopted out or reclaimed by the parents, and two are still alive in the orphanage. How one nun with a couple of half-witted or deaf-mute girls to assist her can possibly take care of 90 to 100 babies, many of whom are sick, and give them the shots, treatments, and medications that I order, is beyond me. I am delighted that she does as well as she does, especially since she really is not a nurse and has just been learning on the job."

The response from his friends back home was overwhelming—they all wanted to help. Many sent him some of the necessities he was lacking.

The months of Gleichman's tour, October and November of 1966, raced by, and at the completion of his contract he embarked for home. Just how grueling the assignment was proved to be evident by the fact that en route home in December, he suffered a mild heart attack and was hospitalized in Hong Kong. When he returned to Denver on New Year's Eve, 1966, he was determined to do something to help the thousands of orphans.

Despite that he was under strict medical orders to rest before resuming his large practice, Gleichman devoted his energies during the early months of 1967 to making speeches about Vietnam before civic groups and local clubs. He was obsessed with the subject and talked about it every chance he had to anyone who would listen.

After his departure from My Tho, several army medics he befriended took over the orphanage visits he had started, and his communication with them from Denver dramatically increased. It started out on a small scale, and packages were sent to the APO address in care of reliable individuals who were trustworthy in getting the supplies to the orphanage.

Realizing there was a need for an organization to help as many kids as it could through honest intermediaries, Gleichman founded the Friends of the Children of Vietnam (FCVN). In addition to talking to fellow physicians, patients, parishioners in his church, and friends, he developed a slide show and gave presentations to organizations which demonstrated an interest. It was a beginning.

Furthermore, it was no mere coincidence when incorporation papers for the organization were filed in March, 1967, that the roster of officers sounded like a roll call of Gleichman's friends in Denver. In addition to himself, they included his lawyer, William Klas; Doris Brown, a patient; Bill Beier, President of the Englewood Lions Club; and Leonard Pike of the First Universalist Church. The group's first office was in the basement of the church, and it became a storage and shipping area as well.

With the overwhelming response, FCVN began to think in terms of brochures and general appeals for gifts. Then the organization suffered a personal loss when Bill Klas, the president of the group, was killed in a light plane crash. Gleichman assumed the presidency himself and moved the headquarters into the basement of 1919 South University Boulevard where he had his office. By the end of 1967, the group was sending supplies to not only the My Tho Orphanage, but to individuals within South Vietnam who had made requests and pleas for assistance. FCVN began to expand on both sides of the ocean.

There was still no indication of the things that were to come or how big and for how long the project would last. There was only the determination to keep it going as long as it filled a need.

In the beginning the support to the orphanages was trivial...a dozen sweatshirts for beggar boys, a case of soap for an orphanage, a few dozen diapers for the children at My Tho. The contributions provided a funnel to Vietnam for the people who wanted to help, and the FCVN efforts were supporting that small effort.

As a result of this support, within a short time, the death rate among infants at My Tho alone dropped fifty percent. Ted Gleichman had begun a movement that soon attracted hundreds of volunteers to the plight of the orphans. Thousands of children would be saved as a result of the involvement of an American doctor who was troubled by the loss of one small life.

As Gleichman's health improved, his practice began to make more demands on his time. For more than a year, the small group continued to send supplies and donations to the orphanages. From time to time it attracted the attention of local Denverites who assisted in the collection and packaging of supplies for shipment. Eventually, as the American military involvement increased, FCVN took a low profile. The Vietnam War became unpopular. The organization remained small, as a part-time endeavor with a few board members and a small treasury. There were no plans to beef up the agency to what it was to become in the future with new directors.

During this period, when Gleichman's involvement was dwindling, two women emerged who were to become deeply committed, not only with the functions of supply, but with the orphans themselves.

LeSanne Buchanan of Denver and Wende Grant of Boulder, Colorado, both housewives, were deeply interested in the children of Vietnam and had a desire to adopt orphans and bring them to America.

Buchanan, a woman of deep conviction, was the mother of three small youngsters; her husband John was a schoolteacher. She felt a reverent gratitude in her role as a parent and needed to expand her good fortune by offering a home to the children of war. So determined in her effort to better the conditions in Vietnam for children, she contacted anyone who could, and would, talk to her about adopting a Vietnamese child.

During the sixties, many organizations, such as the Pearl Buck Foundation, whom Buchanan had contacted, were soliciting funds to maintain the upkeep of children in many foreign lands. But, as far as she could determine, none were processing orphans from Vietnam to homes in the United States. Laws concerning the adoption of a foreign child in 1967 were complicated and enmeshed in red tape and delays.

Ted Gleichman was LeSanne Buchanan's bridge to accomplishing her desire for a Vietnamese child. He put her in contact with Rosemary Taylor, an Australian woman who had been working for several years in Vietnam under the sponsorship of a church group in her country. She acted as an intermediary between adoptive parents and five South Vietnamese orphanages. Although she was not a doctor or a nurse, her reputation for saving children was widespread in Vietnam, and FCVN had been sending supplies to the facilities with which she was affiliated. Taylor was anxious to place some of the abandoned children in good homes, hopefully out of Vietnam, and FCVN in Colorado was receptive to assisting her in adoptions. It was a cooperative effort that benefited both parties. Rosemary Taylor was now considered to be FCVN's affiliate in Vietnam.

Buchanan's written request for a child was favorably received by Taylor, and it was the beginning of a long complex process on three fronts, involving immigration, social services, and the red tape of the Vietnamese government.

The adoption of a Vietnamese child in the United States was unheard of in the late sixties, and a Denver-area social services agency that eventually agreed to do the home study was in a dilemma as to why the Buchanans wanted an Asian child. Their naiveté was ignoring the availability of infant babies on the American scene and thinking there was only a surplus of older, handicapped and hard-to-place children available in America for adoption.

Immigration proved to be even less encouraging. They admitted to delays in accepting applications and interviews, and in discussing their backlog, they made the error of alluding to a family in Greeley, Colorado, who had been waiting five months to begin the immigration process for the adoption of a Vietnamese child. This inadvertent slip of the tongue by the immigration official angered Buchanan to a point where she lost her temper and admonished the agency, questioning not only their efficiency but their morality as well. She demanded to know how the official managed to sleep at night knowing there were at least two children who could die because he did not take a serious interest in his work.

The criticism struck a nerve. Later that same evening, as Buchanan was bathing her children, the doorbell rang. Standing on her doorstep, with a briefcase in hand, was the immigration official Buchanan had reprimanded earlier that day. He apologized and expressed his willingness to begin the immigration process.

"Ma'am, I've been up to Greeley today. I sure heard some strong language..."

It was Buchanan's first tangle with the establishment, and as time would prove, it would not be her last encounter with state and social agencies.

Inasmuch as Rosemary Taylor at that point in time was not licensed or affiliated with a licensed adoption agency, the mechanics involved proved tedious. Immigration requested a special study of the adoptive child, and an official was sent to Saigon from Manila expressly to investigate the background of the orphan up for adoption. Verification that the child had no family was essential. As a result of the long process and the distance between agencies, the Buchanans found they had to start the adoption procedure long before the child they selected was born, and because of the red tape involved, the infant was nine and a half months old by the time he reached his new home in Denver.

Rosemary Taylor personally escorted their baby to Denver with several other children she was placing in American homes. Timmy, as the Buchanans called him, was the first child to have been adopted in the United States by this new "mail-order" process. The Buchanans later adopted two more Vietnamese children.

LeSanne Buchanan found a change in herself as a direct result of the drawn-out adoption process. She wanted a Vietnamese child desperately and began to realize that she must do something to keep him alive until she got him. She began by cutting into her grocery budget and sending small shoe boxes of supplies to the orphanage caring for Timmy. The Buchanans were not well-to-do, and with three small children to provide for, the frequently sent package was a sacrifice shared by the whole family. As a result, LeSanne became more involved and committed to the FCVN purpose, and in her effort to adopt, became associated with more people who were interested in obtaining Vietnamese children. It expanded into a network of people calling each other to exchange information and encouragement to those who found the red tape frustrating. Initially they got together over coffee to discuss their mutual interests and emerged as a group of men and women who truly liked each other.

When it became apparent to this small group that they needed more of an organization to receive and channel money and supplies, they decided to formalize their objectives, and they looked to FCVN as a role model.

FCVN was becoming a defunct organization from a lack of new members and was short on individuals who could donate the time required. But it had it all—a charter, tax exempt status, a good reputation, and invaluable connections. The "coffee group" was so eager and sincere in their desire to bring children to the United States, in addition to supplying provisions for the orphans who would remain there, they approached FCVN explaining their goals and their desire to become involved in the work.

Gleichman's job was done at this point, and he secretly hoped that new blood would come along to follow in his mission to halt the appalling death rate of infants and children in Vietnam. When Gleichman and the remaining board members of FCVN agreed to turn over the reins of their organization to the new group, they had no idea that it would grow to such proportions and that chapters would begin throughout the United States and Europe.

LeSanne Buchanan then became President of FCVN and Wende Grant became Vice President. The old guard was pleased to see the work they had started expand in a new direction. Since they could not provide the time and effort themselves, it was a compliment to see a fresh new group take up the torch and continue with the momentous tasks they had begun.

With the formation of the new group, new goals sprang forth and enthusiasm grew. Friends and relatives of the group became involved, and word of the good work spread throughout the United States through letters and personal calls. Small chapters began to spring up and were organized in many parts of the country. Checks, small at first, then larger, began finding their way to the headquarters in Denver, which was LeSanne Buchanan's living room. FCVN encouraged the development of new chapters, and as a result, more orphanages in Vietnam benefited by the flow of supplies.

Around this time, Wende Grant and Buchanan decided to travel to Vietnam to view first hand what was happening there and to meet some of the people who were involved with the orphanages. They found that it was time to set up a formal organization in that country, to open a local bank account, file the necessary papers with the Saigon government, and to establish themselves as an organization representing their official designation, Friends of the Children of Vietnam.

FCVN had grown into a national organization by 1970-71, and it was now necessary to set up the corporate structure in the country it was servicing.

What Buchanan and Grant witnessed in Vietnam only confirmed their earlier suspicions—which they saw depicted in Gleichman's slides—that the children in that country were in danger. A never-ending stream of unwanted, hungry children turned up at the child care centers and orphanages. The task before them was monumental. Only an experienced corporation with limitless funds would have taken on the project. Yet, due to the naiveté of two women who were impressed with the work done by Rosemary Taylor, they returned home with a new found spirit and determination to push on with a new ferocity to save the children of Vietnam. Seeking out good homes in America for the unwanted orphans became an obsession.

Without any recruitment, the Denver FCVN organization had grown to about seventy members. It was a unique group of dedicated individuals drawn from all professions. They held formal meetings and had an agenda to establish written policies and procedures. But for the most part, it was an exchange of ideas and information about what was going on in the many orphanages receiving support services from the agency.

FCVN was becoming internationally known, and big money started to pour into the coffers. It seemed that everyone wanted to help, and it became easy to join. Strangers showed up to help pack boxes and were invited to join.

Of course, involvement in Vietnam also drew criticism, and many volunteers were burdened with trying to offer explanations and justification to family members and friends who did not understand their fervent commitment to children in the unpopular country. With the availability of so many American handicapped children to adopt, it was difficult for some friends to rationalize why it was necessary to give aid to foreign children and sometimes even children of the enemy.

To complicate matters, FCVN began to attract people who wanted power and who recognized the potential of this young organization in that adoptions were big business and lucrative. Entrepreneurs from various factions attended meetings and witnessed what they felt was a lack of sophistication in business affairs, one of which was not having professional offices. In the absence of formality, it was easy to assume that the functional structure consisted of a group of amateurs who had suddenly found themselves holding the brass ring in the adoption stakes.

With its international recognition, as well as important connections, critics insinuated that the current officers did not have the capabilities to meet the challenge of expansion. Therefore, attempts were initiated to rally new members and outsiders to put pressure for change in the organization. A power base is a foothold on authority and success, and FCVN was to become a battleground of internal strife and division as a result of this influence from outsiders.

The organization was plagued with offers from professionals to head up the agency for a substantial fee. Other individuals promised millions of dollars in fundraising and vowed to establish FCVN as a leader in the international adoption market.

It seemed that everyone had a plan.

All the external interest and influence proved threatening to FCVN. It stimulated a lusty appetite within the group for some who felt that there could be some credibility to the promises and who were convinced that the time had come to take it to another level.

It didn't take much to evaluate and put motives in order. The general feeling was that FCVN had been struggling to get organized and worked relentlessly to get people involved to commit for an extended period of time. Then suddenly, when success and recognition were forthcoming, others wanted to take control.

With all that was happening, and considering the wide diversification of the personalities within the organization, the resentment that surfaced was predictable. There was a consensus among those who had done all the groundwork and suffered the frustrations of slow growth that others wanted to take it from them just as they were finally succeeding. The feeling was suspect and disheartening.

"It had started as a small group of only five couples who wanted to do a totally unselfish thing to help children who had no one to turn to. Then, overnight, it exploded into a bandwagon on which others who had needs of their own to fulfill wanted to jump on." This was the final reflection of LeSanne Buchanan years later when she was far removed from the organization and assessed what had happened during her tenure as president.

The prospect of outsiders coming into the organization to seize control was frightening. Great mistrust developed regarding new people wanting to join, and it began to cause internal stress and disagreement in the once cohesive group. It was disheartening to think of all the energy that was going into political dissension when children half the world away were in need of these adults pulling together.

The five original couples who picked up the banner from Ted Gleichman's group weathered the early organizational frustrations and tried to hang on to fend off the new upheaval. Finally, the power struggle grew to such proportions that it dominated their lives.

Simultaneously, organizational problems surfaced in Vietnam itself. Rosemary Taylor was officially the FCVN Director of Overseas Operations and in full control of the mission from that end. She was totally dedicated and had a well-earned reputation recognized by various governmental agencies in Vietnam, and she was doing a remarkable job under all the pressures and dangers imposed upon her. However, problems concerning policy and procedure with the home office began to surface. Having been there for several years, she was aware of on-site needs and priorities and began to differ with her Denver cohorts who were 10,000 miles away and, most of whom, had never been to Vietnam.

From FCVN's point of view, with an expanded organization and the additional responsibilities it was assuming in the area of adoptions, board members wanted a larger voice in the Vietnam decisions as well as paperwork accountability to substantiate the distribution of thousands of dollars. There was some speculation that the supplies and equipment were not arriving— that they were being pilfered at the docks and that a good percentage ended up on the black market. Equally important were other unresolved issues regarding the adoption process and expenses handled exclusively by the Denver office.

If one were to understand the position of Rosemary Taylor, who was under the stress of the battle zone, and the changes that were occurring within FCVN, it is conceivable that there was some sort of communication breakdown between Denver and Vietnam.

At some point during all the hard politics, Taylor came to the United States. FCVN had set up a press conference in her honor, expressly to give her an opportunity to inform the public about the plight of the orphans. The fact that Taylor did not grant interviews was not considered. She saw the media as intrusive. In the past, Taylor had to physically and verbally fend off aggressive newsmen as she made her way through airports with children. In Denver, the media waited in the conference room, but she herself declined to put in an appearance. There was no explanation given, and the separation of FCVN and Taylor soon transpired.

All the issues would remain clouded and the parties involved would be guarded for years to come. The result was the same, however; everybody began to feel differently about how the organization was managed and about each other. The group's split was inevitable, and it was the only alternative under these grave circumstances. However, the mission of saving the children was to be salvaged at all costs.

On October 27, 1973, FCVN issued a statement of position, which was a formal attempt to justify the reorganization of the agency and to announce the separation of the two major functions, adoption and Vietnam orphanage support.

The reasons cited for the separation were administrative. FCVN emphasized that it had become difficult for the board to meet the needs of an adoption agency and, at the same time, fill the demands of the expanded programs (of fundraising, life support, chapter relations, and a myriad of related functions.)

Therefore, a legal and administrative separation between the adoption agency and other FCVN activities was deemed desirable in the interest of furthering both activities.

Friends For All Children (FFAC) became the name of the new group designated to handle adoptions, and Wende Grant served as its new director, with Rosemary Taylor affiliated as its Director of Overseas Operations. In addition to agreeing to transfer all adoption inquiries, finances, arrangements, applications and paperwork to FFAC, FCVN further agreed to cooperate in assisting the new corporation in securing a license to operate as an adoption agency in the State of Colorado. (FCVN already possessed those credentials.)

Additionally, FCVN did something they had been criticized for not doing in the past—they opened a formal office at 600 Gilpin Street in Denver.

LeSanne Buchanan remained president of the organization, but Rosemary Taylor's new affiliation with the newly-formed FFAC group left a vacancy in the Vietnam operations. A supply officer was a priority but not feasible until the fires simmered down and the right person could be found. The newcomer to Vietnam would have a monumental task restructuring the organization previously administered by Taylor.

Further, there was a difference in philosophy between the women running both organizations. Wende Grant leaned heavily toward the adoption unit and wanted to concentrate on getting the adoptable children out of Vietnam to homes in America. Buchanan wanted to save more than the kids that were adoptable; she wanted to continue to give aid to those children who would never leave Vietnam. They became two halves to make a cohesive whole unit. It should have worked, but it didn't. Some members of the group took sides on the issues and followed the philosophy with which they were most comfortable. The volunteers could not remain interested in the mission by just extending aid and packing boxes because so many of the people involved in this really wanted children themselves. As a direct result, FCVN was to soon resurrect the adoption agency function within their organization. This placed an additional strain on the agreement made during the split.

For awhile both organizations continued to work together, but the pain of the split, the disagreements, and the feeling of competition emerged. FCVN did not find complete fulfillment in just granting aid and procuring supplies. FFAC found that support from FCVN was dwindling. In the past, they had reaped the benefits of FCVN's fundraising efforts. Finally, an impasse occurred. FCVN was already established as an adoption agency with the government of South Vietnam. It made a recommendation and assisted FFAC in getting their own adoption agency status, and when licensing to FFAC was achieved, there was a permanent break in the relationships, never to be mended. As a result of the split, FFAC faced serious financial problems. Rents on the buildings were due, supplies needed replenishing, and a new source of income had to be found. Conversely, FCVN was left without children to fill their adoption applications.

In Vietnam, however, the split was not public knowledge for some time. Many Embassy and government agency people continued to assume that Rosemary Taylor headed up the FCVN operation there and had merely changed the name to expand services to children of all nations. Because of the long years of its operation, FCVN was well known and popular. When the new name FFAC surfaced in Vietnam, it did not register with affiliates, nor was it recognized as a separate entity. The assumption worked to the advantage of the new organization (FFAC), however, this issue placed additional strain on the

already existing conflict between the two groups. Taylor acknowledges in her book, *Orphans of War,* that "the closeness of the name
was later to cause some confusion when both organizations were
arranging the adoption of Vietnamese orphans." FCVN, too, saw the
choice of a similar name as a conflict. FFAC attests the similarity was
chosen to retain the association with FCVN in their continuation to
place children under FFAC's contract in Vietnam. The end result did
not justify the means...both FCVN and FFAC ended up as two separate entities, duplicating services. It was all for naught.

There was little clarification about the relationship between FCVN
and Rosemary Taylor, which was evident when Ross Meador arrived
in Vietnam as the new organizer of the FCVN contingent there. Only
nineteen years old, he had been engaged as the new supply officer in
February, 1974. But because Taylor had been in Vietnam for many
years and had long established herself through lasting relationships
with various agencies as well as officials, it presented problems for
Meador. He was thought of as "the new kid on the street" (and one
with long hair at that), and thus was associated with the flower children—those who objected to the war and America's involvement. Yet
while his acceptance by the "old guard" was slow, it eventually did
come after Meador proved himself through hard work and courageous
effort.

Emotionally drained, defeated, and stressed out from the split, the
original five couples that took over the FCVN organization from Ted
Gleichman's group eventually withdrew altogether, but not before
more internal discontent arose. There were accusations and counter
accusations regarding abuse of power and violations to the policy
structure set down by the group.

There may have been moments in the lives of the original five
couples where they felt a loss and a sense that they missed the "pay
off" of their labor...which was the thrill of bringing the children out.
But ultimately, with all the legal hassles and litigation that would erupt
after the airlift, they may also have realized they were spared from the
stress of that involvement and may have been thankful they relinquished their authority. What is important is that all the families originally participating in carrying on the organization from Ted
Gleichman remained intact and happy; not so with many others who
were involved in Operation Babylift. Many couples were to divorce,
some individuals died young, and many never regained the peace of

mind they had before the whole encounter. For some, the emotion and grief of the project was too great...the pain, depression, anger and even denial of the events themselves, would never end.

Perhaps the time had come for the third wave of heroes to enter the scene—those with thicker skins to weather that which was about to happen. More tragedy, dissension, and trouble would brew over the entire Babylift effort.

LeSanne Buchanan believed that fate had intervened and placed her in that particular place at that particular time. Had she and Wende Grant not possessed the fortitude, the organization may have been lost with the diminished activity of Ted Gleichman's group, Friends of the Children of Vietnam—from which, ironically, FFAC found its beginning.

Years later, in reviewing it all, Buchanan looked back at her departure from FCVN as the end of her usefulness, and she accepted it. "In the realm of reasoning, it very often takes individuals with strong egos—those with overwhelming confidence—to pull off such an event. The humble, the moderately insecure, and those who had no stomach for carrying a big ax, would be trampled upon and would not survive the onslaught of adversity."

Meekness is not weakness. It is sometimes smartness.

CHAPTER V

"MISTER ROSS"

"If a man does not keep pace with his companions, perhaps it is because he hears a different drummer. Let him step to the music which he hears, however measured or far away."

– Thoreau

Although Ed Daly's maverick flight from Vietnam captivated international attention, not all of the Babylift evacuations were as dramatic. Many went unnoticed, yet each was decidedly different.

It was a familiar scene and a vivid one at Tan Son Nhut Airport, one that was repeated daily during the four weeks of April, 1975. Usually a late afternoon shower passed over the airfield. Lingering raindrops glistened like tiny rainbows before they slithered into the puddles below the Pan American Jet. A build-up of young voices heard in the distance alerted a waiting crew that children were racing across the tarmac.

"We're here!" Ross Meador sighed in relief as he edged the vehicle bearing the U.S. Embassy seal closer to the ramp. He had lost count of how many of these trips to the airport he had made during those last days in April.

"Next stop, America!" he shouted above the noise coming from the small bodies, who by now were curiously half-hanging-out the open windows.

One by one the anxious children, some crying, jumped down from the bottom step of the bus, each trying to outmaneuver the youngster before them. It was a gigantic leap, both feet hitting the ground, a game they repeated whenever the occasion of a bus ride provided for it. This time, for sure, the last jump had a more definite significance.

Meador carefully checked the tag of each child to a master list in his hand. As he grabbed the arm of a small toddler about to attempt a feat too high for him, he could not find an identification band. They weren't difficult to remove, and Meador had been careful to fit them so they could not easily slip over the children's wrists.

Halting the disembarking procedure, he hurriedly jumped on the bus and frantically patrolled the floor for a sign of the missing tag. The child did not look familiar to him. Realizing the dilemma, one of the eight-year-olds spurted out, "Mister Ross, he no come from house...he not us. Papasan pushed him through window when we stop on road..and we take him."

The youngster was tugging his arms to demonstrate. "Him go to America, too!"

The look on Meador's face reaffirmed to them that they had played a joke on him, and it worked. Ross was aware that incidents like this frequently happened. He wasn't prepared for it himself.

Meador's first inclination was to gasp, "Oh, my God!" He lifted the still smiling stowaway in his arms. It was obvious the boy was happy to be with the children, wherever they were going. The child was too young to understand and babbled unintelligibly as Meador tried to question him.

"Oh, God..." Meador repeated to himself over and over. He was stunned. He stared down the flight line...searching, hoping a frantic parent would rush forward to claim the toddler. But only the long, empty stretch of runway and the jungle horizon met his eyes.

Futility grabbed him as he turned and walked to the ramp of the plane, slowly measuring each step as a painful mistake in the child's life. There would be no blood ties in the child's future, and, though there would be love and comfort, there would also be an emptiness— a lifetime filled with unanswered questions and perpetual searching. Instinctively, and without words, a volunteer reached for the child and took him back to the bus. The absence of the required documents for each child's departure hindered the grandfather's ploy to get the child on the airlift.

To not place the boy on the plane was one of the heartrendering decisions Meador had found himself making as Co-Director of Overseas Operations for FCVN.

The faint smile he bore was for the children's sake. Inside, Meador was devastated. He had not yet come to terms with the every-day abandonment of children, particularly those with families. During these last days, the sheer numbers overwhelmed him. The power to change a child's destiny was like playing God. There are rules about that sort of thing...but, considering the time, the place...the war,...rules of conduct were discarded.

Ross Meador had been in Vietnam for fourteen months, working for the cause of the orphaned children, when the apocalyptic events began to infiltrate Saigon. He was only twenty years old, but the year had made him feel like an old man. Assuming the responsibility for hundreds of babies was beyond the scope of his experience. It happened quite unexpectedly and filled him with apprehension.

A summer program abroad during high school had given him an appetite to see the world. So serious was his desire, in fact, that he relinquished college in favor of a job at the Salk Institute, where he planned to generate funds for his vagabond adventure. However, his dream of traveling was cut short when he went to Mexico and discovered the expense was far greater than he had anticipated.

There were other ways to achieve his dream. He could join the Army and opt for an overseas tour, or seek employment in an organization with overseas operations. Since he was a committed conscientious objector, the latter was the appropriate course of action for him.

Information regarding FCVN came through a family friend. Excited about the prospect of traveling to Asia, Meador sought further information on the need for childcare workers and escorts through the friend's correspondence with an FFAC staff member. Edie de Chadenedes, who was an early childhood development specialist, was already on site in Vietnam. The response was discouraging. Conditions in that part of the world, with the country at war, were catastrophic. But, more importantly, Chadenedes intimated the shaky position and instability of the FCVN itself. For undetermined reasons, she stated there was "no longer an FCVN organization in Vietnam" and that there had been an abrupt halt to FCVN operations and that a new organization, FFAC, had taken over all the existing facilities.

It was the moment of crisis between Rosemary Taylor's group in Vietnam and the FCVN Headquarters in Denver, Colorado. Since there had been no official announcement in Saigon regarding the split, various liaison agencies continued to associate Taylor's name with FCVN. It wasn't until after the arrival of more FCVN volunteers, and their persistence in Saigon, that the Vietnam agencies came to realize that FCVN and FFAC were two distinctive organizations.

Despite the early discouraging correspondence from Vietnam, the information did not alter Meador's fascination with Asia. He felt a certain destiny magnetically drawing him to a continent where time seemed to stand still. He had a general impression of the job of a childcare worker and fantasized flying all over the world as a babysitter. It captured his imagination to a point where he devised an excuse to hitchhike to Denver to visit a sister (who was attending the University of Colorado) to make a personal contact with FCVN headquarters.

He made his pitch for a job in Vietnam from a gas station telephone booth. Having reached Al Westlake, who was then president of the group, Meador learned that FCVN was going through a restructuring process (the split with Taylor, undoubtedly) and that there were no jobs available until the re-organization was completed.

The response on the other end of the line sounded defeating. But Meador had "wit enough to keep himself warm," and his ingenious contrivance compelled him to boast, "Since I am going to Vietnam anyway, regardless of whether you give me a job or not, I am wondering if there isn't something I can do for you once I am there?"

The statement disarmed Westlake and captured him by surprise. "So, you're going there anyway?" It was an interesting thought. With that, Westlake drove to the service station to meet this aggressive young man who exemplified a certain type of courage. Taken aback by his long hair and youth, Westlake expressed doubt a second time.

"How old are you?" Westlake asked.

"Eighteen. Brainless, with courage," Ross replied.

There was no way of anticipating to what extent FCVN was assessing Meador's potential, so the next approach was to cancel any negative impressions by inflating his credentials.

First, he showed Westlake a letter of reference from the Salk Institute, complimentary but neglecting to qualify his particular duties. Meador also boasted he had medical experience as a nurse's aid.

Westlake was impressed, so he took Meador to the home of another FCVN board member who also came under the spell of the young man's candor and enthusiasm.

What was of value to the FCVN board may not have been the obvious determination of Ross Meador, but rather his aggressiveness and relaxed attitude about going to Vietnam. Additionally, he appeared to be healthy, eager, and not fazed by the low pay FCVN offered or by the dangers of war.

In fact, FCVN was in a desperate posture and in a struggle for its very survival in Vietnam. Rosemary Taylor's resignation left a serious void in the Saigon operation. Chapters had formed all over the country and were working toward the cause of the children in the orphanages. Unless re-organization occurred in Vietnam, there was a possibility that word of the split would filter out unfavorably; confidence in the entire organization was in jeopardy. Or worse, FFAC could sway the stateside chapters to their newly formed group. FCVN knew it was time to issue a position statement, but the immediate emergency was in filling the vacant post in Vietnam.

Along with vacating the Field Director's position, Taylor had taken charge of the four child care centers that FCVN had been financially assisting in Vietnam. FCVN had a waiting list of prospective adoptive parents anxious to receive a Vietnamese child. Taylor's departure interrupted the process since she had control of all the orphans, so FCVN had to re-establish a system of getting orphaned children to fill their adoption requests.

Equally important was receiving and dispatching supplies and equipment to Saigon monthly. Thousands of dollars worth of cargo was sent by the supporting chapters around the world, and many shipments were en route. If left unattended or unclaimed on the docks for any length of time, they would eventually be stolen or pilfered; tons of supplies were hopelessly tied-up in customs. The lack of FCVN personnel in Vietnam was a serious matter, indeed.

FCVN was in no position to haggle. It could take months of screening to find a newly qualified director, and most individuals seeking the job would probably expect a substantial salary for the war zone as well as a contract packed with benefits. Ross Meador was willing to depart as a volunteer, with an expense account, and to accept the volunteer's pittance for the mission. Meador's sincerity also disarmed any doubts the group may have had about him, and the discussion took the direction of: "this is what you will take on...then you will do this..." The comments were directives. He no longer was begging for a job. Reality compelled FCVN to hire him as the new supply officer for the Vietnam vacancy. They did not designate him as Co-Director of Overseas Orphanages just yet; however, it would be a position he was to occupy when an immediate need arose.

Hiring Meador was a practical solution to the crisis and would provide someone there immediately while the FCVN board deliberated and planned for a more permanent solution to the Saigon management problem.

If humor has its place, it certainly existed in Ross Meador's past employment record...the one he boasted to Al Westlake.

Since time was of the essence to get someone into the vacant FCVN position in Vietnam, no further reference or clarification was requested regarding either of his past positions. Meador neglected to define his nurse's aide experience (while he was in the eighth grade he worked in a nursing home, aiding the elderly and running errands for charge nurses). Also, he did not indicate that his job at the Salk Institute consisted of cleaning animal cages. Ross Meador could, and often did, recite the benefactors of his labor in his sleep: 3 goats, 18 chickens, 250 rabbits, 600 guinea pigs, 2,000 rats and 6,000 mice!

Weeks later, Meador was embarking on a new-life journey, one that would give substance to his existence. It would be the adventure that would cause him great emotional pain and place him in the order of heroes. It would be *his* life changing experience.

Flying out of San Francisco, the Pan American plane was filled with vacationers to Hawaii. As it proceeded on to Guam, it was filled with military men and their families, then on to the Philippines with a mixed manifest. A weird realization overcame Meador as the plane flew toward Saigon—except for five other passengers, the 747 was empty. Strangely enough, those passengers were older women who were returning escorts for children departing from Vietnam.

Upon arrival in Saigon, there was no one to greet Meador at Tan Son Nhut Airport. Christie Leivermann, who was on Rosemary Taylor's staff, was there to dispatch the women escorts and took pity on Meador's plight. It was apparent that the young man was not aware of the rivalry between the two organizations resulting from the split. In a gesture of fellowship, Leivermann took him to the FFAC offices at Rathaven Nursery. As a volunteer forsaking the comforts of home and family for the cause of the orphans, Meador was warmly welcomed by everyone.

It didn't take long for Meador to realize he had embarked upon a momentous task. The brief orientation he received before departure was inadequate, and by all accounts, he had good reason to feel he had been "thrown to the wolves." At first he tried to "feel-his-way-around." He didn't know what he was doing and in some manner he was critical of FCVN hiring him. He quickly realized he wasn't qualified for the momentous task. The poor introduction to such a meaningful and dangerous mission would have shattered the average person, but there was a special quality that had Meador not only digging into restructuring the FCVN Vietnam image but remaining in Vietnam longer than he expected. Later he was designated to the Co-Director's position (and would be the last FCVN volunteer to leave the country).

A place to live and a home base was a priority for Meador. FCVN made arrangements with My Friend's House, a non-profit charitable nutrition center in Saigon under the directorship of Don Scott of Massachusetts, assisted by an ex-Jesuit priest and a nurse, Guy and Diane Palmeri. My Friend's House nurtured abandoned children back to health and placed them in orphanages for adoption. The group was hard-working and dedicated. They derived a great deal of pride in saving the little lives and had sustained hope that they, too, would acquire an adoption license. Due to the restrictions of the Vietnamese government and their attitude toward foreign adoptions (they already looked upon the seven agencies already functioning in this capacity with skepticism), My Friend's House found their quest for an adoption license mangled in red tape. Despite the discouragement of not being able to achieve adoption status, the organization continued to do their merciful work until the war's end.

Other Americans pitched in to help FCVN. On the surface they may have appeared to be average people, but in reality they were unique. They left the safety and comfort of homes and careers in a prosperous safe land to seek purpose to their lives in the plight of the war orphans. Most did it without pay. The volunteers didn't receive a salary—just living expenses—and most paid for transportation to Vietnam themselves.

With the slow arrival of the new FCVN staff, exciting things began to happen. Since the four centers that Rosemary Taylor had in operation at the time of the split remained under the FFAC banner, FCVN had to begin again. FCVN recognized the importance of obtaining the support of agencies in Vietnam in order to re-establish themselves. Although they had the approval of the USAID in Washington, the Vietnam office was indifferent. Even after presenting credentials, that included a Vietnamese-approved adoption license issued years earlier (and before subsequent groups obtained one), FCVN was told that "they were not needed, and that there were already enough organizations in the country to care for the orphans." Further, it was stated that these other agencies had access to unlimited funding, and that the U.S. government had (in April 1974) allotted more than seven million dollars to provide for child welfare in Vietnam. The attitude of the official was duplicitous, and despite the lack of cooperation, FCVN prevailed. They not only established other large orphanages and child care facilities, but they reached out into the community to encourage Vietnamese women to keep their babies.

Soon more Americans came to Vietnam to work with the adoption agencies. A compulsion to visit the orphanage at Qui Nhon, from which Cherie Clark's adopted child came, drew her to Vietnam in early 1974. She witnessed a strong emotional encounter that left her with an intense desire that she couldn't escape. She returned to the U.S. to find herself loving the abandoned Vietnamese babies and the beautiful black babies she had seen huddled together in their cribs as much as she loved her own fair children.

She wondered what would become of all the sick, diseased and dying children she had seen. As a nurse, Clark had the capability to do something about it. Her response to the crisis resulted in her returning to Vietnam with her husband and children to aid FCVN in its fight for life. Along with Ross Meador, she was named Co-Director of Overseas Operations for FCVN.

Tom Clark, Cherie's husband, had taken a one-year sabbatical from his position with IBM and was in full support of his wife's obsession to save the forgotten children of the war. After the fall of Vietnam, however, their lives took separate paths. Tom returned to his career at IBM, in the States, but Cherie departed to India where she began her Mission of Hope, a non-profit organization dedicated to saving the abandoned babies of that poverty-stricken country.

Sue Walters was Cherie Clark's younger sister. Walters had been a part of the Clark household when Cherie was president and active in the Illinois Chapter of FCVN. The adoption of the Vietnamese orphans into the Clark family inspired Walters to learn the language and left a lasting impression regarding the misery that must be endured in Asia. For this reason, her appearance in Saigon shortly after the Clarks' arrival was not considered unusual. Sue Walters remained in Vietnam until the end of the war serving as Administrator to the orphanages. She continued as an integral part of FCVN after the fall of the Asian country.

In its attempt to re-establish child care centers, FCVN rented a large French villa on Truong Minh Giang in Gia Dinh which was one of the many readily available in Vietnam. The last remains of a proud French influence, the stately structure was bordered by green lawns overflowing with flowers and trees. The entire compound was surrounded by high concrete walls. Many such villas were available for lease and could be rented for a mere $200 to $300 per month. Though the locals could not afford the fee, they were ideal and reasonable for foreigners. Many villas had large water fountains that graced the circular driveways and were transformed into swimming pools whenever children were present.

A five-story complex on Bu Thi Xuan in Gia Dinh, the northernmost section of Saigon, was converted to a critical care center. Cherie and Tom Clark directed the facility, staffed by other American volunteers and Vietnamese childcare workers. Kathy and Duane Frisbee were among the Americans who threw their energies into saving the children. Kathy was a nurse practitioner who worked tiny miracles in pulling them back to life. Though she was young and lacked experience, she possessed a charisma and outstanding nursing skills. Chris Mosher of California and a young couple from Denver also joined the mercy mission, among others. Their church in Golden, Colorado, along with friends, raised money to send them to Vietnam to aide the children.

The Denver couple (which has chosen to remain anonymous) were Vietnam veterans and had met years earlier in the war. The woman was stationed with the American Red Cross at Chu Lai in 1970 with a mobile unit that used helicopters to transport recreational programs to military bases in the northern section of South Vietnam. It was unusual for a woman to enlist in the war, but Vietnam was the event of her generation, and she was very much aware of what was going on in the world around her. The earlier tour in Vietnam was the deciding factor for her return under FCVN in 1974. She had performed volunteer work at orphanages around Chu Lai and felt then that the orphans were the forgotten people in the midst of the tug-of-war for Vietnam.

She remembered the half-American children and the attitude of the Vietnamese toward the mixed race. The nuns at the orphanage made a special effort to draw attention to her visits. She also recalled her experience with a young 18-year-old woman who had worked at the base who was half-black and the offspring of a French soldier. She was never allowed to marry, attend school, or have a job of any significance. The prejudice the American witnessed as a child on the streets of Chicago between various ethnic groups did not begin to compare with the displayed feelings of the Vietnamese against their mixed-blood countrymen.

The couple was initially assigned to the toddler section housed on one of the upper floors at the Bu Thi Xuan Complex. These children were in the process of adoption and were healthier than most. When the work load permitted, the wife would linger in the intensive care unit of the building to watch Cherie Clark's staff and admire the skills of the nursing team and the facility physician, Dr. Cuong. She had not yet given birth to a child of her own and felt the detachment made it bearable to draw from the courage required each day. Pain and fear were things to be put aside; with so much to do, there was no time for emotions in Vietnam. It was a sentiment to have substance in the months ahead as volunteers were reluctant to leave Vietnam...knowing that the day of atonement—the grieving—was yet to come.

Just when the volunteers thought they were making remarkable progress, there would be a dramatic set-back.

Many of the children rescued by FCVN did not make it. At one point there was an epidemic of crib deaths; fifty-two children died of an epidemic of measles within a few days. (Measles usually is a benign infection with a low mortality rate and one attack apparently confers lifelong immunity. However, particularly in infants, the disease may be followed by bacterial infections that maybe fatal). One of the villas was turned into a hospital environment, sterile and attended by a full-time physician.

It worked well to a point. Then, the workers began to realize that babies need affection and stimulation to promote their human development and to survive. Therefore, a plan was devised to place some of the infants in foster homes with caring Vietnamese families and pay for the child's care, along with free medical service for the entire family.

With the implementation of this new plan, it was discovered that the children did well with a family, any family, and it became obvious that without personal attention, many babies would die, no matter how well they were fed and how clean their environment. There came a certain determination among the workers that each child must have a family. Any family would do, no matter what color the parents were. Not that there wouldn't be problems, but the advantages outweighed the disadvantages. The driving force behind the staff was to keep the babies alive to realize the joy of their own home and parents.

The Delta region was the quagmire of South Vietnam. It was a big marshland with an incredible number of bridges, most of which were narrow and allowed for only one-way traffic. Rocket fire was frequent, and often, as one approached or drove across, the bridges blew up. It was always hot, too, as was most of the country, but because of the multitude of rivers and swamps and canals, the Delta was unbearable. In the northern part of Vietnam the nearby mountains offered some relief, but the low jungle deltas provided only heat and humidity.

In Vietnam, only two seasons exist. To the Americans, they were "wet" and "not so wet." The semi-bearable days of January and February are as dry as Vietnam can ever be, but the heat begins to intensify in April. By July, the hopes for the monsoon rains have become prayers, and downing salt tablets becomes a daily ritual.

When the first rains come, they turn to steam as they hit the dusty streets and the air becomes thick with its heat. The same reaction occurs in the countryside when the rain hits the trees. It will rain every day until November, by which time the mildew has turned a dark green and must be scraped away with a knife. Mildew actually ate one of Ross Meador's shoes once. He had left it on the back porch and forgot about it; later, there was nothing left but a well-fed green blob. Mildew was a defiant creature that crawled up the beams of any structure. Clothing, papers, leather and other articles easily give way to its dominance.

April, 1975, was as hot as promised, but there was different heat overtaking the country...the final days of a hot war.

The Delta had a lot of orphanages. As the war progressed, refugees pushed into the southernmost part of the country to escape the onslaught of the Viet Cong. But the Delta was infiltrated and had fighting, though less intense. Many of the orphanages were protected because of their remoteness, and access was only by waterways or narrow roads forged atop mounds of dirt between canals.

Ross Meador began the long journey into the Delta before sunrise. Often he would be accompanied by a driver or a nurse, heading for the highway that led to the heart of the mysterious terrain overpowered by rivers and swamps. Highway 4 ran from Saigon down the length of the province, then turned south to Can Tho. By day it was crowded with military vehicles, civilians, bicycles and even livestock heading into the Delta. At night, when the Viet Cong were in control, it was all but deserted. Then at daybreak, when the Viet Cong would crawl back into their tunnels or retreat to camps deep in the jungle to rest and prepare for the next night's terror, the South Vietnamese Army would emerge for their daylight patrol of the roadways.

By mid-morning, Meador was wringing wet with the heat and humidity as he traversed the countryside visiting orphanage compounds. The Volkswagen bus was stacked with supplies and equipment which was replaced with boxes of babies before the day's end.

The sight of the FCVN Volkswagen bus bearing its familiar trademark was a welcome relief to the nuns and childcare workers, for it represented help and support. Meador was likened to a 20th-century pied piper, and in a matter of seconds after his arrival, he would be surrounded by the inhabitants of the compound, all simultaneously communicating messages to him.

The trips to the Delta were always fruitful, and the bus would soon be stacked with boxes of babies wrapped in anything the nuns could spare. Villagers would hail him on lonely dirt roads to offer small bundles wrapped in newspapers, still covered with afterbirth—dirty, starving, and all but forsaken. Most of the infants weighed only four to five pounds, and Meador found it necessary to interrupt his hectic trip periodically to prop a feeding bottle at the infant's side if it wasn't too weak to suck. Others he held gently and squeezed rice milk into their mouths.

The trip commanded every ounce of hope and concentration he could muster. Too, he was worried about ambush on the back roads.

Usually the babies were lulled to sleep by the motion of the van on these long trips, but more often it was a symphony of screams, cries, whimpers, and unintelligible babble. And though the terrorists and Viet Cong were threatening, the elements were the biggest enemy to the babies. The heat inside the van was stifling, and fear of shock and dehydration was a serious concern. Frequently, the trips were long and it was a miracle any of the babies survived.

Meador was always exhilarated by making it "home free" as he pulled into the driveway of the critical care center. In fact, it was not uncommon for him to drop over on the wheel into a deep stupor, exhausted from the stress endured during the tense journey.

The staff at the center seemed to develop an instinct for his return. He would start hitting his horn when he was several thousand yards away from the compound, hoping the familiar sound would travel ahead and serve as advance warning of his approach. Every second was valuable to the small lives, the coordination of the staff was remarkable. As soon as the van arrived at the entrance dozens of arms would reach in to rescue the infants from their misery.

Since many of the babies did not have a name when they arrived at the center, the staff immediately rectified the indignity. The designation of a name often articulated a profound insight. Other names were taken from the Bible, from close friends, or relatives from afar, or a name would be a response from a striking inspiration of the moment. FFAC had favorite names like Venus, Faith, Hope and Charity. Even names like Richard the Lionhearted, El-Greco, Victoria, Luke, Mark, Matthew, Esperantha, Elizabeth, Martin Luther King, Jericho and Helen of Troy emerged. Other agencies were more traditional with names such as Leonardo, Jonathan and David. Robert, Thomas, Marie, Andrea, and Danny were equally popular. The staff was aware that a child would be given a new name by its adoptive family, but their designation had special significance and provided encouragement to the workers themselves.

Keeping babies alive and monitoring their progress was a dedicated effort requiring not only skill but also acceptance. The staff at the complex was meticulous in charting each baby's progress, and every effort was extended to give them intensive care. The main concern was to keep food in them, and once they started gaining weight, it was as if the angels were singing. Unless they caught pneumonia, many would make it. Others who could not gain weight would die. The losses were inevitable, and several babies died each day.

Some infants were so small and fragile that IV's would be inserted into their heads where the largest veins could be found. Cardiopulmonary-pulmonary resuscitation was an established procedure. The little patients were monitored 24 hours a day, and Dr. Cuong, the full-time physician, labored long into the night hovering over a small life, only to have it slip away from his grasp.

Death became routine, yet it was always hard on the staff. It didn't matter if the child was a resident for days or weeks or for just a few hours; there was still grief. The death of an infant was especially hard on the volunteers. For all their skill and vigilance, when a baby's little lungs would cease to breathe, it was as if the staff suffered a personal failure. It could happen unexpectedly and without warning. It could be daybreak or night or even mid-day, when all the other happy children were heard out in the courtyard or at play. The sound of their joy was a celebration of life that permeated the death room. It was a dichotomy...as if life and death were occupying the same plane in time.

The climate of Vietnam necessitated immediate disposal of a corpse. If death occurred late in the day, the child was merely wrapped in a blanket and placed in a storage room for the next day's burial. Not everyone was aware of the procedure.

The volunteer from Denver needed to replenish supplies for her unit and late one night went into the storage room, unaware that the corpse of an infant had just been placed on the shelf. Just as she was about to turn out the light and close the door, she noticed that some of the linens looked disarranged. She casually reached over to run her hands on the stack to straighten the lumps, and her warm hand fell on the cold face of the dead infant. Realizing what lay atop the shelf, she was struck with terror that rendered her spiritless. It had triggered a flash-back to her earlier tour in Vietnam, when she witnessed rows of green plastic body bags and other horrors of war. As she slid to the floor of the storage room, she covered her hands with her face and exploded with pent-up emotion.

For the many babies and children who died, there remained the matter of disposing of their tiny bodies. The task of escorting the infants to a final resting place fell to a kind old Vietnamese man who made daily trips to the numerous centers to collect the corpses of infants and children. Placed on his shoulders, in reverent silence, he would carry them in a small box prepared for internment to the cemetery. The white crosses that marked their graves not only bore the names of the children, but also the birth dates (often guessed) and their dates of death. The children were, in the words of a volunteer: "Safe at last."

So secure was the cemetery that the Vietnamese themselves sought shelter in the burial grounds to avoid rockets or fire fights. The Viet Cong held a reverence for the dead and did not desecrate graves; consequently, the burial place for the dead was a haven for the living.

With so much to be done, the Denver couple remained in Vietnam and were able to offer a more stable environment to small children when they were assigned to Thu Duc. They rented a French Villa owned by a Frenchman who had left Vietnam. For a mere $200 a month they had eight huge bedrooms, four bathrooms, a kitchen, dining room, living room and a large sunny playroom. Money sent from friends in Golden, Colorado, allowed the husband to build a playground for the children, and boxes arrived from the States with much-needed clothing. Occasionally, a snowsuit would be among the items, but usually everything was useful. The children who arrived from Saigon were excited. They had been in the city all their lives. They were street kids... smart, and survivors. Some had never seen a butterfly before or had the opportunity to go to school. That, too, would change. It was a serene setting; the only disruption was reams of barbed wire that enveloped all the surrounding houses. It was a ploy to keep neighbors from stealing from each other.

In early February, 1975, the couple returned to Colorado, their three-year-old adopted son would soon follow. With no replacement volunteers coming to Vietnam, it became apparent to Ross Meador that the war was winding down. Short of staff, Meador himself moved to Thu Duc to stay with the 57 children until they were evacuated on Daly's plane.

Life at Thu Duc became routine with Meador; it was a chance for him to stabilize and get to know some of the children. He would often entertain them with stories of America and take them on little trips to town. Committed to his Co-Director's responsibilities in Saigon, the FCVN Volkswagen van was the lifeline to his work. He had a problem with a hole in the radiator that seemed to provide no end to trouble, and repairs during the last weeks were impossible. Even though it was just a small hole, all the water would drain out, causing the engine to overheat and stop running. One day, as he was returning to Thu Duc from town with a van load of kids he had taken to the movies, the engine began to overheat. It was getting dark as they approached a bridge, which, like every other bridge in Vietnam, had at least five guards. Just as the van got to the top of the overpass, the engine stopped, the lights went out, and it started to roll down the hill toward the guards, who instantly began to shoot at it. Before Meador could get a word out to the Vietnamese girl on the front seat to shout at them to stop, she was on the floor. It was an instinctive reaction; whenever the kids heard the rockets they would immediately crawl under their beds or get down on the floor, screaming and devaluating the Viet Cong. "Mr. Ross...Mr. Ross...VC numba ten!" As the Volkswagen took fire, Meador finally convinced the girl to yell to the guards that they were children from the orphanage. When the guards realized who was in the van, they were apologetic, even going to the riverbed and filling their helmets with water, which they poured into the van's radiator.

It was the second day of April, and the silent invisible clock fending off defeat by the Communists was ticking down. Within thirty days the nation of South Vietnam would collapse. The safety of the hundreds of children in the FCVN facilities began to concern Ross Meador to the point of desperation. He began a slow acceptance that Saigon would be doomed in a matter of days, a week, or even just hours. The sooner the children embarked for America, the less risk would be involved in their departure.

Early in the day, he had been to the Vietnamese Immigration Service seeking exit permits for the children and was given excuses for delay in processing the children. Unless he could find some way out of Vietnam, legally or illegally, the hundreds of children whose adoptions were already in progress would never be united with the families that really wanted them.

Word of Ed Daly's daring escapades in Danang had spread throughout Saigon. He was regarded as the hero of the hour and immediately became international news. Without giving a thought to Daly's celebrity status, Meador headed to the offices of World Airways at Tan Son Nhut in search of him. Daly was, after all, a fellow American and the one man Meador felt could help him without the run-around he was getting in diplomatic circles.

Upon arriving at the World Airways offices, Meador heard a congenial gathering—laughter mixed with a discussion of the haunts of the American Embassy. Daly was surrounded by an entourage of secretaries and assistants, but Meador's lanky frame caught his eye. At the tycoon's invitation, Meador poured his heart out, explaining his predicament about visas and getting the children to America. He did it with all the wit and candor he could muster, and he had Daly's complete attention.

Meador had no way of knowing that Daly was already in tune with the plight of the orphans and was arranging for the evacuation of some FFAC children that very afternoon. Daly explained that his present commitment was to FFAC but that he would see what he could do. In the mood to fracture a few more rules, Daly understood the mechanics of the bureaucracy and especially the proliferation that had overtaken during these last days of panic.

Turning to one of his aides, Daly gruffly ordered, "Go down there and pay them whatever it takes to get them to release visas for these kids."

The World Airways President was experienced in the power of the dollar and recognized the pressure the Vietnamese officials put on refugees for high-priced tickets and visas to leave the country.

"We'll get you fixed up, son." He laid a hand on Meador's arm and smiled.

It wasn't the approach Meador had expected, nor understood. The American Embassy and USAID officials, as well as the Vietnamese contingent, were aware of Daly's independence and saw his behavior as arrogant and self-serving. There was even speculation that some diplomatic officials were "out to get Daly"...to cut him down to size. It was perceived that Daly was being watched closely in the hope that he would make a serious mistake.

Meador feared that if he had become implicated with some sort of "payoff" to the Vietnamese officials in an attempt to obtain legal papers for the children, it might ruin any chance for their exit. He was also aware graft was running rampant in Vietnam during these last days and knew that Daly's remark was appropriate for the hour. Nonetheless, he was fearful that the step was a dangerous one. Once outside the airport, he dismissed Daly's aid and, in an effort to resolve the matter himself, went to the American Embassy alone.

In Saigon, an "I'll scratch your back if you scratch mine" diplomacy was prevalent, but it became a mystery whose back to scratch. Much of this "backroom negotiations" and diplomacy was beyond the realm of Meador's experience. He did not follow the U.S. Embassy's conflict with Ed Daly, though he knew it existed. He had also heard rumors that Daly had a "pushy manner" and didn't care what other people thought of him. Therefore, a lot of people were offended and didn't understand him. His humanitarian gestures often met with, "he can afford it," but there were many affluent people who did nothing. Meador was only anxious for the sake of the children and wanted them out of the country without any backlash or trouble. Speaking with the Embassy, he was dismayed when they discouraged him from going with Daly, promising that within a few days a huge transport would be flown in to remove all the FCVN children at one time.

The news of a huge transport en route was encouraging, and Meador had no alternative but to place his trust in what the Embassy was telling him. At the same time, he was well aware of the thousands of people who hounded the agency in an attempt to leave the country and realized that many of them had connections in high places. His instinct compelled him to believe that when the time came, the children would be a low priority; money would talk. He couldn't accept the "don't worry" picture that the Embassy official was painting for him.

Both disgruntled and wary, Meador went back to Thu Duc to secure the orphanage for the night. The sun was going down and the Viet Cong would be on the move. He was the only American left at Thu Duc, and the remaining Vietnamese staff and children depended on him. Away from Saigon, it was quiet in the countryside, and the long night ahead would allow him the time necessary to ponder his next move.

As evening turned into night, most of the very young children were already in bed asleep. Some of the older ones were allowed to stay up in their pajamas and sit out on the porch to hear the stories "Mister Ross" loved to tell about America and the wonderful life they would have there.

Suddenly, a car screeched into the driveway and Tom Clark jumped out. "We're going. We're going...now!"

"What? What happened?" Meador commanded.

"I don't know the details, but FFAC is not using Daly's plane...the flight that was scheduled for this afternoon has been canceled. Daly's plane is on the runway, ready to go in an hour. We can take all the children from here and get them out tonight."

Thu Duc was a forty-five minute drive from Tan Son Nhut. Meador checked his watch. Then, waving his fists and shouting, he quickly decided. "Let's go!"

The children were awakened and instructed to grab whatever they wanted to take with them—that they were going to America.

At first, the children didn't understand what was happening. A fear came over them, with all the shouting and excitement, and they began screaming to one another..."VC, VC...VC come...!" They thought an attack was coming, and the sound of mortar fire heard in the distance only confirmed their suspicions.

It was almost impossible to calm them above the noise and excitement. The younger children began to cry as they were awakened from their sound sleep, and the commotion frightened them even more. The eyes of the older children reflected fear as they were convinced they were in danger.

Meador shouted desperately trying to get his message across. "No...No...No...Go to America!" He was not succeeding. All that he had hoped for, planned for, was going to happen...but not like this. The kids were unhappy and afraid. What could he do to make them understand? He was both exasperated and desperate.

Then, as if by magic, he began shouting, half-singing... "California here I come...right back where I started from!"

It worked. The kids finally started to understand what Ross was telling them. They were really going to America...right now!

It was a sight to behold, one that would warm the heart of any doubting American. Fifty-seven children crammed into speeding vans, holding tightly to each other, heading out into the night and passing both friend and foe in the darkness. Courage was in their voices as they were pitched to the highest degree, singing "California here I come!"

Even in fractured English, the message was clear.

The race against time across the Vietnamese terrain was a danger within itself, but the children were excited beyond their dreams; they were on their way to get parents. They had already learned the words "Momma and Daddy" and repeated them over and over, along with the song. At long last, they had a rendezvous with happiness...and right now, happiness was Ed Daly and World Airways.

Reporters and cameras were waiting as the van pulled up to the main gate. Instantly lights sprang up to focus on the orphans who appeared pathetic and frightened at the unexpected attention. It was obvious that the press had been alerted as to what was about to happen, but Meador didn't exhibit the sensitivity to the press that the FFAC group did. In fact, he hardly gave them any thought. The important thing was that the kids were going to America...they were going.home.

In the confusion at the gate, Meador heard someone shout above the crowd, "GO...go now! Drive right on the airfield, down that way...the plane is waiting. Hurry!"

Not knowing if gunfire would follow, Meador threw his van into gear and raced across the tarmac to the waiting jet. It beckoned in magnificent silence, momentarily outlined by the flashes of mortar fire on the horizon.

Interaction varied from silence to crying as the children were pulled from the van and hurriedly placed inside the plane. Meador was surprised to see that all the seats had been taken out and that mattresses lined the floor. He realized it was not a military plane when he noticed the side walls resembled the interior of a commercial airliner.

Hours earlier the plane was classified as "unsafe" because of the absence of passenger accommodations. Meador was aware of the controversy but felt the risk outweighed the uncertain factors of getting the children out at another time, possibly not at all.

At this point, one of the youngsters was taken from the plane by the immigration guards who arrived unexpectedly. They determined he was too old to leave, despite the fact that his two younger siblings were on the plane. A family was being separated forever.

"Too old. Too old," the guard demanded. "You cannot let him go!"

"You've got to let him go!" a volunteer pleaded. "Let him go-brothers-sister."

"Sorry....sorry....or no one is going! Get him off the plane!" With this, the guard grabbed the boy. Ed Daly tried to keep him aboard by giving the guard a $100 bill, but the guard refused. (Meador later took the boy home with him and managed to provide his escape on a later flight.)

With the door to the cockpit open, a loud strident voice could be heard throughout the plane and to the reporters outside.

"Do not take off, you are not cleared for takeoff. Repeat. This is the tower, you are not cleared for takeoff."

Daly, at the rear of the plane, responded vigorously, "Oh yeah? Just watch me!"

Standing on the tarmac in the wake of the departing jet, Meador remained fixed in his spot as he watched the plane roar down the runway. How he wished he could go with them...if just to see their faces when they reached California. He wanted to see them meet the families who would be taking them home as their own children. But he knew he was still needed in Vietnam; it wasn't his time yet. Besides, he had a valid excuse—he didn't have his passport back from the American Embassy; it had expired and he was awaiting renewal.

Meador's eyes squinted as he followed the jet into the dark night. When he no longer heard the tinted sounds of the engines, he turned to head back to Thu Duc with the young Vietnamese at his side. Tears swelled up in his eyes. He was experiencing a sense of happiness that came each time he saw kids leave during the past year. He was thinking, too, of the children who would not make it to America, or to anywhere.

Upon return to Thu Duc, Meador felt a deep loss. He was happy to have it all done, yet the sight of an empty house gripped him. Toys and clothes were scattered about and a radio was still playing. An open jar of peanut butter and crackers were scattered on the kitchen table. There was a premonition of something wonderful and important coming to an end in his life.

The fact that he might never again see these children became a realization. After the American couple left, Meador had moved to Thu Duc and became both mother and father to the kids. Many a night he would comfort a frightened child. Sometimes his bed would be full of kids by morning. There were also nights he sat holding a sick child until dawn broke through the curtains, the fever finally gone with the darkness.

With the departure of the children, the staff that worked at Thu Duc were out of their jobs, and Meador felt a sense of obligation. He would try to get them on an evacuation plane. He noted that one of the girls was missing. Ahn was a young woman who was the diaper washer of the orphanage. It was a very unglamorous job, but necessary, and it meant a great deal to her to work with the children. She performed this repulsive task with all the smiles of a "Kelly Girl" working for a vice-president of a corporation.

Her absence was not alarming, as Meador assumed that she had just accepted that her job was over and left quietly, probably returning to her village. Much to his chagrin, several days later the *Stars & Stripes*, the U.S. Military newspaper, featured a large picture of a young woman peering out of a window of Daly's plane in Oakland. The headlines, "Freedom Bird Flies Again, Babylift Begins," was an anticlimax to the face of Anh, smiling in the photograph, happy to have arrived with the children in America!

The success of Daly's flight was headlined all over the world, and Meador felt elated that it served as the catalyst to force the issue of evacuation of the orphans to the public's attention. All of Saigon buzzed with details of how Daly defied USAID and the American Embassy once again. To the world, Daly was a hero, and the agencies that opposed him were once again considered the "heavies" in the drama. Daly's initiative helped convince American and Vietnamese officials to face up to the crisis of the orphans.

The Presidential announcement of the implementation of Operation Babylift brought a cheer from the volunteers who were becoming frustrated and despondent. They were beginning to lose hope of ever getting the children out without government assistance. The backlog of adoption paperwork in Saigon was the basic holdup. Children poured into the orphanages without any identification, and before a child could be involved in the adoption process, they had to be officially acknowledged. In some instances a court procedure was necessary before a child could have a document to prove it existed. Once that was obtained, the legal adoption process could proceed and the child was issued a passport. Because all of this took time, the departure of adoptable children from Vietnam was slow and engulfed in red tape. The impending fall of Saigon changed all that. President Ford's declaration would, hopefully, cut the red tape without any repercussions from the Vietnamese government.

With the departure of the Thu Duc children, Meador busied himself the following day at the critical care center. There were hundreds of records to organize, update, close out. Identification bands were made, and children needed to be tagged and identified with the names of the receiving parents. The record process was extensive, yet necessary. The crew worked long hours to accomplish the task in the event that a plane would become available on short notice. The Embassy officials had promised Meador that a C5-A Galaxy would be flying from the Philippines on Saturday to evacuate FFAC children and there would be room for some FCVN babies. They would only have a couple of days to prepare for the mass evacuation aboard the huge aircraft.

On Thursday night, the 120 babies in the house of the critical care center took turns keeping everyone awake with their cries and whimpers. It was as if they sensed the increased tension about them.

Sleep was a welcome reprieve for the workers. But with the sounds coming from the nurseries, Meador found himself awake throughout the night, tossing, unable to find the solitude and quiet necessary to free his mind. Grabbing his pillow, he headed out to the courtyard toward his van. He knew he must get to sleep. It would be daybreak soon, and he couldn't anticipate what the next day would bring—perhaps another short-notice flight and a mad scramble to the airport. In sheer desperation, he crawled into the rear of the van parked in the driveway. He closed the door and managed to slip off into a deep state of rest. When he awoke the next morning, he was surprised at the silence, forgetting his surroundings.

That day, Meador went to Father Oliver's office at Catholic Charities to get their list of the children they wanted to send out. A flight for Australia was scheduled later that day, and Meador went to pick up the children from the nurseries. (A group of parents from Australia had been in the process of adoption and the red tape was cut so that their children could be evacuated.)

By Friday, April 4th, all the adoption agencies in Vietnam were notified of airlifts and were in full swing to take advantage of Babylift. Planes were scheduled for departure every few hours, yet there remained a sense of disbelief among the volunteers...as if the order might somehow be rescinded and they would find themselves abandoned as before. It seemed too good to be true, unreal, and more than they had hoped for.

Then tragedy.

On Saturday, April 5th, the C5-A Galaxy that President Ford ordered for Operation Babylift arrived from the Philippines to evacuate the FFAC children. Then, several minutes after take-off, it crashed. Word of the tragedy was devastating. It was early evening when word came to Meador. Like everyone, at first he thought it was a joke. It was natural for humans to reject such news, and he didn't take it seriously. There were always rampant rumors, and news of any incident around Saigon was often blown far out of proportion.

Meador's first inclination was that it was a minor accident, a delay in the take off—something had been misunderstood. Finally, acceptance came with further verification, and it was announced that sabotage was suspected.

The days following the crash were insane. The death of the children and their escorts traumatized the volunteers and plunged them into deep sorrow...something they were all thought to be immune to...something that was to be held back until all this was over...when they were safe in their respective personal corners.

Meador thought to himself, "I could have died today."

It was as if fate interceded. The truth was, Meador himself would not consider leaving Saigon with so much FCVN work left undone.

Following an unexpected tragedy, there is a sense of defeat... "what's the use?"...no matter how hard one tries, destiny has her way." It is a note of acceptance that is received with shock. Meador was torn between rushing down to Tan Son Nhut to help and a rationalization that the best memorial to those who lost their lives that day was to push to completion the work they had started.

Although totally exhausted, with little reserve left, he worked long into the night, dealing with the papers that were necessary. His eyes were so tired and weary that the words and letters blurred into each other.

Overcome by grief, he managed to hold back the emotions until his head hit his pillow. At that moment, all the feelings he had managed to hold back poured out in a flood of tears. Then he drifted off asleep. Tomorrow would be another crucial day and it would come soon enough.

CHAPTER VI
THE PLANE CRASH

*"It is the human race, not the individual that is wounded here, is out-
raged here...What torments me is not the humps or hallows nor the
ugliness. It is the sight, a little bit in all of these men, of Mozart
murdered."*

— *St. Exupery, Terre Des Hommes*

Ed Daly's unauthorized flight from Saigon, with a cargo of children was the vanguard of an extensive orphan airlift from beleaguered
South Vietnam. He was the hero of the hour and, in evacuating the
orphans, he struck a blow for freedom previously lacking in the
Vietnam saga. In doing so, he touched the hearts of millions of people around the world.

By the time those 57 homeless children arrived in Oakland, shortly before midnight on Wednesday, April 2, 1975, word of the flight and
Daly's unique cargo reached the press and television networks. The
heroic humanitarian act was headlined in the morning papers all over
the world. Interest in the abandoned children of Vietnam sprung up
over night. Sympathetic public opinion and enthusiasm set the wheels
in motion as the White House was deluged with appeals on behalf of
the children. A momentum that was impossible to stop had begun.
Daly's flight stirred the concern of the nation.

President Gerald R. Ford made the official announcement that
Operation Babylift would be implemented and the U.S. government
would assist in the evacuation of thousands of unwanted children.

"It was an announcement of sanity and reason during the final
stages of the Vietnam War, that didn't have much of either," stated a
White House aide present in the briefing room.

Ford was placed between a stone and a hard rock. The 38th
President had been in that spot several times during the past four years.

119

In 1973, after the resignation of Vice President Spiro Agnew, Ford stepped into the Vice Presidency. A year later, when Richard M. Nixon resigned, Gerald Ford assumed the responsibilities of the highest office as well as the closing of the Vietnam War. Ford remained optimistic in appealing to Congress for aid for the Thieu government. "I still think there is an opportunity to salvage the situation in Vietnam."

Many in Congress said no aid would help.

It left Ford frustrated. "It will be up to Americans and history to assess the causes of South Vietnam's reversals," he said, adding: "I think historians in the future will write who was to blame in this tragic situation."

The nation was in desperate need of healing after the political turmoil of the seventies, and the withdrawal from a controversial war. Ford's role as a peacemaker was his destiny. The President wanted peace and harmony for the nation; it had been a long hard storm.

Yet there were some who would not close the chapter on Vietnam. They would use the children, future expenditures on social programs and, worse yet, hate propaganda to object to Babylift. Ford indeed had placed a great burden upon himself.

Though minimal at first, objections came not only from the Communists but from groups inside the United States. Editorials and press releases were generally favorable, yet there remained a segment of citizens that looked deep into the motives. Some came up with conjectural statements as to why we were bringing foreign children to America when there were so many American disadvantaged children in need of adoptive homes.

Officials in Saigon reportedly called Babylift, "Marvelous propaganda, which could be useful to persuade a reluctant Congress to vote more arms and money to keep the war going."

While Communist countries denounced the orphan evacuation in speeches at the United Nations, South Vietnamese diplomats issued an appeal to the American people: "For God's sake, don't close your hearts to the human tragedy of Vietnam."

Stories began to filter down from every reliable source to reveal to the public the true plight of the children of Vietnam, and especially of interest were the tribulations of the Amerasian children, those fathered by Americans.

The United States, unlike Belgium, England, France and Holland, did not make any provision for the children of its servicemen in Southeast Asia. When the French lost their Indochina War in 1954, all Vietnamese children sired by Frenchmen, whether born in or out of wedlock, were entitled to French citizenship. Thousands went to France, where they received a free education. The United States had no similar program. It was as if the children were never born; there were no methods assuming responsibility to even count them, and it appeared that no one wanted to admit their existence. The only survey on record of orphaned children was taken by the Catholic Relief Service just before the last Communist offensive, and it involved only Vietnam's 120 registered orphanages in which 17,500 children lived. Not all orphanages were registered, however, and most of the 120 were located in and around Saigon. Of these 17,500 children, about 8,400 were without both parents, 5,000 only fatherless, 1,800 only motherless and 2,200 had both parents. (The parents relinquished their children for various economic and social reasons.) The registered orphans included 632 of white American blood and 312 with black American blood. Bear in mind, these figures provided by the orphanages only accounted for babies and very young children; children beyond eight or nine years old were usually not in these institutions unless they were retarded.

Since the American forces became involved in Vietnam in the early 1960's, there were no statistics compiled to determine the total number of Amerasian children since many had been born and lived in villages and hamlets far from Saigon. The street children in Saigon alone have been estimated in the thousands, homeless and fending for themselves as early as four or five years of age. After the fall of Saigon in April, 1975, it was conservatively estimated that there were at least 40,000 Amerasian children in Vietnam alone and about 150,000 in all of Southeast Asia.

South Vietnam endured thirty years of uninterrupted war, and it was always a poor country. It was speculated that the country had an orphaned population of at least 1.5 million children. When it appeared imminent that all of South Vietnam would fall under the Communist rule, a panic gripped the U.S. populace and orphanage staffs to save the mixed blood children.

"We want to get these babies out," said a determined nun from one of the orphanages. "In Ban Me Thout, we got reports that the first night after the Viet Cong came in, all the American-blooded babies were killed and those old enough turned into supply bearers."

With the departure of the American troops and the new thrust by the Communists, the adoption agencies functioning in Vietnam were giving top evacuation priority to the American-blooded children for fear of North Vietnamese reprisals against them. Even if the Communists were to give a reprieve to the Amerasian children, most were destined to live their lives as paupers.

Children born of mixed blood know at an early age that they are different from other children. They are often taunted and beaten by their peers, often abandoned at an early age and left to fend for themselves by stealing or begging in the streets. Ridicule is constant, not only from other children, but from adults as well who ask endless questions about their origin. Harassment never ends, and they are branded as second class citizens for the rest of their lives, denied the right to marry, attend public school, or hold jobs. In short, they are destined to live as outcasts in countries where racial purity is extremely important.

With emphasis on the plight of the Amerasians, the response from the public was phenomenal. Offers of homes poured in from all over the free world. Washington's agencies were flooded with calls of concern for the children of war and demands for the United States to render assistance.

On Thursday, April 3rd, at a noon press conference in San Diego, California, President Ford announced that he had ordered a giant C-5A Galaxy Air Force cargo plane to Saigon and that more than 2,000 children would be airlifted to Travis Air Force Base near San Francisco and to other west coast air bases. Additionally, he declared he would cut red tape and other bureaucratic obstacles preventing these children from coming to the United States, and that a special two million dollar fund to fly the orphans out was established.

"This is the least we can do, and we will do much, much more," the President added.

Later that day the Pentagon confirmed that the first C-5A Galaxy was due in Saigon Thursday night from Clark Air Force Base in the Philippines to begin the mass evacuation. The evacuation would begin sometime on Friday afternoon, April 4th.

Ford's plan was to transport the children back to Clark Air Base for 48 hours of medical exams and treatment before flying to Travis.

Many of the children had scabies, skin disorders, diarrhea and infections that needed attention. A time saving evacuation plan for Operation Babylift flights was devised; while the first group received medical attention and treatment, the Galaxy would shuttle between Saigon and Clark, bringing more children out before retrieving the first load and proceeding on to California. A second Galaxy was being ordered into the operation as well. Time being of the essence, the plan called for getting as many children out in as short a time as possible.

Holt International Childrens Services (HOLT), Catholic Relief Services (CRS), World Vision Relief Organization (WVRO), Pearl S. Buck Foundation (PBF), Traveler's Aid International Social Services of America (TAISSA), Friends of the Children of Vietnam (FCVN) and Friends for All Children (FFAC), the U.S. voluntary agencies licensed by the Republic of Vietnam to process inter-country adoptions, were deeply concerned about whether they would continue to get the cooperation of the South Vietnamese government since the orphans were already a low priority.

As the Communists thrust deeper into South Vietnam, the attempt to save the children had become an hour-by-hour agony. With the fall of the Saigon government, it was determined that the North Vietnamese would stop the external support of the children from U.S. based agencies. Then it became a question of what, if anything, these organizations could do about the orphans remaining in Vietnam after the take-over.

There was little expectation that the new regime would allow the evacuation of orphans or Amerasian children to continue after Saigon fell. The relentless Communist drive through the country split apart countless families; and South Vietnam's major cities were crowded with pre-teen beggars and lost children. There was no way the Communists could care for the thousands of youngsters that made up the latest lost generation of Vietnamese. A number of volunteers from charity organizations vowed to remain in Saigon, confident that the Communists would bear no malice to the homeless children. For many others there was disbelief. FCVN, FFAC, HOLT, WVRO, TAISSA, CRS, PBF, and other adoption groups, An Loc Orphanage, and Vietnamese American Children's Fund (VACF) began to gather children from the orphanages to place them on promised flights.

In Washington, government officials were reluctant to talk about the subject, apparently for fear of adding to the tense atmosphere in the threatened South Vietnamese Capitol. Government officials were reported considering plans for what could become the evacuation of one million refugees from Saigon. There was a deep concern not only for the children fathered by the American forces, but also for the many civilian Vietnamese employees of the American Embassy and American sponsored agencies and installations.

The State Department task force was studying refugee evacuation proposals, including ways in which a cease-fire might be arranged to allow safe conduct for as many as one million persons from South Vietnam should the Communists take over, which was imminent.

The U.S. Agency for International Development (USAID) the official disaster relief center, confirmed that personnel were working around the clock to handle the thousands of offers of adoptions and aid to refugees. People were urged to donate money, supplies and their time to local relief organizations.

Vernon Lyons, spokesman for USAID, termed the public response as "Unprecedented. We had the big responses from the public when the Hungarians, Czechs, and Cubans had their crises, but this has been the biggest response to human tragedy that I have seen in my thirty years of experience."

From New York to California, families sat down together to explore the possibilities of adopting a war orphan and to decide if they could manage with another child. Because the situation was so immediate, people were looking into the matter right away.

Friends For All Children, the organization that had just one day earlier refused Daly's offer to fly their children out, received word from the USAID agency, who phoned their central office at Rathaven, that there was a U.S. Air Force C-5A Galaxy at Tan Son Nhut to evacuate 230 children that very afternoon.

Unlike Daly's plane, which was stripped down for cargo, the C-5A was promised to have all the necessary safety features essential for the flight.

In President Ford's announcement of Operation Babylift, he stated that he had directed that the aircraft, and all other aircraft involved in Babylift, be specially equipped for the flights. Oxygen, seat belts, escape routes, food, and emergency medical equipment, would be available for the short flight to the Philippines. With time running out, the organization made immediate preparations to get the children to the airport.

After four days of negotiations with government agencies, commercial and private airlines, (including Ed Daly's flight,) the news of the arrival of the C-5A brought a sense of relief to Rosemary Taylor, the Australian coordinator in charge of the FFAC Vietnam operation. On several previous occasions, the children had been loaded onto buses heading for the airport only to find that the flights were canceled.

The procrastination and indecision was debilitating in itself for all the child-relief agencies in Vietnam, not only because it crushed hopes each time of getting the children out safely, but because it had shattering effects on the routines of the children and staff. Preparations for immediate departure were in "stand-by" status for days. Food, clothing, medicines and supplies were piled up at the entrances of the facilities in the event that the opportunity for evacuation would come. As each possibility evaporated, the staff would again try to establish a routine to settle the children. As a result of the uncertainty, the children were beginning to experience the effects of the tensions and frustrations of shuttling back and forth. An epidemic of crying, restlessness, and discontent infiltrated the care centers. As unpredictable as children are, quite often they got sick on the buses or on planes en route to the United States. They developed everything from spiked fevers, nausea and vomiting, to chickenpox. In several instances smallpox was suspected (it was not) and children were quarantined on arrival at their destinations.

In addition to the disruptions, the workers became exhausted as they labored frantically during the night to prepare the paperwork necessary for the evacuation. The essential name tags were prepared, medical records sorted, identification data compiled and lists coordinated to match the babies with the proper adoptive parents. Many of these preparations had to be done while there was only sporadic access to telephone lines, and much of the information required updating on a regular basis.

President Ford remained in California, making arrangements to greet the orphans at Travis Air Force Base. He and Mrs. Ford stayed close to the situation and instructed aides to give priority to the mission.

Then all of America waited in great anticipation and a new chapter was added to the tragedy of Vietnam.

The C-5A Galaxy, a monstrous transport and the world's largest plane, arrived at Tan Son Nhut from Clark Air Force Base in the

Philippines just hours before, bearing emergency war materials. The plane was hours late arriving, and supply personnel hurriedly unloaded the fourteen howitzers, artillery ammunition and other weapons of war for the hard-pressed South Vietnamese Army struggling against Communist forces near the city.

The mercy mission of the Galaxy flew into Tan Son Nhut with a crew of sixteen Air Force personnel, which included ten medics and nurses from the medical group at Clark Field, located outside of Manila. All professionals, they knew the significance of their role in the historic undertaking that was about to commence.

With the arrival of the C-5A Galaxy, FFAC had to make a decision which children to put on board. It was determined that the healthiest and oldest would make the journey. Those from the Allambie Nursery and all of the Phu My children were prepared for the flight. Fifty of the healthier babies from To-Am and twenty from Newhaven were selected. None of the Hy Vony children were considered well enough for this flight. Many of these children were babies only several months old.

Hy Vong Nursery, the pride of FFAC, opened in 1973 and boasted being the best nurse-to-child hospital in Vietnam. It was established as an intensive care unit because many of the hospitals would not accept children with contagious diseases for fear of contamination in the crowded conditions. Hy Vong was fully-equipped with necessary life-saving and intensive care equipment and in the last days was turned over to the Sisters de Chartes from Tuy Hao. These small, desperately sick babies would not likely endure the long trip to the States.

It was late afternoon before the crew and FFAC personnel began to board the children and prepare for the flight. The flight crew did their best to hurry things along to keep plane #80-218 on schedule for the rendezvous with the President. The Galaxy was on the flight line for several hours prior to the children's arrival. It took hours to unload the supplies for the ARVN. During the equipment unloading operation, South Vietnamese troops guarded the C-5A and continued to remain around the transport and surrounding area while the children were assembled and put on the plane.

It was a clear, hot day in Saigon. Shelling was heard in the distance. Occasionally a cloud of smoke would rise on the horizon and off in the distance the sound of gunfire "tack-tacked" from grassy mounds around the perimeter of the field.

Rosemary Taylor arrived at the airport ahead of the children and her staff members. As Director of Operations in Vietnam for Friends For All Children, she wanted to supervise the boarding procedure herself and to assure every contingency was covered. Too, stalwart as she was, her presence was essential to morale.

One by one she met members of her staff as they accompanied their charges from various nurseries. She saw Margaret Moses, an Australian co-worker, get off one of the buses that brought the Allambie children. The two women looked at each other and without words understood the triumph before them—they were getting the children out. The confusion of departure surrounded them and time was too important for words. Few staff members spoke, concentrating only on getting the children boarded and settled.

In order that there would be some familiarity for the children on the flight, a decision was made about which staff members would accompany them on the journey. Those remaining behind would accompany the smaller babies on the next flight.

Many of the children were screaming in fright as they were carried aboard. The sight of the huge C-5A Galaxy was staggering. Others slept in the arms of the relief workers accompanying them while tiny babies cooed in small boxes, unaware of the drama surrounding them.

There was no air conditioning and the inside of the plane was oppressively hot. The children were the last to be boarded and the heat and bedlam on the upper level was unbearable as Taylor tried to make a count of the babies that were strapped in the seats. She and Christie Leivermann, an FFAC nurse who had been in Vietnam since 1972, were accompanying the Air Force crew in adjusting seat belts to keep the infants from strangling themselves.

In an attempt to soothe the babies who were screaming and squirming in their respective places, the women dabbed drops of cool water on their mouths and wiped their faces.

Leivermann remained on the upper deck to move about the babies freely, making certain they were secure and comfortably positioned for take-off. The small babies were strapped ten abreast in seats that normally held three. The older children were crammed in two to a seat. The top section of the plane where the passenger seats were located, quickly filled up with small babies. The older kids and adults were strapped down in the lower cargo area that had just housed the howitzers. Blankets were stretched out on the steel floor and cargo harnesses substituted for seat belts. It was a scary situation and many of the children were crying. More than 150 people were crowded into the lower cargo hold for what was to be a twenty-hour flight to the U.S. There were no life rafts, no toilets, not enough air sickness bags (which would soon be needed) and no oxygen for emergencies. It had much less to offer than Daly's stretch cargo jet which USAID "thumbs-downed" for the evacuation as "unsafe."

Since there was nothing more she could do on the upper deck, Taylor climbed down the ladder to assist the adults and children crowded on the floor of the vast cargo hold. She noted that Margaret Moses was crouched among the Allambie children, appearing cheerful as she gave them directions, attempting to calm their fears. A battered suitcase of records and documents sat beside her.

Along with 24-year-old German born Brigit Blank, who was an administrative nurse at Hy Vong, was Lee Makk, an Australian nurse who worked at Allambie, and Dolly Van Bui and her daughter, Tina. Sister Ursula, a nun at the Good Shepherd Orphanage in Vinh Long had spent the past sixteen years in Vietnam and had been asked just that morning to accompany the children. It would be her first trip to the West. Understandably, she was excited. Overflowing with happiness, she said goodbye to each sister at the orphanage and asked for the blessing of her superior, Sister Mary, saying, "I'll be ready for anything." It was an omen of what was to come.

Rosemary Taylor was relieved that Margaret Moses, her associate, was on board to organize the operation. Moses was an Australian-born teacher, 36 years old, who had been in Vietnam for five years. She was fluent in French and well-liked. They shared a loyalty and friendship, along with professional support, that strengthened FFAC to become the organization that it was. Although Taylor felt that their paths would probably cross again many times in the future, she later wrote that at the time "she felt an unusual sadness at the parting."

The inside of the C-5A, which stood as high as a six-story building, took on the atmosphere of a nursery as supplies, toys and children were intermingled. The women escorting the children sat along the side of the plane continuously caring for the small babies lined up in small boxes.

The babies and children were noisy. Most were scared, continuing to wiggle and tug at the seat belts or harnesses holding them. It was a situation they did not understand, and all the confusion of strangers moving quickly in all directions frightened them even more.

Finally, when the last of the orphans had been secured in position, the pilot contacted the tower for clearance. Slowly, the engines of the huge jet transport fired and the monstrous plane thundered down the runway. At 4:03 p.m., it took to the air. Twelve minutes later the nightmare began.

Stunned by the chaotic scene of departure, Taylor and her staff write that they were vaguely conscious of leaving the airport. They drove back to their orphanages already planning the next evacuation. A few observers remained to watch the plane ascend into the horizon until it appeared as a speck.

As the huge plane thrust forward, reaching climbing altitude, inside the plane some of the children stopped crying and with wondrous eyes became fascinated with the feeling that accompanies the sense of flying. The fact that they were cuddled together may have been a comfort to them.

The children calmed down and acted "beautifully" on take-off, observed the escorts, who scanned their charges looking for signs of trouble. A concern was that the children might pry themselves loose from the seat belts or harnesses.

The plane was striving for a cruising altitude and was at 23,772 feet, four miles high, when suddenly, without warning, the door locking system failed. The huge clamshell loading doors at the rear of the plane blew off. There was a loud explosive, rapid decompression in the cargo compartment, and a sudden swoosh of air out of the cabin. Crew members back near the doors were sucked out of the aircraft.

Objects flew around. Blankets, eyeglasses, pens, clothing and toys. Even the plastic-lined pillows exploded. Bodies were tumbling; screams dominated. Pieces of insulation were ripped off the ceiling of the plane while clothing tore off passengers and various articles were dislodged. The disruption continued for several minutes until the air flow stopped. Within seconds of the decompression, many in the cargo hold had passed out. For others it was like suffocating, gasping for air and not getting it. For some there was a strong pain in both ears and terror for all.

The huge gaping hole in the back of the plane was revealed by the sunlight streaming through from the west. Once the decompression hit, the babies on the upper deck quieted down immediately.

On the flight deck, pilot Dennis Traynor reported to the tower at

Tan Son Nhut that he had lost control of his steering mechanism. (Presumably because the flying doors had severed hydraulic control cable lines leading to the tail. When hydraulic failure occurs, the flaps or landing gear won't come down and steering power is lost; it's like trying to steer a car without power.)

The plane was fifteen minutes from Tan Son Nhut. The engines were throttled immediately to turn back to Saigon and attempt an emergency landing.

Back on the ground, the observers who, just minutes earlier, had watched the plane disappear on the horizon, suddenly noticed a tiny speck in the sky growing larger. The plane was coming back.

As the pilot banked and headed back to the airport, the crew frantically tried to assess the damage, determining that the aft pressure door failed and blew out for some reason. In blowing out, the door damaged the elevator, and as a result, there were problems controlling the aircraft's rate of descent. This became critical to the point that the pilot almost lost control as he made the turn into the airfield.

There was very little oxygen at their altitude. The passengers were getting groggy until the oxygen masks had dropped from their containers above the passenger seats. There weren't nearly enough masks to go around, so the escorts and Air Force personnel aboard moved quickly from child to child administering oxygen. It was necessary to keep their own masks on, otherwise they would become drowsy and pass out from hypoxia. Some of the children appeared to be getting drowsy and were soon revived as the sharing procedure continued.

The masks in the cargo hold disintegrated and fell apart. Few worked, and the adults used them for themselves, then shared them with the children and babies who were turning blue. Children were passing out, and most people in the cargo hold at the time of descent were unconscious.

The consensus was that everyone would die, but the crew reassured the passengers that they were not to worry, the plane was returning to Saigon.

Although the plane was losing altitude, there was time to discuss what to do on impact. Everyone was instructed which doors to use for exit, and responsibilities were designated in the minutes the plane was descending. During all this confusion, the staff continued to administer oxygen and prepare the babies for emergency landing. Making sure all were secure in their seats by padding them with whatever was left from the decompression was the only recourse left before impact.

For a moment the crew thought they were going to make the tip of the runway. They didn't.

About a mile and a half short of the airfield, the plane lost altitude and skidded into a rice paddy at 309 miles per hour, twice the speed of a normal landing. The craft bounced back into the air, then suddenly rebounded across the Saigon River. It continued to skip across the tall grass like a flat rock on a pond, unable to stop. Then came an explosion that sounded like a hollow thud. The plane hit an embankment where its wing broke off and a fuel tank in the other wing ruptured on impact.

When it was over, the cockpit was lying about 100 yards away from the fuselage and the tail section about the same distance in the other direction. Huge towers of black smoke could be seen in Saigon, seven miles away. The time of the crash was 4:45 p.m., just 42 minutes after take-off.

The scene inside the plane was horrible. Many of the seats were ripped off the floor and turned upside down with children still strapped in them. One of the crew was trapped beneath metal debris while one of the escorts lay with her back broken, her ear severed. Another was hanging upside down, his leg twisted around metal, an eyeball hanging out and his head laid open as blood gushed out. Everyone seemed to be bleeding, and while shrill screaming was everywhere, most were unconscious; many were dead. There was smoke and fumes which made the rescue hazardous and breathing difficult for the survivors.

Many passengers slowly regained consciousness in the rice paddy, their bodies covered with mud. There were babies everywhere, crying. Many bodies were naked, racked with multiple injuries, and unable to move. When the plane crashed there was nothing to hold onto and the force of the impact dislodged everything.

Fire trucks and other rescue vehicles were unable to get to the crash site because of the narrow road that could only be traveled by foot, nor could they drive through the swampy field to get to the wreckage. Fearing sniper activity from the Viet Cong, more than one hundred South Vietnamese militiamen were ordered into the area to provide security for the rescue operation. Helicopters were dispatched to the scene, and American rescuers with sledgehammers and crowbars rushed to the burning wreckage. Crews dropped from helicopters and waded through the mud, trying to find survivors along the mile-long swath. Bodies were buried deep in the mud, and children were still trapped in the plane's cargo hold.

As children and babies were pulled from the plane, many were catatonic. Most of the children were badly hurt, while some showed no visible signs of injury. There was a sense of relief that some of the children were alive, even though they acted lifeless and dazed. A possibility existed that perhaps some of these youngsters had suffered brain damage due to the lack of oxygen during decompression. Later, they received a cursory medical exam, and many flew to the United States a day after the crash. Conversely, the crew was rushed to a military hospital for intensive observation.

Helicopters from Air America and the South Vietnamese Air Force picked up survivors and rushed them to the Seventh Day Adventist Hospital just outside the main gate of Tan Son Nhut. When the U.S. had troops in Vietnam, the hospital was operated by the military and treated thousands of wounded soldiers. It was now seeing the biggest disaster since the departure of the Americans.

Stunned Vietnamese soldiers and Americans worked side-by-side, carrying the mangled bodies of babies to the helicopters. With years of war behind the men, they had become somewhat accustomed to removing the dead bodies of comrades and death was an everyday thing in the war-torn country. It was a different matter, however, to lift the lifeless bodies of young children and babies.

Headless bodies were buried in the mud, pools of blood trailing from the corpses to the gullies. Pages of a Donald Duck comic book flipped in the wind in the rice paddy where the remains of the Galaxy were lodged. Along with the baby bottles, boxes of diapers, a flight manual, cushions and clothing, all sorts of melted unidentifiable objects were scattered about in the burning grass.

The horrible sight was beyond description. The bodies of some headless children were wrapped in ponchos and put aboard the choppers and flown to the hospital morgue.

As in any disaster, the loss of life brings a feeling of desolation and waste. Survivors somehow balance out the bad with the good, and the rescuers were grateful that there was life emerging from the wreckage. Some of the passengers got out through a chute in the top of the plane, but the children and adults in the cargo area didn't stand a chance. As it plunged to earth, the impact had flattened the cargo hold of the plane where about eighty of the orphans were strapped in.

Some of the children were unaccounted for, many of whom had been sucked out of the plane when the cargo doors blew off. Most passengers were strapped in, yet because the decompression tore off their clothing, a hospital doctor said almost all of the dead brought in were naked, their bodies charred or mutilated beyond recognition.

Few of the crewmen were seriously injured. All but one were found alive by nightfall. There could be victims anywhere in the tall grass and at dusk when the rescue operations had succeeded in getting out survivors. Search parties continued through the night despite the dangers. With Viet Cong in the area, the rescue crew faced the threat that searchers would be an easy target and the casualty list would increase.

The huge fuel tanks on the wings of the plane ruptured on impact, touching off a fire that still raged when darkness fell and smoke continued to billow from the cockpit the next day. Fire engines were unable to reach the site, a mile from the nearest road and adjacent to the Saigon River, where the soil was muddy and impassable to vehicles. The narrow foot path remained the only lifeline to the plane from the ground.

There were 342 people on the plane. Of the 228 orphans, 78 were killed, 150 survived. Some 20 adults were also pulled out alive from the wreckage. Most of those below in the lower cargo hold, an area 20 feet high and 120 feet long, were killed. The death count was recorded as 172. Of the 94 escorts, dependents, and Air Force personnel killed, some were unaccounted for and were either dead in the fields along the route of descent, or trapped in the pulverized smoking wreckage. An undetermined number were sucked out of the plane when the doors blew and decompression occurred.

Many of the babies who survived the crash displayed no injuries, physically or emotionally. As one handicapped boy was carried from the plane, he still had his brace on, saying only that he wanted to go "potty"!

Several of the adult women were in a daze and remained silent, unable to communicate for a long time. When they finally spoke, all they would manage was a repetitious mumbling, "the plane went down, the airplane went down."

A crewman who survived, an Air Force Reservist from California, was stunned by the drama and could only shake his head in disbelief. He had flown to the Philippines with his reserve unit in what started out to be a weekend exercise, a chance to see Vietnam and help with the Babylift.

The area of the crash, near the Saigon River, was partially controlled by the Viet Cong, but there was no immediate indication or evidence to support the theory that the C-5A had been shot down. There had been fighting in the area only the night before. As an additional precaution, back-up for the one hundred Vietnamese militiamen already in position were rushed to the scene to secure the area as helicopters, an inviting target for the Viet Cong, continued to ferry out the living and the dead through the night.

Rosemary Taylor and the others were informed of the crash within minutes and hurried to the hospital where they found crying babies covering the beds and floors. When Taylor saw Christie Leivermann emerge from the ambulance, mud-spattered but appearing unharmed, she instinctively knew that Leivermann was the only survivor among the orphanage staff. Margaret Moses was dead, along with Bridget Blank, Dolly Van Vui and her daughter, Tina, and Dolly's two adopted sons, who were also in the cargo hold. Sister Ursula and Lee Makk, the nurse from Allambie, had also perished. Ilse Ewald, the chief nurse administrator, was in a state of despair as she learned of the death of her daughter, Monique. Ilse was sending Monique back to the States to live with friends until she could be taken back to Germany.

There was no time for grief or hysteria. Taylor and the others scooped the babies up and prepared to get them back to the nurseries as quickly as possible.

It was the first crash of a passenger plane from Tan Son Nhut, which at the height of the Vietnam War was the world's busiest airport. It was also the first fatal crash of a C-5A, the world's largest plane.

Upon receiving news of the crash, a Congressman urged temporary grounding of all C-5As because the plane "had not performed up to specifications."

The headquarters of the 18th Air Force in the Philippines refused to comment on reports that the controversial swept-wing C-5A had been delayed on its departure earlier from Clark Air Force Base due to mechanical trouble, where it was rushed into service under Ford's plan.

The presidential order directed that the Air Force assign the Lockheed-built C-5A Galaxy (which had been embroiled for years in controversy) to the Babylift rescue. In aviation circles it was known that the locking system frequently malfunctioned on its giant cargo doors that were so wide, three jeeps could be driven through them abreast. In 1971, an Air Force report even called it "a monster system that could lead to catastrophe." But, in the spring of 1975, it was considered that a successful rescue mission would bolster the plane's image, even though this cargo plane was not especially equipped for emergency evacuations while others nearby were.

There were four fully-equipped medical planes in the Philippines which could have been used instead of the C-5A, but weren't. One survivor, who was a sergeant in the medical corps, indicated at the time that there were three DC-9's and a C-141 on the ground in the Philippines which were medically equipped. Additionally, the crewman stated that he was briefed how the mission was supposed to end. Although it was indicated that the future Operation Babylift flights were to proceed to Clark Air Force Base in the Philippines, the C-5A, #80-218, was to proceed to Travis Air Force Base in California and President Ford was to meet the plane. The President was to take the first baby off as a gesture of support for the airlift and publicly tie him to the baby evacuation which accounted for why the C-5A was dubbed "the President's plane" as it departed from the Philippines.

Built by Lockheed Corporation in Marietta, Georgia, the Galaxy first flew in 1968 and had never been involved in a fatal accident. Two of the 81 planes (built at a cost of $55 million each) burned while on the ground, and a third was destroyed by fire the previous year after making a crash landing forced by a mid-air fire in one of its four turbofan engines. There were no injuries in any of those incidents.

The C-5A, which is still in use today, is 248 feet long and has a 223 foot wing span. With a maximum payload of 225,000 pounds and a top speed of 550 miles per hour, the plane has a normal crew of five and can carry as many as 15 in relief crews. The upper deck can seat 90 troops and the main deck can carry 270.

The Air Force officially began flying the plane in July, 1970, and it made a valuable contribution to the Vietnam War by hauling heavy equipment speedily to the war zone. It had been plagued by wing cracks from time to time, but continued to fly under weight restrictions.

The Galaxy was grounded for a time in 1971, after one of the four engines tore loose as one of the planes was preparing for take off from Altus Air Force Base in Oklahoma. The first crash of a C-5A was near

Clinton, Oklahoma, on September 27, 1947.

In addition to the theory that the plane crash may have been due to Viet Cong anti-aircraft fire, speculation began to emerge that it may have been due to sabotage. It was possible, during the confusion that surrounded the plane during loading, for someone to sneak aboard and plant an exploding device. Military sources in Saigon felt that to be a strong possibility and said it existed because the cargo doors of the C-5As were built so that the pilot controls should not be affected if the doors blew out. A team of investigators was summoned from Thailand the next day.

The rumor of sabotage was popular, and additional rumors to support the theory were rampant. Officers familiar with the design of the C-5A, who supported the concept of the large transport, said it was possible that a saboteur could have placed an explosive charge inside a passage leading from the cargo compartment to the plane's tail. Other Pentagon sources, who said they were keeping an open mind on the possible cause, pointed out that the C-5A was guarded by the South Vietnamese while on the ground.

In time, government investigators agreed the probable cause of the disaster was due to a defective latch on the door of the rear loading platform. What occurred resulted from the pressure that built up inside the cavernous holds and cabins, while outside the air pressure gradually diminished as the C-5A climbed to 23,000 feet. At that point, the pressure from within had grown too great and the improperly latched door blew out, followed by the ramp and other pieces of gear.

The explosive ejection severed the elevator control cables leading to the plane's tall T-shaped tail. To keep the plane from going into a dive, the pilot had to maintain a speed of 325 mph while turning back to Saigon. Then, on landing approach, the giant jet pitched and crashed.

Coincidentally, two Air Force photographers were aboard the ill-fated plane and took pictures of the damaged tail area while the plane was still aloft. But after the crash South Vietnamese soldiers looted the wreckage and destroyed both films as well as the flight-data recorder. The looters also stripped an injured flight engineer pinned in the wreckage of his watch, wallet, shoes and pistol. They pilfered anything of value from the victims and from the plane itself.

During the rescue operation it became evident by the actions of the

South Vietnamese soldiers that they were angered by the orphans leaving their homeland. One of the soldiers bitterly commented, "Too bad some of your souvenirs broke."

The feeling of resentment would emerge many times in the days to come when Vietnamese nationals showed anger at the loss of the children, the future of their country.

Major Dennis Traynor, the pilot who escaped unhurt was dazed and covered with mud. He recalled the events leading up to the crash and said he was eighteen minutes from Tan Son Nhut Air Base when he had to turn back. A Pentagon spokesman commended the pilot on keeping the plane level and bringing it in for a crash landing, lauding "It was a remarkable demonstration of flying skill."

The choppers continued back and forth for hours bringing the dead and living to the Seventh Day Adventist Hospital. One small boy was the sole survivor from the lower cargo deck. Officials of the adoption agencies hurried around the courtyard of the hospital trying to put the uninjured children into vehicles to return them to the familiar facilities they had left a few hours before. As one van pulled away, jammed with 22 babies and small children with escorts, it crept slowly past a trolley being pushed to the hospital morgue. The bodies were covered in green canvas bags and as they passed the children were silent. They did not speak. They did not cry.

The records of over one thousand FFAC orphaned children were being sent back on the flight and were destroyed in the crash of the Galaxy, along with 172 children and adults dead. It is doubtful if there were duplicate records.

When some of the children were returned to the orphanages, it was clear that thirteen of them were not orphans. The orphanage nurses said they didn't know them as they had no orphanage necklace I.D.'s and, most strikingly, no scabies, lice, furunculosis, diarrhea, or any of the other diseases which commonly distinguished the children of the orphanages. Further, no one at the orphanages recognized them. Speculation was that they were children placed aboard the flight by high officials. Often, during the evacuation, their children were among the orphans and met at the other end by family members or friends. It was a dependable escape route, and during the last hectic days of the war, when rules of procedure were broken to meet any eventuality, children were smuggled aboard the many flights departing from Vietnam.

News of the crash sent a shock wave throughout the United States where hundreds of families awaited the arrival of the first plane load of official Operation Babylift children.

The representatives of the agencies involved were numb with the news regarding the crash and the number of dead. Those who had been at the airport to see the Galaxy take off just minutes before were still in the area when it was attempting the emergency landing. The scene was one of horror, leaving them helpless on the ground, defenseless with the tragic sight before them. Bystanders were screaming, crying uncontrollably, and years would pass before many would be free of the pain, or could even discuss the incident. Many still have trouble today.

A new life in America—it was full of hope and promise for the orphans who had little chance at a normal life in Vietnam. Many of the children on the plane had come a long way in battling not only abandonment, but intolerable illness. An unfortunate act of fate destroyed that one chance of getting the life they deserved. Expressions of horror and shock came from agencies all over the world. The crash devastated the hopeful beginning of America's evacuation effort. Telephones of the adoption agencies were jammed throughout the country by prospective parents inquiring and anxious for news of their adoptive children who may have been on the plane. In Boston, actor Yul Brynner and his wife Jacqueline, like many other anxious couples, were keeping close to the telephone to find out if the infant Vietnamese girl they adopted was among those aboard the ill-fated plane. The crash of the Galaxy was to have far-reaching effects on those involved in the evacuation for years to come.

A White House aide at the presidential quarters in Palm Springs, California, awoke the President.

Upon hearing the disheartening news, President Ford said,"Our mission of mercy will continue. The survivors will be flown here when they are physically able. Other waiting orphans will make the journey. This tragedy must not deter us but offer new hope for the living." He added that he was "deeply saddened at the loss of so many innocent lives on the first official U.S. orphans evacuation flight from Saigon, but the airlift will go on."

Several weeks after the crash, Sister Ursula's body was shipped to Thailand to the Good Shepherd Convent there, en route to her home in Malaysia. Friends were asked to identify the body, even though it was doubtful that an identification could be made as 24 days had lapsed since the crash. To the astonishment of everyone, the sister's body was intact and serene. For those who knew her, she was well-remembered for distinctly tilting her mouth to one side when telling something funny. That was the expression they saw on the body.

A mother's heart was broken. Mrs. Moses, Margaret's mother, had been visiting her daughter in Saigon since Christmas. Infinitely proud of Margaret's humanitarian work in Vietnam, Mrs. Moses had extended her stay to help at the orphanages. When she learned of Margaret's death in the crash, she departed quietly on board a convoy to Australia, not only as a grieving mother, but as an aid helping children in need. Hers was a grief that did not speak, and a broken heart that found solace only by continuing her daughter's mission.

Edward J. Daly, President World
Airways, Inc.
Courtesy Western Aerospace Museum

Daly visiting the many
orphanages in Vietnam – 1971

Refugee evacuation from
Danang, March 1975

Maverick airlift from Saigon, April 2, 1975;
orphans aboard World Airways DC8

Daly (second
from left) at
Yakota with visi-
ble injuries from
Danang rescue
*Courtesy Stars &
Stripes*

Dr. Theodore K. Gleichman,
founder of the Friends of the
Children of Vietnam
Photo Courtesy Kay Gleichman

Dr. Gleichman,
en route to
remote villages
*Photo Courtesy
Kay Gleichman*

Ross Meador . . . a friend to the children of Vietnam

FCVN Bui Thi Xuan Critical Care Center, Saigon
Photo by Ross Meador

"Mister Ross"

FCVN van transporting infants from the Delta
Photos by Ross Meador

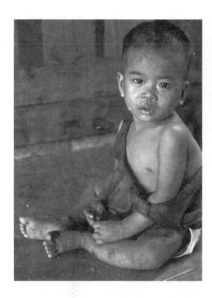

Orphans of Vietnam
Photos by Ross Meador

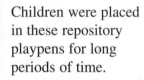

Children were placed
in these repository
playpens for long
periods of time.

Their crib was their world

Disabled children at Phu My Orphanage
Photos by Ross Meador

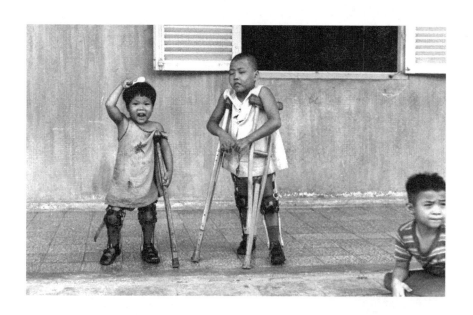

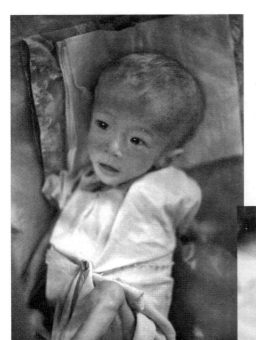

With no motivation for life, abandoned children just stopped living. Deformities, too, were common.

Photos by Ross Meador

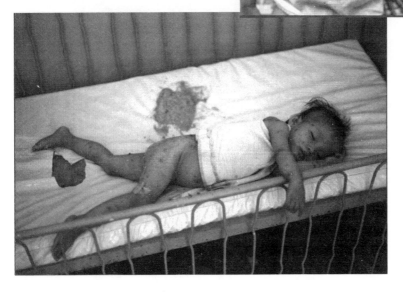

147

Orphanage at Vinh Long.
Healthy children found life more
tolerable.
Courtesy Ross Meador

Aerial view of C-5A Crash, April 4, 1975, Saigon
Courtesy Air Mobility Command History Office
Scott AFB

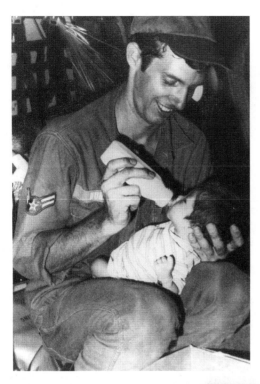

Airman feeding orphan en
route to Clark AFB,
Philippines, April 1975
Courtesy Gerald R. Ford Library

Infants transported to Clark
AFB on military transport,
April 1975
Courtesy Gerald R. Ford Library

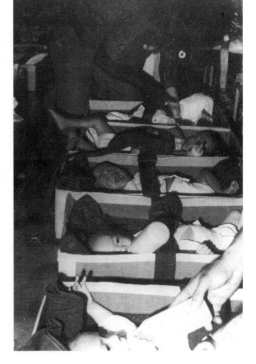

President Gerald R.
Ford welcomes
orphans, San
Francisco Int'l
Airport, April 5,
1975
*Courtesy Gerald R. Ford
Library*

President
Ford with
Babylift
orphan
*Courtesy Gerald
R. Ford Library*

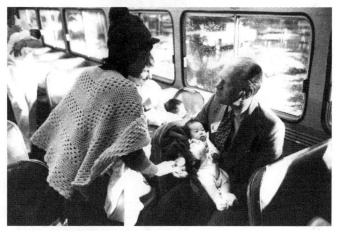

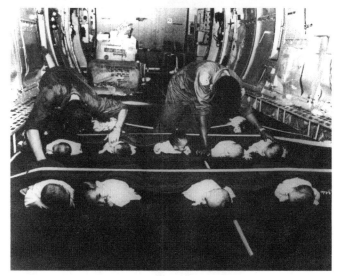

Operation
Babylift
transporting
orphans to
Clark AFB,
Philippines
*Courtesy Gerald
R. Ford Library*

Air Force crew assist
orphans boarding C141 at
Tan Son Nhut
Courtesy National Archives

If we're lucky . . .
maybe when we
wake up we'll be
home.

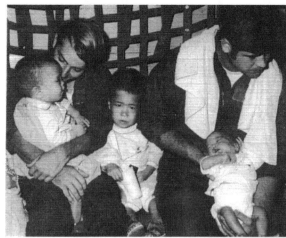

Orphans being cared for aboard C141 en route to U.S.
Courtesy National Archives

Harnessed cartons became cradles – combat crews became surrogate "mothers."

It sure is a long way to America.

Orphans arriving in the Philippines
Courtesy National Archives

Operation Babylift processing center, Clark AFB, Philippines
Courtesy Ross Meador

Evacuation from the roof of the U.S. Embassy, Saigon
April 29, 1975
Courtesy Ross Meador

Operation
Frequent Wind,
evacuation
aboard *USS
Midway*, April
29, 1975
*Courtesy Ross
Meador*

USS Midway
crowded with
ARVN
helicopters that
arrived with
pilots and their
families from
Saigon, April
30, 1975
*Courtesy Ross
Meador*

Orphans arriving Continental Care Center, Denver, April 1975, escorted by Lowry AFB personnel
Courtesy Bernie Mantey

Continental Care Center
2201 Downing Street
Denver, Colorado

Fitzsimons Army Hospital staff assists Babylift

The indomitable piano looms in the background as a little fellow helps himself to the juice bar.

Orphans
departing
to their
new
homes,
Continental
Care
Center,
May 1975

All a girl needs is
a new dress . . .

Shirley Barnes, Continental Administrator comforts a crying baby.

Shirley, Nuyet, and friend on leg.

Volunteers came in all sizes.
Blair Barnes, age 8

Volunteer Esther Hahn and friends
Photo Courtesy Rev. Hahn

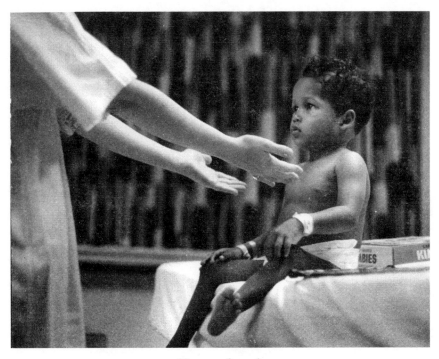

You are loved.
Photo Courtesy Bernie Mantey

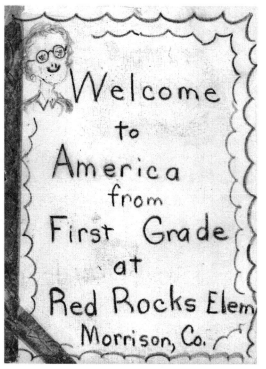

Friendship Portfolio of drawings created by Gertrude Borup's First Grade class, Red Rocks Elementary School, Morrison, Colorado. May, 1975

Amen.

May 15, 1989

Dear Ms. Peck-Barnes:

Thank you for your letter of May 1, 1989, in reference to "Operation Babylift" and indicating your plans to write a book on this historic rescue mission.

I have read the summary of your proposed book, which is most impressive. It certainly brought back vivid memories of those difficult days in 1975. I congratulate you on your proposed documentary.

Regrettably, I must decline your request to write a Foreword. Since leaving the White House I have been heavily over committed and as a result have mutually pledged with Mrs. Ford to cut back drastically. I support your endeavor, but cannot respond affirmatively to your request that I write a Foreword. I hope you understand.

You have my very best wishes for success on this most worthy project.

Best regards,

Gerald R. Ford

A letter from President Gerald R. Ford

THE WORLD'S LARGEST
CHARTER AIRLINE

WORLD AIRWAYS, INC. OAKLAND INTERNATIONAL AIRPORT · OAKLAND, CALIF. 94614

CABLE: WORLDAIR, OAKLAND
GENERAL OFFICES: (415) 577-2000
RESERVATIONS: (415) 577-2500

January 17, 1983

Ms. Shirley E. Barnes

Dear Ms. Barnes:

Thank you for your letter of January 10, 1983 requesting an interview.

I am enclosing some information regarding the "Baby Lift" that we put together. After you have read it and if you have further questions, I ask that you submit them first in writing. I will then decide if a personal meeting will be necessary.

Warmest regards.

Sincerely,

WORLD AIRWAYS, INC.

Edward J. Daly
Chairman of the Board

A STANDARD OF EXCELLENCE · A WORLD OF DIFFERENCE
Member National and International Air Carrier Associations

Although in failing health, Edward Daly sends his technical support
and warmest regards for the book.

GARY HART
COLORADO

COMMITTEES:
ARMED SERVICES
ENVIRONMENT AND PUBLIC WORKS
BUDGET

COLORADO OFFICE:
1748 HIGH STREET
DENVER, COLORADO 80218
(303) 837-4421
COLORADO SPRINGS (303) 635-0001
PUEBLO (303) 544-8277, EXT. 375

United States Senate

September 24, 1984

Ms. Shirley Peck-Barnes

Dear Ms. Barnes:

Thank you for taking the time to inform me about your
intentions to travel to the Socialist Republic of Vietnam as
part of your efforts to write a documentary about "Operation
Babylift." I appreciate knowing of your plans to undertake this
important project.

As you may know, I share the concern millions of Americans
have expressed about the fate of the children who were the target
of the humanitarian assistance provided by "Operation Babylift."
I applaud your efforts to remind the citizens of all nations
about the terrible price children pay when they become the victims
of a war, and I will look forward to seeing the results of your
inquiry.

Thank you once again for calling my Denver office.

Sincerely yours,

Gary Hart

THIS STATIONERY PRINTED ON PAPER MADE WITH RECYCLED FIBERS

Senator Gary Hart acknowledges author's request to visit Vietnam.
Hart's office sets up Vietnam Mission appointment

163

PERMANENT MISSION
OF THE SOCIALIST REPUBLIC OF VIET NAM
TO THE UNITED NATIONS
—
20 Waterside Plaza, New York, N.Y. 10010
(212) 685-8001

PHÁI ĐOÀN THƯỜNG TRỰC
CỘNG HOÀ XÃ HỘI CHỦ NGHIÃ VIỆT NAM
TẠI LIÊN HỢP QUỐC
—

5 December 1984

Ms. Shirley Evelyn Barnes

Dear Ms. Barnes :

    I would like to inform you of the message I have
just received from Hanoi regarding your request for permission
to visit Vietnam. The message is that your request has been
given due consideration by the relevant authorities, and that
due to problems we have at home in making necessary arrangements,
final approval of the request is not yet available. It is expected
that you will be able to make the trip in the first quarter of
1985, hopefully in January.

    In the meantime, I will stay in touch with you and
notify you of the final approval once it is available. Please
let me know anything further that I could be of service to you.
I solicit your understanding for the delay on our part.

Most sincerely,

Tran Trong Khanh
Press Secretary

Correspondence from Tran Trong Khanh, Press Secretary to the
Permanent Mission of the Socialist Republic of Vietnam to the
United Nations.

PHẢI ĐOÀN THƯỜNG TRỰC
CQNG HỜA XÃ HỘI CHỦ NGHĨA VIỆT NAM
TẠI LIÊN HỢP QUỐC
—

PERMANENT MISSION
OF THE SOCIALIST REPUBLIC OF VIET NAM
TO THE UNITED NATIONS
—

20 Waterside Plaza, New York, N.Y. 10010
(212) 685-8001

June 24, 1985

Ms. Shirley Evelyn Barnes

Dear Ms. Barnes ,

First of all , I must apologize to you for this very belated
reply. I was almost overwhelmed with the inflow of nearly 100 American
correspondents who came to Vietnam this time to cover the 10th Anniversary of the end of the war. Therefore, it is not until now that I
am in a position to write replies such as this one .

In the meantime, I have tried my utmost to make your trip to
Vietnam possible. Although , as I said to you, it appeared that the
approval was forthcoming, I have failed to get it until this moment.
I understand of course that,without the trip,your book will not be
complete or perfect the way you have desired. In saying this to you
I feel no less frustrated. But I hope you will understand .

Again, thank you very much for your warm disposition and for
the nice photo book you have sent to me. I sincerely hope that your
book will be laudable anyway.

Wishing all the best, I remain .

Yours sincerely

Tran Trong Khanh
Press Secretary

Letter from Tran Trong Khanh

165

Chapter VII

THE AIRLIFT

"Babies are precious little gifts to mankind. They shouldn't be left in boxes or dirty old oil drums... they should be in pretty little cradles or baskets of warm boughs."

Author unknown

Operation Babylift had many fathers. A sequence of events during the last months compelled both the United States and the Vietnamese governments to respond to the tragedy of the smallest victims of war. The abandonment of so many children was unprecedented in the history of both countries and options for a solution were running out in the spring of 1975.

OPERATION BABYLIFT – Saigon, Late March to April 15, 1975

Following the departure of the American troops in 1973, the failing Vietnamese government was overwhelmed by the stress and setbacks of the war. The country was on a course of economic destruction. The ceaseless flood of refugees into Saigon, and the unrelenting abandonment of children, were issues that Vietnamese officials had neither the manpower, or the funding, to stem the tide. And, though it was a major objective of both the Ministry of Social Welfare and the adoption agencies to curtail abandonment by providing services, it was too minimal for what was needed.

The adoption agencies recognized that finding homes for the orphans in the West was an equitable solution to saving the lives of babies who otherwise would perish in the war-ravaged country. With orphanages bulging and the availability of so many homeless children, American interest in adopting a Vietnamese child drastically increased.

In the early months of 1975, as the Communists thrust deeper into South Vietnam, the attempt to save the children had become almost an hour by hour agony. Prospective parents were concerned that Vietnamese orphans already selected for adoption faced not only real physical danger, with the increased hostilities, but would not be able to leave Vietnam expeditiously under the lengthy Vietnamese exit and U.S. immigration procedures.

With airlines hesitant to book chartered flights, for which a large advanced deposit was required, the agencies also had a concern for the only other available option—that requests for departure on Military Airlift Command (MAC) planes would unduly interfere with other priority evacuation plans. As a last resort, the adoptive parents and agencies jointly requested assistance from the U.S. government to expedite the movement of the Vietnamese orphans who were already approved for adoption in the United States. The unauthorized maverick flight of World Airways President Edward J. Daly was perceived to be a decisive act; the public outcry that followed was the catalyst for both Washington and Saigon to "to do something...and quickly."

Conversely, efforts were being made in Saigon even before Daly's daring flight. In late March, as the situation in Vietnam deteriorated, the United States Agency for International Development (USAID) entered into negotiations with Dr. Phan Quang Dan, Deputy Prime Minister in charge of resettlement (concurrently Minister of Social Welfare) on the question of evacuation of children who were already in the adoption process. The Deputy Prime Minister was sympathetic to the issue and on April 2nd prepared a letter to the Prime Minister of Vietnam requesting authorization for the agencies to move approximately 1,400 children who were then residing in child care centers in Vietnam. The Prime Minister signed the following letter, which was to become the basis for the Vietnamese government's cooperation in the adoption airlift. This letter was hand-delivered to the appropriate adoption agencies:

April 2, 1975

Dear Mr. Prime Minister:

At the present time, approximately 1400 orphans have been brought to Saigon, and are being cared for by international welfare agencies prior to being taken to foreign countries where they will be placed with permanent adoptive parents. At present, operations of the Ministry of Social Welfare and Hamlet Building and the Interministerial War Victims Relief Committee have been severely hampered by some complicated situations, among which requiring immediate resolution are the problems the orphans cited above which must be handled in conjunction with many other important difficulties that we are faced with. Moreover, the whole question of collective emigration of this number of orphans mentioned above is further exciting world opinion, particularly in the United States, much to the benefit of the Republic of Vietnam.

Right now, there are two 727's belonging to World Airways that have been waiting all night at the Tan Son Nhut Airport, prepared to transport free of charge the emigrating orphans. Mr. Daly, the President of the above mentioned airlines, is an international figure. The American Ambassador has also interceded with me to permit the orphans to leave the country together. He stressed, in addition to this emigration issue, how a million refugees and war victims fleeing the areas taken over by the communists would help to turn American public opinion regarding Vietnam, particularly the orphans arriving in the United States, given extensive TV and press coverage with narrated reports from witnesses of the situation, would have considerable influence

If you agree, Mr. Prime Minister, to approve the emigration of the orphans mentioned above, the Ministry of Social Welfare and Hamlet Building will coordinate with USAID to carefully monitor and control the international welfare agencies' implementation of this operation.

Respectfully,

Phan Quang Dan

In compliance with the letter, a procedure was immediately established to effectively carry out the departures. Each agency was required to submit a list of its children to Dr. Dan's office. After verification that the children were properly certified as adoptable (abandoned or formally released by the closest surviving relative or guardian), Dr. Dan, or the Chief of the Cabinet, would sign the list. It was arranged that this list would be sufficient authorization for departure of the children from Vietnam under the Ministry of Interior. It was also agreed that escorts (except Vietnamese, French or Chinese nationals) would be allowed to leave, even without individual exit visas. In practice, however, it turned out that airport immigration officials were not fully informed of these understandings, particularly regarding escorts. Therefore, it was often necessary to work out final details after the children and escorts arrived at the airports. Often this confusion caused further delays and disrupted the children to the point that it endangered them. USAID soon advised the agencies to use only those escorts with individual exit visas. The restriction dramatically reduced possible escape routes for orphanage workers who had hopes of going to America on the Babylift flights.

Two other agencies, USAID, and ADRR (The Associate Director of Relief and Rehabilitation) received the agency lists at the same time as Dr. Dan's office, and upon approval from the Vietnamese government, quickly arranged air transportation; USAID and the Embassy arranged bus transportation from agency to airport. The ADRR staff participated in assisting with escort exit visas, loading buses, getting Vietnamese immigration exit stamps, accompanying agency groups through airport formalities, and in loading the children on the airplanes.

Then, unexpectedly, a crisis arose. On or about April 8th, the Ministry of Interior noted that more than 2,042 orphans had been evacuated, exceeding the 1,400 authorized. Since no quota was designated for each agency, an inequity existed. The question was raised, as it soon would have been in any case, as to whether the airlift could continue. Dr. Dan informed USAID that he would continue to authorize small departures on a group by group basis. Orphans from the An Loc Orphanage, along with FCVN, PBF, and CRS, were then authorized to move some 300 children who were unable to make the earlier flights.

APRIL 16 - 28, 1975

With the instability of the government and the changes erupting in the cabinet, Dr. Dan was no longer in a position of authority, and there was serious doubt that the existing airlift procedure would continue. Several agencies continued to submit additional lists for the new Minister of Social Welfare (Tran Van Mai) but he made no decisions. When the ADRR urged the new Minister to continue the procedure, and specifically to authorize the lists already in his hands, he reneged and said that any decision would have to be made at the Prime Minister's level. At this point, the seven agencies were frantic. As the Vietnamese government further deteriorated, it became evident that no continued formal authorizations of the movements of adoptable children could be expected. The Minister had, however, indicated verbally that the MSW would not object to, or intercede to prevent, further movements. On this basis the ADRR advised the adoption agencies that USAID would arrange transportation of those children remaining, with the clear understanding that all agency personnel would depart with, or shortly after, the children, and this would end U.S. adoption activity in Vietnam. Operation Babylift was completed on April 25, 26, and 28th.

President Ford's announcement and implementation of Operation Babylift quickly put the evacuation in motion. Funds were made available to the MAC and the Department of Defense (DOD) by the Agency for International Development (AID) for transportation and operating costs in reception/processing centers at military bases in the Pacific Area and on the west coast of the United States. The transportation and reception budget was estimated at $2,000,000, while an additional $600,000 was allotted for medical services.

Flights departed daily from Saigon's Tan Son Nhut Airport to Clark Air Force Base in the Philippines. It was the major intermediate processing center in the Pacific area, where the orphans rested and were provided necessary medical services, including hospitalization if required. After a preliminary immigration screening and clearance, they were usually transported within 24 hours to the reception centers in the United States. Refueling stops at Anderson Air Force Base in Guam, and Hickam Air Force Base in Hawaii, were also geared to render assistance if any child required medical attention or hospitalization before continuing on to the Continental United States.

Three major processing and reception centers in the United States were located on the west coast bases of the Presidio in San Francisco, Long Beach Naval Support Activity in California and Fort Lewis in Washington. The Presidio was the first center to be activated on April 2nd and would handle sixty percent of the orphans processed through all the centers.

The Presidio became involved initially at the request of Charlotte Behrendt, Ed Daly's daughter. Ms. Behrendt reported that several hundred orphans were airborne on a World Airways aircraft from

Vietnam and would be arriving at Oakland International Airport on or about 2200 hours on April 2, 1975. As a result of the abrupt change in plans in Saigon (FFAC's cancellation) Daly departed with only 57 of FCVN's children. With Operation Babylift officially on the books, the U.S. Army Forces Command at the Presidio was directed to provide accommodations and facilities for the temporary care of the Vietnamese orphans arriving in the United States from Southeast Asia. Although the Presidio was the first center to be established to receive orphans as a processing center, and because it processed the majority of them, it also experienced the most problems. Since there had been no precedence for this type of operation, those involved at the Presidio had to resolve procedures on an ad hoc basis. In addition, flights were not well spaced, and the large numbers of orphans who arrived in a short period of time overwhelmed the staff and facilities. (Within a four-day period, from April 5-8 inclusive, 819 orphans were processed at the Presidio.)

Harmon Hall, Bldg. #649 was designated as the primary site for the reception and housing of the children. It was a large gymnasium-type facility and consisted of several large rooms on either side of a very large court. Approximately 350 mattresses were placed end to end in columns of twenty. At the end of each column a medical examination table was set up. There was only one bathroom for females and one for males, and washroom facilities proved to be totally inadequate for the activity that was subsequently generated. Two additional buildings, #617 and #910, were organized and equipped to accommodate the overflow.

The military plan called for the Presidio to assume responsibility for communication facilities, housing, food service, transportation equipment and supplies and security. It responded par excellence. To coordinate and assume overall responsibility for all other aspects of the administration of the operation, namely the identification processing and release of the orphans, medical service, volunteers, records, internal communication, inter-agency liaison, etc., an ad hoc planning committee of volunteers emerged. Subsequently, they developed into an incorporated organization known as Orphans Airlift, Inc., and assumed a controlling role rather than a supportive role in the operation.

The Board of Directors of this organization served as a resource group and was made up of affluent business and politically influential leaders of the Bay area. Without resistance from the Presidio or from representatives of the seven official adoption agencies who had legal custody of the arriving orphans, Orphans Airlift, Inc., literally took over and developed a power infrastructure that was never challenged. Manpower for the management group was provided largely by the recruitment of many volunteers, including a group of Veterans. During the course of the operation, and within the organization itself, conflict, dissension and power struggles developed, causing unnecessary delay, confusion and frustration. The scenario had a familiar ring to what many adoption agencies were experiencing within their own organizations. Throughout the airlift, conflicts would arise between the Orphans Airlift group and the adoption agency personnel who, although they knew the children best, were completely disregarded in their processing and care.

In the USAID report of 1975, Orphans Airlift, Inc. was given good marks: "Although the performance of Orphans Airlift, Inc. lacked luster and sophistication, problems developed that could have been avoided in the absence of any other jurisdiction willing to assume overall control and responsibility for the entire operation. In retrospect, it can be concluded that the group made a substantial contribution to the success of Operation Babylift."

THE FIRST FLIGHT

Operation Babylift had a disastrous beginning with the crash of the C5A Galaxy on April 4th. However, FFAC quickly rebounded from the disaster and chartered a flight the following day. Sadly, it took the tragedy to convince Pan American Airways that the orphans needed a fully-equipped plane, and only after a Connecticut businessman stepped in with a downpayment of $150,000 against the total cost of $230,000 for the flight.

Although the C5A was the first designated flight out of Saigon under the program, the FFAC Pan Am 747, with 324 orphans aboard, would be the first flight to arrive under the U.S. government sponsored airlift. The Pan Am flight became known as the "President's Plane," having the distinction of being met by President Gerald R. Ford at the San Francisco International Airport. Except for a refueling stop at Yakota AFB, Japan, the flight came directly from Saigon.

On this same day, Holt also sponsored a Pan Am chartered flight, which arrived in Seattle with 376 orphans, including 28 sponsored by the Pearl Buck Foundation. Most of these orphans were in good physical condition and were scheduled for onward movement to various points in the United States. Unlike the FFAC flight, which processed at the Presidio, no reception facilities were utilized for the Holt manifest, although Fort Lewis Army Base was on standby. These first two chartered flights were arranged by the organizations themselves as private charters, but because of the circumstances which existed and the financial problems the agencies were experiencing, the charters were picked up and financed under Operation Babylift.

The FFAC Pan Am flight was configured for transporting children with special supplies aboard. Cardboard cartons lined with pillows and red airline throws were used to box the babies safely. Milk and formula, along with cases of diapers, plastic bags, clothing and blankets, were also plentiful.

With all the rumors of possible sabotage of the C5A, only the eleven FFAC escorts and the Pan Am crew were allowed on the plane. Christie Leivermann, the nurse from Minneapolis, Minnesota, who had survived the C5A crash a day earlier, admirably boarded the Pan Am jet without any visible hesitation.

Unprecedented, the caring of so many children on the long flight presented a marathon of feedings and changing diapers. Tempering the tears and fears of the older children grouped in first class would be an ongoing effort in itself. Each tiny baby was placed in a low-sided cardboard box that slipped under the seats of the long cabin, later to be pulled out like dresser drawers. The larger babies were in large boxes wedged between the seats. With so many people handling babies, there was an understandable worry that when a baby was taken from a box, was it fed, or had it missed a feeding? The same confusion occurred when a baby was also asleep and passed over when feeding bottles were distributed. There was a constant stream of wails and cries from babies and children throughout the flight and an ongoing search for signs of dehydration and respiratory disasters. Odors of vomiting and soiled diapers permeated the cabin, and the aisles were consistently crowded...not only from the volunteers, but with children who wandered the length of the plane, bored, restless and curious.

Arrival at Yakota AFB produced a detail of medical officers on board to examine the children and to render whatever assistance was needed. It was consistent with the Air Force stopover support and part of the Operation Babylift massive relief effort ordered by President

Ford. FFAC was visibly upset, insisting that they didn't request medical help. Despite the fact that FFAC held custody of the orphans, the army doctors proceeded with their orders to check the children. (It was a wise precautionary measure. Babies died on subsequent flights en route to the United States; ramifications of such occurrences could conceivably hinder the operation.)

A heated discussion erupted when the doctors selected twenty of what they determined to be very sick children in need of hospitalization. In addition to chickenpox, some of the children were found to be dehydrated and in need of nourishment. FFAC stood its ground, insisting that the children the army chose to hospitalize had superficial problems well-known to their nurses. The medics were directed away from, and missed, the tiny babies tucked in the back section who were dehydrated and in respiratory distress. Leivermann was prepared to put them on IVs upon departure of the military medical team. Wende Grant, the FFAC Director, threatened to cancel the remainder of the flight in retaliation for what she perceived as the army's interference, and she demanded hospitalization for all 324 children. The doctors relented and negotiated, hospitalizing what they considered to be the two emergency cases.

A two-month girl, who had what was considered to be a "boil" by FFAC, was diagnosed by the doctors to be suffering from malnutrition, dehydration and a dangerous abscess that could spread to the bloodstream. Another two-year old, whose eyes were crusted and closed, was also removed with severe conjunctivitis, a disease that, if untreated, can lead to blindness. (Both girls received medical attention and were sent to the U.S. at a later time.)

In addition to a variety of ailments, doctors found that many children had chickenpox, the mildly serious childhood disease that is highly infectious; it is possible that more children contracted it later.

Adding to the mayhem, Captain D. W. Salsberry of the Pan Am crew emerged to announce that reporters were waiting to come aboard to photograph the children.

"Absolutely not!" challenged Grant.

The pilot went on to explain that he had received a cable requesting the news coverage from the "highest U.S. authority…from the *very* highest authority," he added.

Grant stood her ground again. The captain, relenting on the request, retreated to tell the newsmen that they could not board his plane.

"Wonderful man," Grant wrote years later. "I should have expressed my gratitude. He was to be the last person for weeks who recognized my responsibility and authority as Director of the agency holding custody of those 324 children."

Captain Salsberry was indeed in tune with his cargo. Earlier, as the aircraft approached Yakota, he called ahead for 40 orders of fried rice for the older children. The request was answered by the Air Base Wing Chief of Services, Lt. Col. Bobby Lay and SM Sgt. O. Higgenbothem, non-commissioned officer in charge of the commissary at Yakota. The two men got the rice from the commissary and rushed to the military dining hall to cook it themselves, putting the fried rice into paper cups they scrounged from the terminal cafeteria. Also sent on board were additional supplies and cans of air freshener; other Air Force personnel raided their children's playrooms and came up with bags of toys.

Upon departure from Yakota, volunteer Red Cross nurses from the base, who joined the flight to the U.S., took charge of the perpetual feedings and changing of diapers, which came as a relief to the already over-burdened escorts and stewardesses.

Although the children and infants on the flight lacked passports and entry visas for the U.S., they were eligible for the parole power that was invoked under Operation Babylift. However, one of the Red Cross nurses had been instructed to fill out U.S. Immigration forms I-94 for each child. Since many children had multiple bracelets attached to their arms, each depicting different information, it became a dilemma to construct the forms. One bracelet could bear the child's orphanage name, while another the birth name, or the name of their adoptive parents. Additional bracelets contained the formula the baby was taking, or other information. Further, as babies were lifted from their beds, for whatever reason, often they were not returned to the same boxes. Later, there was to be massive confusion and delay at the Presidio when many children bore the same name, "Hy Vong", which was the nursery from which they came—not their identity. Too, it was apparent that the FFAC staff was grossly irritated by the questions and actions of the volunteers, especially when one arose regarding infusions into those very sick babies as opposed to hospitalization at Yakota.

Arrival at San Francisco was shortly after 10:00 pm. Rigid security measures were invoked at the airport since President Ford was scheduled to meet the plane. The plane taxied down the floodlit tarmac and into its berth. The stairs were wheeled into place, yet there was no movement for what the exhausted escorts considered to be an excessively long delay. (Standard airline safety procedures require a complete shut-down of engines before doors are opened and passengers are allowed to disembark.)

The medical team was the first to board. Additional stairs were simultaneously placed at the rear door where Leivermann and others soon emerged carrying infants to the waiting ambulances. Within minutes, President Ford and his entourage appeared and boarded the plane. Shortly thereafter, he emerged from the plane, smiling and carrying a child. Flashbulbs popped and the media were positioned all around the tarmac to capture the moment all of America had anxiously been awaiting.

According to one disgruntled volunteer: "During all the confusion of the President's appearance, the rest of the children and escorts had to remain on board to have him meet us...greet the children...to be thanked...I wasn't sure which." However, all the attention generated by the President's appearance in no way hampered what was occurring in the tail section—an orderly quick flow of very sick babies being taken to hospitals throughout the Bay area.

Daly's daughter, Charlotte Behrendt, also boarded, much to the chagrin of some escorts who expressed they "couldn't imagine why." What was discounted was that Behrendt had coordinated arrangements days earlier for supportive services to meet her father's plane, the one that FFAC was to use, then canceled. It would not have been unusual for her to be there...she was highly supportive of FFAC and was there to assure that all the procedures were carried out according to schedule. Considering the months of anguish they had just experienced, and the fact that they had not slept during the past thirty hours, the sensitivity of the staff was understandable. Further, President Ford, who authorized Operation Babylift, met the plane representing the American people, who were not only overwhelmingly supportive of his actions, but in no uncertain terms were happily picking up the tab for the rescue.

Long lines of volunteers entered and exited the plane carrying crying and screaming children to the buses that would transport them to the Presidio. The scene was surreal. Grant had expected to be greeted by her own staff of volunteers, and in the confusion of witnessing strangers taking control, demanded to know "what was happening?" She was abruptly told to "sit down!" Grant found relief in the involuntary tears that flowed. She had envisioned this differently...that familiar faces would be there to feed and care for the babies. And although a few of her counterparts had arrived, there were not nearly enough to handle the volume of children. Orphans Airlift volunteers were hurriedly doing the job. By the time the plane landed, all supplies of infant formula and clothing were exhausted. Time was of the essence, and the frightened, hungry children were in need of immediate attention. It was a time when "any arms" would do.

Usually, the orphans who were abandoned and referred to the agencies for adoption were those in the poorest of health, but the adoption agencies, under normal circumstances, nursed them back to good physical condition prior to departure from Vietnam. However, the abrupt departure of many children who were in the process of rehabilitation, and the manner of transporting them in large groups, increased the incidence of sickness and need for hospitalization. The children who arrived on the first flight had the following characteristics: Of the 324 aboard, approximately 200 were under the age of two. One-third of them had diarrhea on arrival. Ninety-nine percent of them were crying, dehydrated and in need of nourishment. Thirty were immediately removed from the plane, identified as seriously ill and dispatched to waiting ambulances and transported to pre-determined Bay area hospitals. Notably many were from the Hy Vong Nursery and deemed to be too sick to be placed on the C5A Galaxy a day earlier, yet were placed on the Pan Am flight.

With seven adoption groups receiving hundreds of children daily at the Presidio, it immediately became apparent that the sponsor's identification system would not withstand the rigorous disruptions. In addition to constant changes in personnel children were moved for medical treatment, feedings and bathing. Operation Airlift immediately set up their own identification system that included a portfolio for each child containing an immigration form, footprints, medical information and photograph. Irrespective of every precaution taken, there was still confusion and a scramble for data. Sponsors spent hours wandering between mattresses trying to identify and locate their children.

Although the situation was not ideal and there were many mistakes made on the part of all parties involved, it was apparent that an enormous effort had gone into organizing the arrival of the children and in providing for their care. Nevertheless, simple oversights occurred. While the babysitters themselves wore heavy sweaters in the cool, drafty court of Harmon Hall, babies accustomed to the 90 degree temperatures of Saigon lay on mattresses clothed in only diapers and undershirts. Chaotic as it was, FFAC was at least appreciative that they had a place to house the children until further arrangements could be made for travel to their adoptive homes. The final insult came when a doctor who had been on the flight admonished Wende Grant: "This is a medical disaster," he declared, then gave an ultimatum. "You have twelve hours to remove these children from the Presidio." He insisted that more flights were due and that the doctors were exhausted from working several days without sleep to keep pace with the children that were brought to them in such poor health. He went on to cite a litany of their illnesses, declaring that some of the babies had pneumonia and others were on the verge of it.

Exhausted, overwrought, it was a threat Grant didn't need to hear. He was actually reprimanding her for saving children's lives. "The operation in Vietnam had been a disaster for eight years!" she informed him, uncompromising. Children, sick, dying, abandoned...she had seen it all. Babylift was the last hope of saving at least a few.

There was some substance to the doctor's frustration, however. During the four-day period of April 5-8 inclusive, some 819 orphans were processed within a 72 hour period at the Presidio. The facility had processed 1,313 children under Operation Babylift, with the hospitalization of 186 children for a total of 1,186 days. The Long Beach Naval Support Activity Center processed 452 orphans, with 82 hospitalized for a total of 868 days. Fort Lewis, in Washington, processed 224 orphans, with 42 hospitalized for 176 days total.

Considering that 51% of the orphans were under two years of age and that many of them were in poor physical condition, the medical services provided during Operation Babylift were very effective. Of the 2,547 orphans processed under the program, there were nine deaths, seven whose ages were known to be twenty weeks of age or younger. Burials were carried out by the concerned processing centers: Clark Air Force Base (3), Fort Lewis (2), Long Beach (2), Guam (1), and the Presidio (1)...with the permission of the known sponsoring agencies under the auspices of Operation Babylift.

It was a sad footnote to the heroic efforts of Babylift.

SUMMARY — USAID Operation Babylift Report, April–June 1975

Operation Babylift was initiated on April 2, 1975 with the intended purpose of providing transportation from Vietnam to the United States of approximately 2,000 orphans who were being processed for inter-country adoptions by the following U.S. voluntary agencies approved by the Government of Vietnam for that purpose.

The agencies were:
Holt International Children's Services (HOLT);
Traveler's Aid-International Social Services of America (TAISSA);
Friends of the Children of Vietnam (FCVN);
United States Catholic Conference (USCC);
Friends For All Children (FFAC);
Pearl Buck Foundation (PFB);
World Vision Relief Organization (WVRO).

A total of 2,547 children were processed under Operation Babylift. Of this number, 602 were en route to other countries, leaving a total of 1,945 for adoption in the United States. Not included in this figure were earlier recorded figures: 1974 there were approximately 1,362 adoptions completed by seven MSW authorized agencies. The early months of 1975 would dramatically increase that figure to some 3,939 orphans who arrived in the United States.

A total of 46 MAC or MAC-chartered flights were involved in Operation Babylift. Many of these were used to shuttle the orphans from Saigon to Clark Air Force Base in the Philippines. Twenty-six Operation Babylift flights, and six not under the sponsorship of Operation Babylift, brought orphans to the United States. The six included three unauthorized World Airways flights and three regularly scheduled Pan Am flights which had small numbers of orphans aboard.

The USAID report relied on information received from the adoption agencies, which brings out a number of interesting facts about the orphans processed: Over 91% were under age of eight; 57% were male and 43% female; and 20% were racially mixed.

The USAID report was compiled to be a summary of Operation Babylift for the files of the Agency and for future reference purposes. It is based on the best information available and from those who played a key role in the operation. Understandably, there are some differences in the statistics as reported by the various elements, and the report is considered to be *dated.*

CHAPTER VIII
THE LAST DAYS

Friend after friend departs:

Who had not lost a friend?

There is no union here of hearts

That finds not here an end...

– James Montgomery

A vibrant spring, bursting with the hope of a renewal of life, unfolded for thousands of refugees who escaped to the northern hemisphere during the last days in April, 1975. In the small Asian country of Vietnam, there would be no such hope. Each day, South Vietnam lost more territory to the Communists. A massive Communist force of 140,000 enemy troops had closed in on Saigon from all sides with staggering speed, then abruptly halted its advance. The battlefield lull was undoubtedly a tactical pause. The North Vietnamese Army demanded that all U.S. military personnel leave Vietnam. The Americans, in turn, wanted to get as many Vietnamese co-workers out as quickly as possible. The Communists would soon put an end to the game.

Saigon, bulging with refugees and retreating South Vietnamese troops, was at the mercy of the Communist forces, who had enough artillery at the edge of the suburbs to utterly level it if they chose to do so. The unexpected relaxed vigilance at the gates of the city indicated that the South Vietnamese government had one last chance to surrender, and in doing so would avoid total military defeat and devastation. In essence, the South Vietnamese were being asked to give up without further fighting. Additionally, a Communist demand was made that the Saigon government must have no holdovers from the old U.S.-supported regime. It was "unconditional surrender."

Despite the grim picture of inevitable defeat, the orphanage representatives continued to work frantically to save the children. These volunteers were among the last westerners to leave the country, something they did all too reluctantly. No sooner was an orphanage emptied, closed and its charges shuttled to the airlift when, in the absence of its staff, it was refilled with abandoned children.

Hysteria overtook all reasoning regarding the fate of the children. The savagery of the Viet Cong was expected toward pro-American South Vietnamese, yet there was no conclusive evidence that the Communists, as victors, would butcher any of the babies fathered by Americans.

Two decades earlier the French had left a crop of babies, including many fathered by black soldiers from France's African colonies, but the Communists had not singled them out, nor their mothers, for persecution. A social stigma existed in the North as well as in the South against mixed blood children as a direct result of the internal view of racial purity by the Vietnamese themselves.

Yet the frustration that their work was far from over found the orphanage volunteers scrounging for a spark of encouragement from the Communist insurgents. Had there been some hope that their presence would be welcomed under the new regime, it is probable that they would have continued in their mission to work with the children. If the Red Cross had some assurance of their safety, many of the westerners would have remained. Instead, rumors of a blood bath were rampant. Weeks earlier, with the fall of Cambodia to the Khmer Rouge, the fate of hundreds of French citizens was still uncertain.

The U.S. interception of Khmer Rouge radio transmissions substantiated a blood bath in Cambodia in which orders were issued to kill all Cambodian Army officers and their families. A round of executions had been carried out. Foreigners who were allowed to leave the country remained silent once across the border into Thailand, agreeing not to discuss their ordeal to ensure the safety of those still left in Phnom Penh. A news blackout prevailed as Cambodia had no telephone or telegraph communications with other nations since the Khmer Rouge takeover. The fate of several Americans believed to have taken refuge in the French Embassy in Cambodia was unknown. The Americans in Saigon recognized that they could easily find themselves in a similar situation with the fall of South Vietnam.

At least eighty journalists from around the world, who were

allowed by their home offices to decide for themselves, gambled and remained to continue reporting the story after Vietnam fell. Among them were three Americans. Within hours after Saigon's fall, much to the journalists' surprise, it was possible to wander about the streets without feeling any threat or animosity. It was a quiet end after all.

Throughout the month of April, 1975, as all hope diminished for a peaceful settlement, both foreign and U.S. adoption agencies urged their staff to leave the country. Many volunteers defied the orders to close down their operations and held out until the last days. Then, reluctantly, and always with tears, they packed their suitcases and left. "We just left...we got into a cab and left," one volunteer sobbed. "We just left...there were the crying babies, sick children...little supplies and what little staff remained had no funds to continue without us..."

Ross Meador was among those reluctant to leave. For more than a year he had been FCVN's Co-Director of Overseas Operations. He had been directed by the Denver Headquarters to dispose of all its equipment and supplies and to leave Vietnam. Each day he told himself, "tomorrow, maybe tomorrow." It was as if he had some physical restraints keeping him there. The real weight was in his heart. He could not, or would not, leave Vietnam with so much left undone. In delivering the remainder of his supplies to various nurseries around the city, he noted that they were bulging beyond capacity. There was no hope for control.

For the past fourteen months, Meador had seen the pain and suffering inflicted on the most innocent of all...the very young. There existed in his mind a continued state of denial that man could sanction such devastation. Only with the departure of all the FCVN personnel, with no new replacements forthcoming, did it became apparent to him that the war would soon be over.

During the last days, life inside the orphanage compound at Gia Dinh was comparatively normal, except for the echoes of rockets at night. The only visible signs of combat edging closer was the increased number of military convoys in the Saigon outskirts.

Early one morning, Meador awoke in his second-floor bedroom to the rumble of heavy vehicles and looked out to see four tanks and ten truck convoys full of bombs passing the gates below. He had never seen a bomb before, and the realization that the war's end was near left him shaken. He could not believe it was happening before his eyes. America was too strong to allow this tiny country, so heavily invested with American lives, to fall victim to the Communists.

"No," he rationalized like so many others. "The Marines will sure-ly land again!"

Yet, no Marines came.

Only the Marine guards at the U.S. Embassy, the DAO (Defense Attaché Office) complex, and the airfield facility remained. The only Marines to come later were those flown in to secure "Operation Frequent Wind," the final evacuation.

When the Americans left Vietnam two years earlier, they stock-piled warehouses with supplies and equipment. The South was supe-rior in every respect to the North, and it was envisioned that the con-flict between the two segments could continue for years. No one was prepared for the rapid deterioration that occurred in the spring of 1975.

Nguyen Van Thieu, who was the President of South Vietnam for ten years, repeatedly encouraged his countrymen to fight for every inch of Vietnamese territory. Then, taking U.S. intelligence officers by surprise, he failed to advise the American government in advance of his decision to evacuate half of his country. He issued unexpected orders for South Vietnamese troops to withdraw from several provinces.

Thieu's decision to give up the territory was a gamble that he could improve his country's defensive posture, and he clearly hoped it would be the last retreat. But the surrender of half his country was the tragedy that led to the ultimate defeat.

The withdrawal came as a surprise to the Vietnamese people them-selves. Many of the troops became discouraged, and soldiers rapidly deserted the Army, hastily shedding their uniforms and retreating south or into hamlets in the hills. Many ARVNs also deserted to evac-uate their wives and children who accompanied them in the field.

Thieu reminded his countrymen that the Americans signed the Paris agreement that promised aid to South Vietnam. Nixon had pledged that when, and if, North Vietnam renewed its aggression, the U.S. would actively and strongly intervene. It was a common belief throughout Saigon that the Americans would come back to save the country from the Communists.

Meanwhile, Congress was divided in its feelings regarding the American involvement in Vietnam. There were numerous, futile attempts to get support from the legislators for additional aid to South Vietnam, even after the withdrawal.

Every whisper of Communist atrocities was transmitted back to Washington in the belief that the stories of savagery might help win further support. Congressmen and cabinet members embellished the blood bath predictions with figures exceeding hundreds of thousands of Vietnamese that might be massacred in the takeover.

With the intent of renewing the American military buildup in Vietnam, a South Vietnamese official attempted to reveal the undisclosed Nixon promise to aid Vietnam. He released two letters written in November, 1972, and January, 1973, in which Nixon promised that the U.S. would take "swift and serious retaliatory action" and "would respond with full force" if Hanoi violated the Paris Peace Accords. Nixon's public statement in 1973 that the U.S. "will not tolerate violations of the agreement" did not reflect the strong words in the earlier letters.

American diplomats were enraged by Thieu's charges and venomous attack that Saigon was losing the war because of inadequate American aid. The fact was that the U.S. left five billion dollars in military equipment for South Vietnam when the last soldier packed his bags and went home in 1973. Saigon had 600 fighter-bombers and 900 helicopters, thousands of tanks and artillery pieces, and enough light arms to equip a ground force of 700,000 men.

Additionally, the U.S. provided millions of dollars of spare parts and hired American technicians to take care of the equipment Saigon couldn't maintain by itself.

Even if American appropriations were falling, South Vietnam's arsenals were stocked full when the offensive began. The Pentagon hadn't even spent the $175 million of the 1975 appropriation for ammunition when the shooting ended.

The rout that put Saigon in its sad predicament was the result of Thieu's poor leadership and the default of his officers.

It was common knowledge that graft and corruption dominated the poor country, even during the French and American operations. It ran even more rabid after the withdrawal of American troops in 1973, particularly in the military.

President Thieu had survived a decade of intense but disorganized political opposition while fighting the devastating war. When his withdrawal order served only to deteriorate the South Vietnamese defenses and demoralize the people who fought to defend their country, it became apparent to all that Saigon was in grave danger. It was the last stronghold. In the final hours of his presidency, Thieu went on National Vietnamese Television, made America the scapegoat, and heaped scorn and blame on the U.S. He never accepted any blame for himself for the clumsy decisions that ruined his Army and lost the war for South Vietnam in a single month.

Thieu vowed to stay and fight as he announced his resignation, "I resign, I do not desert. From this minute I will put myself at the disposal of the new President and the people. I will continue to stay close to you all in the coming task of national defense."

The valedictory was patriotic, but hollow. Within five days of his promise to the people, Thieu flew off into exile to Taipei, departing from South Vietnam (along with fifteen tons of household baggage and personal effects).

Thieu was replaced by his aging and feeble Vice President, Tran Van Huong, a nearly blind Confucian scholar. Almost immediately, the Communists declared Huong unacceptable as a negotiator. There were grave questions whether the South Vietnamese should defy the Communists and fight if necessary, or force Huong to step aside and make way for a new chief of state more acceptable to the conquerors at the gate. Huong attempted to set up negotiations with Hanoi, who in turn refused to meet with one of his ministers. When it was obvious that Saigon would have to replace him or face destruction, Huong stepped down in favor of a burly ex-general, Duong Van Minh. "Big Minh" was a man whom the Communists considered more acceptable to meet their demands for a peaceful takeover.

An escape epidemic began to grip the population; the topic of discussion seemed always to be *when* are you going? Leaving Saigon was the only alternative to an impending Communist victory. During the first week of April alone, nearly one million refugees flowed into the city, mostly by foot. This influx of people sent terror through the rest of the population as there was no place else to run. Dusty district roads and coastal highways were choked with countless thousands of frightened civilians clutching their possessions and fleeing their hamlet homes to the last sanctuary of the country.

Ross Meador had given only minor consideration to his own safety. He was too involved in the welfare of his Vietnamese friends, the locals who gave support and assistance to FCVN. A perpetual fear existed for those assisting the Americans that they would be singled out and dealt with harshly with the Communist takeover. It was a terror that was understandable in light of the stories that drifted to the South from refugees who told of reprisals by the North Vietnamese forces.

During the final weeks, a public announcement declared that any Vietnamese obtaining an American sponsor would be airlifted to California. Immediately, the FCVN office became swamped with friends and strangers alike seeking asylum and requesting sponsorship. It was agreed that the agency would accommodate a select group of close friends. Yet one difficulty remained. Even though Americans agreed to sponsor the airlift, the Vietnamese government refused to allow any citizen to leave without an exit visa, the cost of which was driven up from one million piasters ($1,333) to $20,000. It was never clear what happened to the collected revenue. The collapsing Vietnamese government gave no accountability of the income or the financial assets.

In any event, the average Vietnamese could not even afford the price of an airline ticket to freedom, let alone a ransom for an exit visa. Meador began to seek means by which he could get some of his friends to America. Frequently, they were sent along to the airport as escorts for the children and then smuggled on the planes. But risking a last minute immigration check was always a threat, and guards were carefully reviewing any documented approval.

Meador devised a relatively simple plan. There was only one entrance gate onto the airfield, and it was heavily guarded by five well-armed Vietnamese MPs. Once inside the air base, the chances of getting stopped were slim. If he could make it to the runway, the U.S. military contingent assured him they would take over from that point.

Getting the Vietnamese nationals through the checkpoint without papers was risky. Meador was depending upon the fact that he was a familiar figure driving the FCVN van and that he would be recognized as an American. Failure could produce serious consequences. If they were caught, he would have no alternative but to claim diplomatic immunity. It would be a lie, but the only one he could perpetrate. As for his Vietnamese friends, they would certainly face immediate imprisonment and later, perhaps, death in the hands of the Communist victors who took drastic action for desertion and treason.

Despite the risks involved, a decision was made to attempt an escape on a departing evacuation flight scheduled to leave at dusk. Five escapees were placed on the floor of the FCVN van, covered with blankets and suitcases. The gates of the orphanage compound were opened, and the van moved slowly through the crowd congregated around the entrance. Each time a vehicle left the orphanage compound, Meador worried. There had been several incidents where refugees attempted to halt the van and shouted, "Take me, take me," fully aware that the cargo inside was headed for the airport.

Meador tried to appear calm as he drove through the crowded streets, as if he were on a late errand to make some deliveries. But the FCVN van heading down Vo Tanh Road toward Tan Son Nhut Airport stood out like a mirror catching the sun's reflection. The direction alone was a dead give-away. There was always fear that the van, with its easy admission through the gate, would propel marauders into action. Several times before, en route to the air base with children, refugees hung onto the van and often tried to climb atop it to gain access to the air base.

It took every muscle in his body to remain calm and disciplined. Something did not feel quite right on this particular trip. Drawing closer to his destination, he was battling within himself whether or not to abort the mission or "run the gate."

Tan Son Nhut was ahead and already in sight on a well-lighted security approach.

"We're almost there," he called to the people hiding in back of the van.

Suddenly, a shot rang out. Looking into his rearview mirror, he saw a young Vietnamese man making a desperate attempt to grab onto the van and board it from the rear. Meador stepped on the accelerator and at the same moment, another shot whizzed by within inches of his face, missing the exterior mirror. Then, from out of nowhere, a pursuing Honda motorcycle pulled up along side the van. The window open, Meador noted a middle-aged Vietnamese wearing dirty army fatigues and a look of desperation on his face.

"Pull over, I go too!" The gun was pointing directly at Meador's head.

Within a split second, Meador reacted by jerking the wheel sharply to the left, hitting the motorcycle and sending it into the ditch beside the road.

Meador chose not to look back. He was too shaken, and if the guards at the gate sensed he was nervous, they might arrest him and find the human cargo beneath the suitcases.

There was a shift change in guards at dusk, and for some reason, Meador had sensed that the evening crew was more paranoid than the daytime guards. More doubts raced through his mind...what if the guards on the watchtower saw the incident?

There was no more time to think. He was already at the guard gate and the ARVN MPs were surfacing from the structure. Meador noticed the manned machine gun nest above; the sweat began to pour down his face...his glasses became blurred as the moisture trickled over them.

Then he panicked. Instead of slowing down, he raced past the group of soldiers.

A shot exploded, motors started, and he heard them shouting all at once, "Halt...halt!"

The feeling of defeat came over him and he stopped the van with a screech, indicating he knew they meant business. The soldiers clamored up to him, rifles firmly pointed at the cab. They were all talking at once, as if they did not have a leader among them. The suspicion and authority in their voices made him wonder if they were angry enough to order him out of the van and then proceed with a search. If only he hadn't panicked and raced on through, he could have spent the night (on the field) and drove back out in the morning, after a change in the guard detail. The thought came too late.

As some of the military police began to wander near the van, Meador made another snap decision and hoped it was right this time.

"I must go," he demanded to himself. With that, he threw the van into gear and re-traced his way back out onto the highway, praying that the soldiers would not make him their target of the night. They did not.

A safe distance away, Meador stopped to free the stowaways from their concealment. It was a narrow escape, and fear and dejection left them wringing wet. They would try again tomorrow, in the daylight, with the van filled with children.

The following day, during the height of traffic going in and out of Tan Son Nhut Airport, the scenario was repeated, only this time the bus was jammed with children and suitcases, concealing the stowaways. The children were instructed to be especially noisy and disruptive—and it worked. The guards waved the bus through the gate without incident.

Daily trips to the air base were becoming a matter of routine dur-

ing April, 1975. The frequency factor made the FCVN van easily rec-
ognizable, and acknowledgment by the guards began to result in a
friendly wave as the van gained entrance through the gate, especially
with a cargo of visible children.

Frequent trips to the hospital with sick or injured children made
Meador a familiar visitor. During one such visit, when he brought a
16-year-old boy who had broken his arm, Meador was recognized by
an American doctor as the orphan's benefactor. The doctor knew
FCVN would soon be leaving Vietnam with all the children. The
American proceeded to take him into his confidence regarding an
escape plan he had brain-stormed. He wanted to provide a safe exit
for his Vietnamese colleagues at the Seventh Day Adventist Hospital,
rather than see them remain in Vietnam where they faced a lifetime of
labor or re-education camps. The main problem, he felt, was getting
through the gate at Tan Son Nhut.

Meador was asked to bring some very sick children to the hospital
to be placed on the medical-evacuation flight to the United States. The
children would be used to detract attention from the group of escapees
that would be disguised as patients. More importantly, the children
would have the benefit of professional medical care on the airlift. The
plan was put into action a few days later.

The Vietnamese physicians stood firm in their duty until two days
before the fall of Saigon. The Communists had surrounded the city
and shelling around Tan Son Nhut was increasing. The hospital was a
short distance from the air base; it was time to leave.

When the children arrived at the hospital, the participants were
ready for the scenario to begin. With all the theatrics of a Hollywood
script, the doctors had prepared themselves as patients. They had
tagged, bandaged and attached IVs to their arms to look seriously
injured, and to further the appearance of authenticity, blood was
poured to drip from the dressings along with stains of medications.
Then, when all was ready, orderly but hurried, they were carried out
past the hospital guards on litters to the awaiting ambulances.

With sirens blaring and lights flashing, the ambulances left the
hospital emergency entrance, commanding everyone out of their way.
Weaving in and out of traffic to the short distance of the gate at Tan
Son Nhut, Meador took up the tail end of the convoy and enjoyed
every minute of the charade, laughing and shouting cheers.

"And why not?" he thought. It was one of the very few humorous incidents of the whole damn war!

When the convoy hit the gate at Tan Son Nhut, it was an impressive sight. More importantly, it was going off without a hitch. The MPs parted like the waters of the Red Sea. The ambulances were flagged through the gate. Sirens brayed as they raced across the tarmac.

The medevac plane was waiting in readiness. The pre-flight check was complete. Oxygen and all necessary emergency equipment was standing by for those who needed it. The departure schedule was synchronized with the arrival of the patients.

Within moments of the arrival of the convoy, however, the medevac realized the prank—the "patients" were really healthy hospital staff members. When the initial shock wore off, the crew recognized it was a clever plan and perhaps the only one that would have worked since the medical professionals were closely monitored at the hospital. The brotherhood of Hippocrates swung into action as the actual seriously wounded were placed aboard. As a result of the plan, it was almost a one-on-one ratio during the flight to the United States, with the Vietnamese doctors administering to the sick all the way.

All of the children Meador had in his facilities had been evacuated by mid April, yet the last days were hectic as mothers threw their children and babies over the orphanage compound walls in hopes that they would be taken to America. The workers often ran after a mother, placing the child back in her arms, pleading with her to keep the youngster—that life would be better somehow. Frequently a baby would be found dead as a result of being tossed over the high barbed wire walls, and falling directly on to the concrete. It became a vicious cycle, patrolling the walls and running after parents, encouraging them to keep their children.

Frightened Vietnamese parents signed waivers permitting adoptions of their children, fearing a rocket or a bomb might kill the child. The progress of the advancing Communists convinced them that all of Saigon would be destroyed. As a result of the chaos of the past several weeks, many children had been lost. Some died of starvation and dehydration or over-exposure. Others were trampled to death in a lunge for a place on a helicopter, plane, or truck. Some were drowned as they fell or were pushed off crowded barges or boats, and there was no way to determine how many were shot by soldiers who were desperate in their own escape attempts.

The exact number of children killed and wounded in the war is unknown. Only those who were in the hospitals were counted. As for how many were killed instantly, died in transit, or were too injured to be moved and died in inaccessible areas, it is not known.

The few hospital wards available were overcrowded with injured children, usually two to a bed, or lying on stretchers on the floor. Loss of limbs was common, as were napalm burns. Bodies riddled by steel fragments, as a result of children playing with explosives was also an everyday occurrence. Other children were killed or injured from running into the line of fire to retrieve parachutes from dropped flares, or tripping mines as they played in the fields. Many were victims of military vehicles barreling down country roads, or from rockets blasting through villages and city streets, leaving death in its wake. No place in Vietnam was safe.

When children were wounded, only a small number were fortunate enough to benefit from the care of several organizations operating in Vietnam. To name a few, The Children's Convalescent Center in Saigon did skin grafts. There was Children's Medical Relief Internation, USAID, Caritas, Internationational Rescue Committee and COR-Committee of Responsibility, an American funded group of doctors and laymen, who negotiated with the Vietnamese government for almost a year, to allow severely wounded children to be flown to the United States for treatment and rehabilitation. Both countries resisted the effort, believing that the children should be treated in their homeland, rather than uprooted. Eventually 76 children were permitted to fly out for treatment to various parts of the U.S. Part of COR'S agreement with the Vietnamese government was that all the children would be returned to Vietnam.

There were thousands of homeless children roaming the city, and Ross Meador felt helpless. Thu Duc and the Critical Care Center at Gia Dinh were vacated, and the one remaining villa near the airport on Truong Minh Ky, where he stayed, was the last facility holding supplies and equipment.

During the last threatening days, Meador would climb up to the roof of the villa and watch the war; with a 24-hour curfew in effect, there wasn't much else to do. He could see considerable smoke from the airport and at the same time hear sounds of a huge firefight from downtown Saigon. It seemed like a chain reaction.

It was a sight to watch the F-104s scrambling out of Tan Son Nhut to disperse to various points around the city, and the night of April 28th was filled with the concussion of distant bombs striking Bien Hoa and other bumps in the night from mortars, rockets, and artillery.

Everyone had gone. The Clarks left on Saturday, the 26th; and were the last of the FCVN American Volunteers. Meador had always felt Cherie was exceptional in her dedication to the children, but because the Clarks had small children of their own, including several Vietnamese, it was Meador who elected to stay behind to disperse the seemingly endless stream of supplies and equipment. He anticipated that he would remain in Vietnam for several more weeks.

Additionally, over sixty Vietnamese staff workers from various FCVN facilities were counting on his influence to get them out on the airlift. There were hundreds of Americans still in Saigon and many more Vietnamese who held "sensitive" jobs with U.S. agencies that had exit priority. It was understandable that the common Vietnamese citizen would be at the bottom of the evacuation list. Meador was holding back hundreds of dollars in the safe at the villa for any back-up he might need in transportation, or even bribery, to get the 66 Vietnamese out of the country.

On the 29th the city of Saigon was in utter chaos. People were becoming so desperate that looting was out of control. In addition to a 24-hour curfew, road blocks were everywhere, and it was unsafe to leave the security of home. Crowds of looters gathered and broke into buildings and compounds they suspected of having anything of value. It became obvious that it was up to the individual to protect his own possessions.

Alarms sounded all over the city as looters ransacked shelves and carted off foodstuffs and medicines. Word had spread that the U.S. had abandoned Saigon's giant Newport PX. As a result, the building swarmed with pillagers. Armed and drunk Vietnamese police lingered nearby, watching with amusement. Occasionally, as a shopping cart passed by them, they would pluck a few choice items for themselves as "an exit toll."

The orphanage compound was not armed. There never seemed to be a need to keep guns and ammunition within the confines. But after several previous threats to his life, Meador was obliged to accept a small pistol from a departing friend. The gun was all but forgotten, however, remaining hidden in a dresser drawer...until early on the morning of the 29th when Meador was awakened by a banging on the front gate. He was still rubbing the sleep from his eyes when he stepped out on the balcony and saw a group of men breaking into the compound. Quickly, he yelled a warning and ran inside to get the gun, a .38 caliber pistol, then ran back to the balcony. The intruders had already managed to break the chain on the gate and were running inside the compound.

He yelled another warning in Vietnamese, but the men did not disperse. Suddenly, in desperation, Meador began firing over their heads. The attackers did not expect armed resistance, and the reverberating shots within the compound walls terrified them as they turned and fled.

His ears still ringing, Meador stared at the gun with both shock and amazement. Though he hadn't hit anyone, he became aware of the threat to their lives. In scaring the intruders, he also managed to scare himself.

The gun still in his hand, Meador dropped to his knees and slithered down beside the balcony posts. Totally alone, he was in a state of confusion. The very idea of pointing a gun at another human made him sick.

"No sir, not me," he had often exclaimed. "They'll never get me to fire hot lead into another guy I don't even know! They'll have to lock me up first."

Even as a young boy, Ross Meador had always considered himself a pacifist. He could settle his arguments with quick wit rather than with quick fists. The excitement of hunting trips with his uncles left profound guilt. He was apt to blast a small rabbit out from beneath a cactus in which it sought refuge, and even some birds were sacrificed so that he could watch billowy feathers float to earth. "Ross, the Hunter," had ended by the time he was fourteen. During high school years he campaigned against war.

Although Meador did not know much about Vietnam, he did realize that Americans were in a foreign country killing for what he felt was not a good enough reason. The political machinery of the Vietnam War disgusted him further, and an enormous sense of compassion for the Vietnamese emerged. He somehow felt responsible and thought if he just yelled loud enough, painted signs big enough, and wrote letters often enough, he would have had an impact on history.

None of this happened. Youth presents itself with a series of black and whites. A twenty-year old Ross Meador was to learn on the balcony that morning that there were also gray areas to life. He himself responded to the strongest of human instincts, the desire for self-preservation when his own life was threatened.

Fear raced through his mind. He sat there for a moment longer, not stirring. Would they come back? He must get dressed and do something, but for the moment, he would take a long look at himself and his life. Everything was no longer just black-and-white. The moral and political questions Meador once had answers for appeared more complex and possessed facets that he did not see before. It was a self-realization and he was "finding himself" on a balcony in the middle of a hot war.

Doubts began to grip Meador about how much longer he could defend the villa. Along with the early morning break-in attempt it became clear that the final stages of war had begun. It was obvious that the single Vietnamese guard, along with the two childcare workers, Hung and Bac, were hardly a deterring force. The presence of the cartons and equipment in the courtyard would continue to attract looters. Perhaps the time had come to face the facts squarely and to conclude that the job of getting the supplies to the many orphanages that needed them, would remain unfinished.

Visibly shaken by both the intrusion and confrontation with the crowd, Meador felt compelled to go into town for a good breakfast in the hopes that it would calm him. Cautiously, he left the compound and saw the real evidence of war's end—hundreds of refugees camping along the highways. There was also an eerie absence of traffic. Soldiers and barricades were everywhere. Driving down Truong Minh Giang toward the USAID building he sensed that he was being watched very carefully through the sights of guns and could feel the moment to moment threat to his life.

Many streets were blocked and he was compelled to drive in the opposite direction on "one way" streets to get to his destination. Nothing stirred. Aside from the occasional groups of soldiers, there were no civilians to be seen in this business district of Saigon. Meador felt it was fun breaking all traffic laws, sort of like Charlton Heston in the "Omega Man." But unlike Heston, he was careful not to speed lest the soldiers interpret it as hostile action and begin shooting at him. It took patience, but he found a round about way to the USAID hotel. Finding the restaurant open was even more of a surprise with a staff nervously attempting to appear normal.

Alone in the dining room, about halfway through his meal, Meador saw another American enter. The stranger was obviously upset and half-commanded him, "Let's go!"

"Where?"

"Get a flight bag, that's all you can take. It's total evacuation...if you want to go, go now!"

A further explanation was not necessary. Meador reacted immediately and ran to his car, determined to make his way over to the USAID Building #2, the closest point designated as an evacuation assembly center. He could not control the angry thoughts that raced through his mind. A day earlier USAID had said "that it didn't look like total evacuation would come for several more days," and committed to making a point of informing Ross when the time came. He listened to the American Radio Service (FM 99.9 MHZ) constantly, waiting to hear the words: "It is 110 degrees in Saigon and still rising," followed by the music of Bing Crosby singing *"White Christmas."* The message was to be broadcast every fifteen minutes, for approximately two hours. It would be the coded message meaning a total evacuation via airplane and helicopter was in progress. Along with thousands of other Americans, Meador never heard the message. In fact the United States Mission to Vietnam prepared a standard instructions booklet for emergency situations; attached was a map of Saigon and a list of 21 civilian assembly areas and 4 U.S. Defense Attaché Officer designated assembly points.

Meador's heart was pounding at the possibility of complete desertion when he found the USAID Building door locked and no one in sight. As he turned to leave, a combat marine who, fortunately for Ross, was making a last check of the building, instructed him to go to the American Embassy. Tan Son Nhut was under heavy fire and all evacuees were being directed to the Embassy compound.

Once again, Meador found himself facing the harrowing experience of driving through a maze of blocked streets, making his way by trial and error until the American Embassy came into view. Meador had been to the Embassy on many occasions. It was a large American compound that looked like Middletown, U.S.A., with big trees, manicured lawns, and houses and apartments over-run with servants. The parties he attended were a nice diversion. Usually it was a lot of drinking and small talk with members of the diplomatic corps.

"I'm sick of working and I want to go home," a secretary chanted.

"What do you mean, this is a party," Ross responded to her complaint.

"Working party. I'd get fired if I didn't go to these every night."

Meador was somewhat of a novelty...still a teenager (19) and surrounded by dignitaries. They were intrigued by his stories of the orphans and what FCVN was trying to accomplish. He recalled, too, that there was a never-ending flow of politicians coming to Vietnam. On one such occasion, an American General invited an FCVN volunteer to a reception he was hosting for a visiting Congressman, who came to Vietnam for one of the many "fact-finding" tours booked by the Embassy.

"Why are you here?" The volunteer asked, making small talk.

"To decide if we should be here or not," he responded.

"How long are you going to be here?" she tried again.

"Two days."

As Meador approached the Embassy he could see Marines pacing on top of the fifteen-foot walls. It was besieged by hundreds of people desperate to get in. Meador had no trouble getting through the big metal Embassy gates. Fortunately, when he left the villa that morning, he threw his bags into his car, concerned for his effects if the looters would return to the compound during his absence. The intuitive action proved to be a smart move, and now he was heading into the Embassy restaurant building to join up with fellow Americans as well as the USAID officials who neglected to contact him regarding the emergency conditions.

Meador mingled with small groups of people who shared his predicament of having left important things undone. He expressed his concern for Hung and Bac back at the villa and how he had promised he would take them when the time of total evacuation was announced. Meador elaborated how he had hundreds of dollars locked up in the safe, and he was concerned that he was the only one who knew the combination. His counterparts laughed at his seriousness—as if it was the last thing to worry about. In reality, the money was not important, but Meador did want to apologize to the Vietnamese nationals whom he had promised to assist in getting on the airlift. He felt a sense of guilt that they would not share in the freedom that Americans take for granted all their lives.

The Embassy dining room was crowded with clusters of people standing and waiting in groups for the helicopters, all eager to discuss their experiences. Meador felt angry for some conscious violation of moral and penal law, either by positive action or by neglect of duty. All he knew was that he must get back to the villa to set things right. There was just too much left undone. It bothered him to stand in the midst of the American Embassy, helpless.

Hurriedly, he pushed his bags to the side and walked toward the exit, almost running. A tall, combat-garbed marine stepped directly in front of him. His clinched jaw indicated he was reading Meador's mind.

"Don't go anywhere, buddy. They're getting ready to weld the front gates now. Once you leave the compound, it isn't likely you'll get back in."

The crowds outside had grown to riot proportions. It was just a matter of time before the Marines would be forced to take action against the thousands of nationals who would struggle to storm the walls in an attempt to gain freedom.

It felt like the final insult to an already difficult morning. If there were a possible chance, Meador would have risked returning to the villa, but the convincing came not from the words of wisdom from friends, or the marine's threat, but from the sounds of gunfire and screams from outside. There seemed to be little point in risking his life for the impossible. Instead, he dashed across the parking lot to his car to retrieve a backpack which contained a bottle of rare cognac. He had accepted it as a bribe/gift from neighbors in hopes they would get a seat on the FCVN staff evacuation plane which was scheduled for departure in early May. That hope faded with the fall of Saigon.

Sitting under a table as rockets fell outside the Embassy, Meador thought it seemed appropriate...the time...the place...to uncork the French brandy. It was a devil-may-care gesture, or at the very least, a salute to just being alive.

There was nothing more Ross Meador could do. If he hadn't done his job in the past fourteen months, then it had all been a waste. But he couldn't accept that thought. So many children were alive because of his involvement—not that they would ever know it—but that, too, didn't matter. There was something much more significant...he knew it in his own heart...that whatever the future had in store for him, at least during these months in Vietnam, a love of mankind reached into the depths of his very soul.

The waiting and uncertainty, wondering if the helicopters would get in and out, added to the tension of the fire fighting in the streets. Someone came through and said that the Ambassador had ordered the large tamarind tree in the parking lot cut down, making way for the choppers to land. Little was it known at that point the importance the tamarind tree had played in the American evacuation.

For weeks the Defense Department had wanted to step up the pace of evacuations in Vietnam. They had, however, been stymied by the attitude of the U.S. Ambassador, Martin Graham, who along with U.S. Secretary of State, Henry Kissinger, feared that such an announcement might ignite widespread panic and possible retaliation against those who were getting out. There was a concern for hasty action, and the Ambassador was determined not to push the South Vietnamese government over the brink with premature withdrawal. While the U.S. was concerned with drawing any attention to an evacuation, other countries were more practical. The British, Italians, Canadians, Australians, New Zealanders, and the Laotians hastily closed their embassies and fled Vietnam. Along with abandoning their indigenous employees, they left behind some of their own countrymen who eventually relied upon U.S. evacuation efforts to get out of Saigon.

Several weeks earlier, Admiral Noel Gayler, Commander-in-Chief of the U.S. for the Pacific, headquartered in Hawaii, made a secret visit to Saigon. During that time he urged Ambassador Martin to have the large tamarind tree in the rear parking lot cut down to clear a landing zone for the "Jolly Green Giants" (helicopters) in the event of evacuation. Martin ignored the advice. To him, cutting down the tree represented the final acceptance of defeat and withdrawal, and he was (constitutionally) unable to "declare evacuation" until the official word was received from Washington. Cutting down the tree would indicate the Embassy *was* preparing for final departure. Unbeknown to the Ambassador, for days, staff at the Embassy had been sneaking out with axes and chipping away at parts of the tree trunk not visible to him. General Smith, the Defense Attaché, also denied permission to chop down two tall flagpoles in the front of the DAO building.

Now that the direct order for evacuation had come to Martin and the Marines were finally sawing down the giant tamarind, the beautiful landmark was being sacrificed to save lives. So too were the two flagpoles, supposedly preserved to be available for a possible flag-lowering ceremony.

During these last hours, drained of all emotion, Ambassador Martin decided he wanted to return to his home to gather his belongings and pick up his black poodle, Nitnoy. His chauffeur's efforts to get through the gates failed as the crowds pushed and the Marine guards were nearly overrun. So, Martin left by way of a back gate and walked the three blocks to his house. Returning to the Embassy compound an hour later, he led Nitnoy on a leash at a normal pace. He wasn't panicky; his gait was one of dignity and calm.

"You know the old man," one of his aides explained. "He doesn't like anyone to think he is ruffled by anything."

The time for symbolic gestures ran out.

Ambassador Martin would be one of the last to leave the Embassy the following morning.

There was nothing the evacuees inside the Embassy could do but sit around and exchange stories. All had a common feeling of how thankful they were to be at the compound. Outside, all around the perimeter, people were dying, and the clear sounds of shots and mortar fire left little doubt that this was the last safe place in all of Saigon. Of the hundreds of people huddled in the compound, each had a tale and all shared the common bond of wanting to leave the doomed country.

Father Merganhangen from Danang had spent a week on a boat coming to the city in hopes of getting on the airlift with his group of refugees. It was obvious that several had come from other cities. One small nun relayed how she had walked through the fields and jungle for five days with small children. The long trip from the central highlands on meager rations was a desperate attempt to get to freedom. Just as they were about to arrive in a safe area, the nun related how they were captured by a band of Viet Cong who later released them.

Another nun told of her capture by the Viet Cong and their heavy interrogation regarding Americans she knew and with whom she had came in contact. She was required to write down their names and all she knew about them. All during her captivity she was threatened with rape and death.

An American soldier who had stayed in Vietnam after his tour of duty huddled his small Vietnamese family together, along with other relatives he did not want to leave behind.

There were stories of armed and drunken soldiers looting, robbing people and shooting wildly. When there was no bounty to take, people were shot right on the spot. Homes were looted and priceless possessions smashed on the streets. Randomly, vehicles were confiscated and the inhabitants molested, leaving the streets littered with bodies and debris as a result of the soldiers' violence.

Ross Meador thought of his parents and how he wished he could get word to them that he was safe. He had written them several times, indicating he would be coming home soon and offering excuses why he had to stay longer. He was not alone in denying that the end was near. Thousands of other Americans procrastinated and stayed in Vietnam until the very end, despite the urging of the U.S. government to evacuate.

The warnings came during the first week in April, at the onset of Operation Babylift. Now a sea lift was also underway and continued through April 29th when thousands departed by water.

Vietnamese nationals associated with the U.S. forces in sensitive areas, such as CIA, interpreters, clerks, and those considered "high risk," would have top priority for airlift or sea evacuation. They were considered to be in the most danger after the Communist takeover.

Thus, there was a plan conceived in the Pentagon of "thinning out" the numbers who would require transportation in any last-minute exodus. The U.S. officials had the anguished realization that it would be impossible to rescue all of the thousands of South Vietnamese who had staked their lives on America's commitment to their country. There was fear that the evacuation of the last Americans in Saigon would turn ugly and bloody.

The early April flow was slow. By April 20th, the evacuation totaled 5,000, far short of the estimated 170,000 Vietnamese refugees forecast by the officials. In addition to a reluctance to leave, several other things hampered the evacuation process. The U.S. Embassy was restrained by Vietnamese government restrictions on who could leave the country. Vietnamese officials were imposing red tape on certain professionals by delaying processing procedures. There was also an unwillingness on the part of many Americans to leave Vietnamese dependents and friends. This holdout stagnated the operation of getting as many Americans out in the early stages.

Finally, in an attempt to speed up the evacuation process, Attorney General Edward H. Levi announced that he was using his "parole power" to waive immigration restrictions and allow up to 130,000 refugees from Vietnam and Cambodia to enter the United States. The parole power was previously used in the 1950's to admit 40,000 Hungarian refugees and again in the 1960's to admit 675,000 Cubans.

The parole power tool was used to admit tens of thousands of Vietnamese whose lives were considered to be in danger if they were left behind. This triggered an even bigger crush to leave the country. Coinciding with this declaration, the South Vietnamese authorities relaxed most of the exit formalities, resulting in an increase in the interest to leave Vietnam. Thousands of Vietnamese, who had reconciled to stay behind, tried desperately to get their wives and children on the airlift. Parents even forged birth certificates, placing their children in the hands of anyone with an exit visa.

It was soon apparent that there were more Americans in Vietnam during the last hours than anyone had anticipated. The lines increased and stretched longer by the minute. The large evacuation that had taken place five days earlier was just a portent of what lay ahead. People ignored all the early warnings to leave Vietnam.

Directives from Washington ordered that all but essential Americans were to be out of Vietnam in the last week. It was then that the Embassy suddenly realized it had made a serious miscalculation since its evacuation plans had been based on a figure of about only 7,000 Americans. When retired U.S. diplomats and army deserters began showing up with their Vietnamese wives, children and in-laws, Embassy officials estimated the number of Americans and dependents to be evacuated as closer to 75,000.

The Ambassador accepted that the time was over for bureaucratic niceties. To expedite the paperwork for evacuation, a movie theater at Tan Son Nhut Airport was turned into a vast processing center. Affidavits that, until then, had taken weeks to obtain, and which had been previously scrutinized, were fixed on the spot. Each time an American name was called, a Vietnamese family (sometimes his own, sometimes someone else's) trailed nervously behind the applicant. Immigration requirements were all but ignored as documents were forged to ridiculous proportions. Relatives of a Vietnamese wife were listed as children, and even unmarried American personnel signed for the responsibility of strangers, listing them as dependents. To keep South Vietnamese police and airport workers from interfering, U.S. officials promised that they, too, would be evacuated.

On April 26th, 6,000 people left Saigon in forty-six C-130 and twenty-eight C-141 flights. They were ferried directly from Saigon to Clark Field in the Philippines for further transport to encampments at Anderson Air Force Base on Guam and to Wake Island. The Vietnamese departing on the huge aircraft outnumbered Americans twenty to one.

So threatening was the Communist thrust that thousands tried to beg, buy, or steal their way aboard jets for the flights to the U.S. bases. It was every man for himself. Vietnamese were handing over thick rolls of greenbacks to get on the list. Anyone who had any connections for getting people out stood to make a bundle of money from the tragedy.

Thousands of upper and middle-class Vietnamese who didn't qualify for U.S. evacuation tried to get out any way they could. The demand for hard currency shot the black market rate seven times higher than the standard rate. Fear was also the great equalizer. Wealthy families arrived at Tan Son Nhut in chauffeur-driven limousines to wait in line for hours under the broiling sun, alongside crooked bureaucrats, street vendors, peasants and Saigon bar girls clinging to their half-American illegitimate children who they felt would justify their passage out of the country.

The lines of people staggered around buildings and moved slowly. It was necessary for Marines to walk down the long lines with buckets of ice water, reviving the dehydrated evacuees.

The Pentagon was geared up for a "resentment situation" and attempts by either Communist forces or South Vietnamese troops to block the final American departure. Incidents were occurring that indicated to intelligence sources that the South Vietnamese troops were frustrated over the defeat of their country and were directing their anger at the Americans whom they felt were abandoning them.

On April 28th, four U.S. Cessna A-37 Dragonfly attack jets, flown from Pleiku Airfield by angered South Vietnamese defector pilots, invaded the airfield at Tan Son Nhut, destroying several aircraft on the ground, including a U.S. Air Force C-130. The runways were littered with shrapnel and rendered useless. The explosions rocked the countryside and were felt throughout Saigon. As a result of the near presence of war and defeat, there was an outbreak of small arms fire in the city as jittery soldiers shot their M-16's into the air. The city was a powder keg. Anything could set it off.

During the last weeks of the war, the lack of unity or patriotic arousal of the Vietnamese people was obvious. There wasn't the slightest sense of rallying against the forthcoming invasion that would be expected of a country about to be invaded. Neither government troops nor the civilian population built fortifications or even anti-tank ditches around Saigon. There weren't even sandbags available. There were no swarms of volunteers or systems set up to handle the wounded that would be expected, or even calls for blood donors. Emergency stations or fire wardens, as would be needed, were not established. Everyone dreaded a Communist victory, yet there was no outward display thwarting the invader or unity among the Saigonese. An aftermath conclusion was that South Vietnam lacked the leadership to relate to the people or to unite them in a common effort for survival. Many officials were too busy preparing to leave Vietnam with their loot and had no interest in making a last stand or concerning themselves with the masses. The exodus was like an avalanche.

In the Ham Nghi Marketplace, pools of blood streamed across the sidewalks as a half dozen shoppers were killed or wounded as a result of an explosion. In other areas of the city, similar explosions tore into crowds. Everyone's nerves were on edge with the Communist troops only 45 miles from the capitol. In an effort to calm the situation, government loudspeakers blared out patriotic speeches and made appeals for order. Too late for any real preparation and organization of the crisis, this only set the Saigonese on edge even more. Fire fighting and rockets erupted every night. Even the eyes on the billboards along the streets were shot out from target practice.

Rumors were running rampant. Newscasts were contradictory. There were runs on banks, and black market prices soared. Fire fighting was everywhere, and it seemed that the South Vietnamese were venting their frustrations over their agony of losing their country.

The Vietnamese Air Force, too, was disintegrating as planes were commandeered by crews and refugees scurrying to fly out of the country. The majority of planes flew to Thailand, abandoning the war. Soldiers swarmed the runways, fighting to get on any departing plane and shooting their weapons in all directions when they were unsuccessful.

Tan Son Nhut was constantly under fire. In addition to the bombing by angry Vietnamese pilots, over 150 rockets and newly placed North Vietnamese 140 mm guns opened up on the air base, destroying aircraft and setting buildings on fire. Not totally satisfied with reports from events happening at Tan Son Nhut, Ambassador Graham Martin decided to make the four mile drive out to the airport to take a look at the situation first hand. What he observed was a complete disaster. Any use of the airfield was impossible. The shells raining down on the airfield sealed Saigon's fate and forced Martin to make the painful decision to send away the C-130s waiting overhead and begin the final evacuation by helicopters. Determined to review the situation at Tan Son Nhut himself, Martin not only risked his life but wasted valuable time. The Ambassador had a son killed in the war...he was not going to give up.

Upon his return to Saigon, Martin contacted Secretary of State Kissinger and, along with Admiral Noel Gayler, conferred on the final consideration; evacuation. When it was decided that the military situation had deteriorated beyond recall, the earlier "Options One, Two, and Three," which involved transport planes flying out of Tan Son Nhut were no longer possible. They had to go with "Option Four," the much riskier and precarious helicopter evacuation and the last available exit from Saigon.

Up to the last minute, President Ford hoped for a peaceful settlement in Vietnam. Ford was in a briefing when a call came to him from Ambassador Martin, reporting that option four was the only way out of Vietnam. At 10:51 p.m. on April 28th, "Operation Frequent Wind," the final evacuation of Vietnam, was put into motion.

During the last day, there wasn't anything to do but wait inside the crowded Embassy compound. The Americans seemed to have more patience. It was the Vietnamese who were restless and uncertain. They began pushing toward the door leading to the parking lot landing area, and only the sight of Marines in full combat dress seemed to improve their behavior. In those final hours, people started coming out of the woodwork. Everyone who had worked at the Embassy brought their families and extended families. Employees, contract guards, servants...all showed up with dozens of people with suitcases. As a result, Marine guards and Embassy officials did not carefully examine documents as the refugees were let through the gates. "It was a monstrous mess," claimed an official as he saw the crowds increasing around the pool area.

Ross Meador had been one of the early arrivals at the Embassy and managed a place in line to be evacuated on one of the first helicopters.

Thousands outside the gate would kill to be in his spot at the head of the list, that close to to freedom. Then, just as Meador was about to move into the landing zone area, his eye caught sight of Father McViegh, Director of Catholic Relief Services. Dedication to the orphans was reflected in the attitude of the organization's workers and in the humble physical surroundings of the Catholic Charities offices. Several desks were crammed into a small office, devoid of air conditioning and any other visible signs of convenience. Even more astonishing, the staff seemed the most cheerful of any of the relief agencies.

Father McViegh was with a large group of Vietnamese that included several small children who were crying. Their twisting, turning bodies and irritable behavior indicated that they were unmanageable, and they began to attract the attention of over-taxed evacuation officials. The priest had one nun with him who was unsuccessful in containing all the little arms and legs, scampering in all directions.

Then Meador did the unexpected thing. He grabbed his bags and headed back to the end of the long line where Father McViegh greeted him with a thankful smile. This act of sacrifice could easily have cost Meador his life since the conditions were to deteriorate even more drastically.

Strangely enough, the group he was assigned to was the family of a transportation official who had originally resolved much of the dock cargo and customs problems Meador had faced when he first came to Saigon.

Outside the Embassy buildings, behind the parking lot and in the swimming pool area, several thousand Vietnamese waited with piles of suitcases and bundles of clothing. Along with several generals were South Vietnamese senators, diplomats, a former Mayor of Saigon, the police and fire chiefs, and all their firemen. As the evacuation progressed into the hours, many of the firemen postponed their departures to fight the small fires erupting within the Embassy compound. They had accepted they would be among the last to leave, and as a result, many of them were abandoned when a halt was called to "Frequent Wind." Vietnamese Embassy employees had their families with them. Everyone was apprehensive, wondering if they would get on the flights. While waiting for the choppers, hundreds of other Vietnamese pushed into the Embassy cafeteria and helped themselves to everything from candy and food to bottles of California wine. Within an hour of the announcement of evacuation procedures, the Embassy gates were besieged by thousands of people, desperate to get in.

Finally, the first chopper came into the landing area in the parking lot and a cheer went up. But as it came in, it drew ground fire from outside the compound. Manned machine guns were visible in the helicopters circling above as the Marines tried to seek out the insurgents. Evacuees on signal scurried aboard, and everyone was quite relieved when it took off safely.

Twenty minutes later, another helicopter came in, also drawing ground fire. While it was loading on the ground, several rockets landed nearby and everyone in the Embassy was instructed to lie on the floor. The VCs started shooting surface-to-air missiles and anti-aircraft guns at it, and as the chopper took off, it faltered and started to drop into the trees. But at the last second, the strength of the engines pulled it out and it headed toward the sea. It was becoming obvious it could be hours before everyone got out. Then it began to rain, and the scene became quiet for a short time.

Word spread that the helicopter landings in the parking area were canceled. Thereafter, evacuation would be in smaller choppers from the roof of the tall Embassy building. That meant the evacuees would have to climb six floors to the top of the structure.

As time passed, the fighting in the area increased, and at one point, Meador counted eleven helicopters over the Embassy. He wished they could all just come down and pick him up. He was tired and becoming apprehensive with all the delays. Firefighting, was increasing and he could see Marines positioned in the parking lot, shooting from the wall surrounding the compound.

The Embassy was not the only specified assembly point for escape. Several helicopter evacuation sites were designated throughout the city. Since Tan Son Nhut's runways were no longer usable, the tennis court at the U.S. military compound was cleared to make a giant pad for the Jolly Green Giants. The perimeter was fortified with sandbags as Marines lined the area in a prone position, their camouflaged uniforms blending into the tropical greenery. It was a weakly defensible position, but reasonably secure to protect the landings.

The entrance to Tan Son Nhut was littered with abandoned American cars and motorcycles obstructing the highway, and it was becoming difficult, if not impossible, to maneuver near the air base. Americans were turned away by resentful Vietnamese guards who were firing into the air and shouting obscenities and demanding, "We want to go, too!"

In desperation, the evacuees had to retreat to Saigon to find open evacuation assembly points which by now were dwindling because of the heavy attack. An increase in rockets made it life-threatening to move about the city. Of major concern were the mobs which interfered with the evacuation; traffic could not move through the jammed streets. A bus convoy had been put into effect to get Americans to secret gathering and staging areas. But that, too, broke down, forcing eight busloads of evacuees to abandon attempts to reach the Defense Attaché Office, a well-guarded stronghold on the sixth floor of the Brinks Building. They were eventually able to find haven in the Embassy compound. Thereafter, it was up to each person abandoned at the outlying staging areas to transport himself to any evacuation center.

To add to the terror, South Vietnamese troops and mobs were harassing American evacuees, and Air American UH-1s were forced to lift some of the desperate from scattered locations around the city when the bus transportation ceased.

Evidence of further lack of realistic planning was apparent throughout the crisis. Vietnamese personnel who had been employed at the U.S. Embassy had been instructed to move to "safe houses" and ordered to remain in telephone contact with officials at the U.S. Embassy regarding their whereabouts. But they were subsequently abandoned when events at the Embassy became hectic and telephones were no longer answered. It was apparent that the American Embassy staff was not prepared for such an evacuation, especially one requiring helicopter airlift of thousands of people from the Embassy roof. The original plan allowed for only several hundred Embassy employees to be evacuated under "Frequent Wind."

The scene outside the Embassy was escalating into a riot as hundreds of Vietnamese tried to claw their way over the 15-foot concrete wall surrounding the compound. There was no relenting as the Marines continued to push them off.

In full battle garb, Marines used their rifle butts, pistols, feet, fists, and clubs, to beat the panic-stricken Vietnamese back. The desperation of the people was beyond reason. The failed attempts resulted in the tearing of flesh and a shattering of their bodies as they fell back on the cruel pavement. Inside the grounds, CIA agents, State Department employees, and security guards roamed the Embassy compound, armed.

Occasionally, groups of other Westerners seeking refuge pushed nearer to the wall after an all-day futile search of the city, looking for a marshaling point to be picked up by helicopters. After being turned away at the docks and airport, they now pushed their way through the screaming crowds massed at the gate that had been welded shut. They knew if they could get close enough, the Marines would take them over. Aware that the Westerners would get sanctuary, the Vietnamese clung to them like a raft adrift on an ocean, and to further their own escape, even helped shove them through.

A young woman clawed desperately at a newsman, screaming to go with him. Soon the men who were pushing to safety were stripped of their possessions, a watch gone, a camera, a wallet and even clothing torn from their backs. Inch by inch the Marines reached into the crowd, fighting off the nationals and struggling to grasp and drag them up by their arms over the wall.

A baby was thrust into the arms of a marine just as he reached down to pull-up an American. The faces of the crowd below did not reveal to whom the baby belonged.

"Take it, I've got to fight," the marine yelled as he thrust the tiny baby into the arms of someone on the other side. Moments later a pleading Vietnamese woman shoved a bag of greenbacks into the guard's hands. Jewelry and other treasured possessions were offered up in the sea of desperation that stormed the walls.

An apocalyptic carnival air began to emerge...Vietnamese soldiers, youth and even police had stripped and stolen scores of abandoned U.S. Embassy cars, wildly driving them around the city until they ran out of gas. Others looted apartment buildings in which Americans lived, then waited on the sidewalk with their booty of TV's, air conditioners, furniture, typewriters, and electronic equipment, for cohorts in cars and trucks to pick them up.

The orphans roaming the streets of Saigon were also caught up in the moment. Those old enough to hold their own joined in the looting, while the smaller ones were pushed aside. Terrified, they fled to hiding places. Crying children were everywhere.

Chaos reigned on the streets of Saigon and spilled over into the Embassy compound. Inside, people were waiting their turn to board the helicopters landing on the roof, one after another amid the rocket fire and firefighting.

The Embassy staff, busy with the mechanics of neutralizing the building, calmly destroyed code machines with hammers. Files and desks were emptied and rooms became littered with papers. Documents were fed into shredders. Telephones rang and no one answered them.

The Ambassador, a tall graying man, moved about freely. Graham Martin was an indomitable man, but his face was drained and expressionless. Occasionally he would stop and talk to people as he entered and departed through hallways. He had the same concern as everyone: "Would there be time enough to get out?"

U.S. military officials were confident that if all went well, they would not only succeed in evacuating the thousand or so Americans in Saigon, but also an additional thousand foreigners in nine to twelve hours. As the night dragged on, they realized their estimates in both numbers and time were naive.

"Operation Frequent Wind," the helicopter evacuation from Saigon, was the biggest helicopter lift of its kind. It would extend into an 18-hour operation that would eventually carry 1,373 Americans and 5,595 Vietnamese to safety to the most powerful U.S. Naval armada assembled since the Christmas 1971 bombing of Hanoi. Over forty U.S. warships stretched out in a crescent-shaped 100 mile-long-task force. Rolling gently in the swells of the South China Sea, the evacuation armada stood ready for the last American operation of the Vietnam War.

Aboard the cruiser Oklahoma City, Vice Admiral George Peabody Steele, Commander of the U.S. 7th Fleet, waited for the signal from Washington before commencing with "Operation Frequent Wind." Closer to the Vietnamese coast on the carriers Hancock, Midway, and Okinawa, 700 U.S. Marines stood prepared to help the Americans shoot their way out of Saigon if necessary. The Marine pilots of 70 "Jolly Green Giant" helicopters, who only a couple of weeks earlier had plucked the last handful of Americans out of the terrorized Cambodian capitol of Phnom Penh, geared up to do it again, this time from besieged Saigon.

The departure process was going slowly. Only one helicopter (a CH-46) at a time could make the landing on the roof of the tall Embassy building. The heavier CH-53s also had to maneuver one at a time in the cramped parking lot. When it became obvious that the evacuation would reach far into the night, two choppers brought in more Marines to beef up the Embassy's defense.

Ross Meador and the Vietnamese family finally reached the front of their line, the entrance to the parking lot. They were instructed to walk around the edge of the pavement, staying close to the wall, then run to the next Embassy building when signaled. As they were receiving their instructions of the path to follow, they heard a tremendous explosion. A rocket had landed directly in the area where Meador had parked his car.

Then the marine gave Meador a nod. He grabbed his bag and the six-year-old boy in his arms and darted out, hugging the side of the building as instructed. At the next checkpoint, a marine signaled him to cross over to the main building. Then, with a prayer, he tightened his grip and made a desperate dash across the open area to the main Embassy building. The sound of shots, rockets and screams followed his every step. Marines, crouched down at the entrance, reached out and grabbed him and the child and quickly pulled them inside. He was breathless, but there was no time to rest. He was directed to the stairwell and only then realized that he still had a long climb ahead of him. The building was six stories high, but each crowded stairwell consisted of two flights, interrupted by a landing. Several times, Meador was delayed by Marines because the family he was with were not Americans and, therefore, were on the lowest priority scale. His hopes sank each time that others were motioned ahead of them.

Darkness was falling outside. An array of vehicles was lined up around the building so that their headlights would illuminate the Embassy grounds and aid the pilots in locating the helipad on top. An explosion rocked the front of the compound. A passerby on a motorbike had thrown a grenade into the crowd, wounding the refugees outside the walls. Though many were wounded, no one dared venture out to help them.

The air-conditioning had gone off in the building and it was a slow climb for Meador, going one step at a time as it was vacated. He was surprised when he recognized the Embassy staff who had priority but who waited their turn in line. Finally, he reached the top floor. He had carried the little boy all the way and found himself hot and tired. At the very least, he wasn't hungry. Earlier, he and numerous others, had emptied the kitchen of the Embassy restaurant where they waited all day for the helicopters. He sought a resting place before he was able to attempt the last set of stairs to the roof. Suddenly, the electricity went off; the stairwell went black. Frightened, several women began to scream uncontrollably.

While he was catching his breath, Meador noticed a marine bolt up the steps and thrust a piece of paper into the hands of the officer in charge of the roof top, who then lit his lighter to read the note. A serious expression washed over his face in the dim light. Meador grew concerned...he felt a last terrifying chill...that perhaps the flights had ceased altogether. Instead, the officer gave commands to others on the roof for more weapons.

"Three units of United States Marines down there and they can't stop a goddamn riot!"

He was referring to the three platoons of about 130 Marines that were flown in from the coastal rescue ships to join the beleaguered men on the Embassy compound walls. Several hundred more were combat ready, awaiting orders to be helicoptered in if needed.

Now it was Meador's time to escape. The door to the roof was open. It was dark now and noisy outside, and hotter than he had ever remembered Vietnam to be. The small family was crouched together, waiting for the helicopter above them to land and for the marine's command to run for it.

Just as they went through the final checkpoint, a burst of automatic weapon fire held them back. Though only a few feet away, it seemed as if they would never reach the chopper. They waited a long time, and when it seemed that the signal would never come, the marine bellowed, "OK, MOVE! NOW!"

This was it.

Meador half-carried, half-dragged the terrified little boy and his bag across the windy roof. He found himself scrambling and stumbling over bodies and bags. Everyone was trying to get in at the same time. Within seconds the chopper was full.

Meador headed toward the rear of the helicopter and thought he heard more firing on the roof. He noticed that the little boy's family was not with them. He had not looked back at the sound of gunfire. Then, just as the helicopter was about to lift off, he recognized the faces of the boy's parents and their other children as they appeared in the door. The people nearest them grabbed and tugged at them as the helicopter began moving. A suitcase containing all of their worldly possessions had broken open as the parents dashed across the roof.

With their other children, they crawled to where Meador was crouched. Their tearfully forced smile transcended all language barriers and communicated that they were thankful. They had not forgotten Meador's sacrifice—that he could have left hours earlier under less dangerous circumstances.

Suddenly, they were airborne, and the lights of Saigon were below them. The rear hatch of the helicopter was partly open, and as Meador looked out the tail, he saw the burning city below. Off to the northeast he could see the Long Binh ammunition dump exploding. His first reaction was excitement, then he noticed seven huge fires burning, all in close proximity to the Embassy. The Star Spangled Banner atop the building was still waving in the wind.

A silence prevailed among the refugees whose attention was drawn to the two Marines manning 50 caliber machine guns on both the port and starboard sides of the bird.

Moving over the city, they could see air-to-air combat, ground to air activity, and even a tracer within 500 feet of the helicopter's tail. The tracers (a round of ammunition, specially treated with a chemical causing it to glow in the dark when fired so that its flight can be followed) continued for several minutes but fell short of their target. The air base at Bien Hoa was in flames as a result of massive artillery assault. North Vietnamese shells had just slammed into the air base at Tan Son Nhut. There was devastation all around. The chopper continued to zigzag in an unpredictable pattern to avoid mortars and ground fire. How absurd it would have been for Meador to be shot down on his way out of Vietnam. (Miraculously, not one of the 120,000 Vietnamese or 20,000 Americans evacuated in the last weeks was lost to enemy action). Only when they were heading out over the water did the gunners release their grip and move back from their guns.

There was just enough light from the rocket blasts to make out the grins and "thumbs-up" sign from the helicopter crew.

The whole sky was dotted with choppers, and once over the water, they all seemed to be headed in the same direction toward the American fleet. Below, fishing boats crammed with refugees, their lanterns glowing from the horizon, almost resembling a floating city.

Holding the small boy in his arms, who had miraculously fallen asleep during the most important night of his life, seemed to be the only real thing to Meador at the moment. It was symbolic of all the children he had held before. At Thu Duc there was always a lonely child on his lap—holding one more during his departure from Vietnam seemed significant and natural...and somehow less traumatic.

Meador continued to watch the lights of Saigon growing smaller and dimmer. The events of the past fourteen months flashed through his mind, and he was sad. Though he felt older...wiser...leaving Vietnam was leaving a home he had grown to love.

Finally, an aircraft carrier was in sight, and only then did Meador realize he had made it. He was among the last ten non-military Americans to leave the roof. When he felt the slight bump of the skids setting down on the *Midway,* the realization hit him...his great adventure had come to an end. Anything thereafter would be considered ordinary—nothing would compare to the exhilaration he felt in having his life spared.

The drama continued to unfold back at the Embassy. At about 11:00 p.m. there was a lull in the helicopter lifts. A rumor had spread that after midnight, the Viet Cong would start shooting the helicopters down. Up to this point the fire fighting concentrated on the ground.

The fact was that the CH-53s were temporarily grounded because the air crews had been flying more than ten hours under the most difficult circumstances. The task force commander was becoming increasingly concerned by this late hour and the effect that the dangerous night flying conditions and fatigue would have on his pilots. The plan was to resume the flights at daylight. But Marine Brig. Gen. Richard Carey, the landing force commander, argued vehemently that by daylight the Embassy would be in the hands of the North Vietnamese Army. He insisted that his pilots keep flying. As a result, the choppers resumed the evacuation flights with the pilots flying 16 hours straight, when regulation time was not to exceed four hours in the air.

Additional support busied the sky as carrier-based Navy fighters provided air cover. Ten F-4 Weasel planes, equipped with electronic gear designed to search out SA 2 missile batteries, crossed the skies.

This night would long be remembered as "the night of the helicopters." As long as the choppers continued circling above the Embassy, the evacuees below clung to a hope of escape.

Then, "Tiger...Tiger...Tiger" was transmitted from a departing helicopter. It was the code message informing the fleet that the

Ambassador had left the Embassy under the direct order of the President of the United States. "Operation Frequent Wind" ended soon after Ambassador Martin, and his wife, climbed aboard Lady Ace 09 at 4:48 a.m., with the American flag neatly folded and placed in a brown paper bag. Only 21 lifts remained for the senior Embassy staff and Marines before the evacuation was terminated.

After the departure of Martin, the Marines at the gate got word to pull back into the courtyard, then into the Embassy lobby, where they bolted the door and went up the elevator. Locking the elevators on the sixth floor, the Marines went up to the roof and blocked the door with everything they could find, including their own flak jackets, personal packs, fire extinguishers and heavy wall lockers that had been used to store weapons. Some 420 evacuees grasped what was happening and looked to the roof, waiving papers; they knew the men were still there. Dawn was breaking and looters were already in possession of the lower floors of the coveted building, trying to make their way up the tear-gas-filled stairwells.

When the helicopters returned, Marines discarded personal gear so that instead of the usual fifteen, more men could climb aboard. Finally, the last eleven men waited for what seemed like an eternity. It was full daylight, and after all the frantic hours of mob control, there was nothing to do but wait for the U.S. CH-46 Sea Knight to return. The men crouched down for the last assault...not knowing if the mob below or the Viet Cong on the adjacent roofs would pick them off. An hour lapsed before the last helicopter returned. At 7:53 a.m., M. Sergeant Juan R. Valdez, the head of the Embassy guard unit, was the last marine to step off the Embassy roof, in what was still the Independent Republic of South Vietnam.

Two American Marines, Lance Corporal Darwin, Judge of Marshalltown, Iowa, and Corporal Charles McMahon Jr., of Woburn, Masachusetts, were killed a day earlier at Tan Son Nhut by rocket and artillery bombardment. Two Marine helicopter pilots, Captain William Craig Nystul of Coronada, California, and First Lieutenant Michael John Shea of El Paso, Texas, also died on April 29th when their chopper crashed into the sea near an aircraft carrier during the evacuation. These men were the last Americans killed in action, lending a final tragic note to America's 30-year involvement in Vietnam.

Though the final evacuation was concentrated at the Embassy, 10,000 more Vietnamese left their country by sea, undertaking voyages of great hardship in feeble boats, sampans, barges, rafts, and anything that could float. Many transferred at sea to the U.S. Navy vessels, and others made it all the way to the Philippines or Thailand. Some of the helicopter landings were life-threatening to observers as well as to the passengers. Pilots, upon unloading their human cargo, were compelled to lift off and ditch into the rolling sea, discarding millions of dollars worth of helicopters as casually as beer cans in order to make room for later arriving choppers. Other fixed-wing transports landed in Thailand with plane loads of refugees, and thousands more headed into the jungles to hide from the invader.

Ross Meador did not go home to America. Leaving the carrier *Midway* in Bangkok, he sent a telegram to his parents informing them that he was safe. He did not know when he would return home. He only knew he needed time to grieve—to let go of what he felt and did and saw in Vietnam. His life would be changed forever.

"Somewhere," he thought. "Yes, I'll find a place...where there are children...there must be something I can do"

It would be many months before he would return to the valley in Ramona, California. It would be years before he could let go of the emotion.

"Someday," Meador promised himself, "I'll write about all of this. I'll tell the world about the plastic card carriers, those in high places who went to Vietnam on their two and three-day fact-finding tours...those who really didn't give a damn about the war or what this was really all about.

I think I'll call my memories, 'Peace, Love, and Pistols.'

Well...maybe."

CHAPTER IX
ON COURSE WITH DESTINY

"Books come into existence from various motives, but if nothing of the personality or life of the author enters into them, they are written to little purpose. They may possibly bring fame and money; they will not bring conviction."

– Bouton

The Vietnam War entered my life during a spring blizzard that descended upon Denver late one evening in March, 1975. The storm forced commuters to inch their way homeward in the wet, heavy snow, and the remarkable drop in temperature, typical of Denver, was making the late traffic hazardous and wearisome.

Somewhat angry with myself for not leaving the office earlier, I gripped the steering wheel and tried to make the best of the situation by tuning into a station warbling music of the forties and fifties.

Suddenly the music stopped. I turned up the volume...

"We interrupt this program for a bulletin. The news from Saigon tonight is that the city is in a state of panic as the military situation in Southeast Asia is rapidly deteriorating. American diplomatic officials are evacuating their families as the Viet Cong troops race to the Capitol."

The newscast continued, describing how thousands of orphaned and abandoned children were wandering helplessly throughout Saigon. The Denver-based Friends of the Children of Vietnam, an adoption agency which had been operating the orphanages in Vietnam for the past seven years, was accelerating its efforts to evacuate the Amerasian children, those fathered by American soldiers, to the United States.

Australia had refused to admit the children in transit. Therefore, hundreds of orphans were to be brought to Denver as soon as the

Vietnamese government issued the necessary exit permits. Cheryl Markson, Executive Director of FCVN, expressed concern in getting the children out of Saigon before the Communist takeover. But the organization faced a dilemma in housing and processing the children once they were brought to the United States.

"More news on the hour..." The music resumed with a blast.

Hearing that bulletin was like a detonator lighting the fuse of a time bomb of memories. My senses began to float...I could see, smell, and touch the past. "Okinawa...Korea...Indochina." The three countries and their similarities raced through my mind.

During the Korean War years, I was offered a job with the Department of Defense. It was an assignment to the Staff Surgeon's Office of 20th Air Force at Kadena AFB, on the island of Okinawa. It was a life changing experience that never left me. I hadn't reminisced about the early 1950's for a long time, but hearing the news from Vietnam brought total recall of those events.

The Korean War peaked when I was on tour of duty in the Pacific. The stories of the plight of those children drifted back to the island, which was a part of the military contingent; the planes from Kadena were flying missions to the war.

Helen LaPlante was a friend who worked for the Army District Engineers and had just been reassigned to Okinawa from Korea. "Smokey" was a photographer and had encountered hundreds of orphans in the course of her work. She was an unlimited, factual resource for the tribulations of the children in Korea, and she often spoke of how the orphaned children of war wandered aimlessly everywhere...in cities, in the countryside and in villages, looking for protection, a haven or some sign of hope. Ragged and suffering from malnutrition, most had scabies, infected open sores, inflamed running eyes, and many had lost limbs. They lived in boxes, abandoned shacks or found refuge by laying against any protective structure, even cuddling down in ditches drenched with water. The elements, too, were their enemy. Korea was cold. Their frail bodies wandered in packs like homeless animals, and they often fought each other to dip into refuse and garbage cans of mess halls for survival.

Thousands of children had been abandoned during the early days of the Korean War; it was impossible to grasp the magnitude of how to care for them. The mechanics of war, the retreating of armies, and concern with military objectives took precedence over human suffering or needs. It had not been uncommon, upon daybreak, to find the bodies of children at the doorstep or huddled against the fences of the American camps. Cold, lonely and confused, the children knew the Americans would bury them, and in their desperate hours, they crawled to what they perceived as their last hope.

Thousands of children had been lost to starvation, infection and the bitter winter before a mass effort was made to harbor them from the ravages of war.

The children of Okinawa were spared much of the fate suffered by their Korean counterparts. During World War II, the American occupation came swiftly, and almost immediately, orphanages and shelters were established by charitable organizations to care for the homeless. But poverty continued to exist in the villages for some years after the war, and entire families endured severe hardships. Our medical group often provided voluntary services to the local indigenous hospital and orphanage. I recalled my boss, Colonel Jack Bristow, who was an ophthalmologist, dictating reports of his surgeries. It was the first time I transcribed the word "enucleation"...the surgical removal of a child's eye. I was deeply touched by one so young to lose so much...so early in life.

For the American personnel stationed in the Pacific, there was a sense of futility in attempting a recreation stint at the beach, or even sight-seeing in the village, without an invasion of curious and hungry children. No sooner would you unpack your gear and sprawl out under the sun, when, in a matter of minutes, they would emerge out from behind rocks, shrubs and trees. Children, as if afraid or ashamed to be seen, would converge on a picnic like an invasion of ants. From the shape of their bodies, they were obviously hungry, and many were suffering from rickets and possibly tuberculosis. The mere sight of them made a relaxing picnic away from the base seem like an extravagant luxury for the American personnel, so the remainder of the afternoon would be spent trying to befriend the children and offer them food or yen.

A brief trip to Nagasaki would be another self-deprecating experience. After a year on Okinawa and a bout with a tropical illness, I was eligible for R & R (Rest & Recuperation) leave. At the invitation of a friend to visit Itazuke Air Base in Kyushu, I hopped the only transportation that was available to the area at the time, which was a Flying Tiger cargo plane in the middle of the night. Don Teeters, the pilot, flew out of mainland China with the AVG (American Volunteer Group) during the war and stayed on when the Flying Tigers converted to a cargo airline. It was a star-studded night and Teeters invited me to join him on the flight deck for the trip. As I sank into the co-pilot's seat, I conceded that there were advantages to being the only passenger and leaving at an ungodly hour. Upon arrival at Itazuke, I learned that my friend, Lt. Noble David, was ordered to inspect a small American radar site above the hills of Nagasaki. A medical officer, Nobby invited me along with the hope that once his assignment was completed, there would be time to tour the historic city.

Due in part to the devastation and political ramifications resulting from the atomic bomb explosions in Hiroshima and Nagasaki in 1945, no American occupation forces were stationed in the area, except for an occasional small radar site. During my visit in 1954, nine short years had passed since the war's end, yet the death and destruction wrought by the bomb, which brought the imperial nation to its knees and gutted its very soul, was still a fresh memory and quite evident.

Fully aware of the Japanese attitude and resentment of the occupation forces, (just a few years earlier we were the enemy) I warily decided that I would accompany Nobby to Nagasaki. En route to our destination we were confronted with cold stares and an occasional aggressive chant "Go home, Americans!" (In years to come I would travel extensively throughout the world, and often in strange places, but never again felt such isolation as I did on that long train trip.

Upon arrival, Nobby departed for his assignment and I registered at the Kanko Hotel, which was the only American-type inn in the area. I was the only guest at the hotel and had some concern about being alone in a hostile city, where there were no Americans, little English spoken, and where my foreign appearance was sure to be cause for speculation.

Nevertheless, early the following morning, I ventured out into the maze of narrow streets and marketplaces. A small group of children were conspicuous in the courtyard in their chattering and noise. My unexpected appearance brought an abrupt silence to their activity, as if a curtain had suddenly ascended on an unsuspecting audience.

Some of the smaller tykes peeked out from behind older siblings, and I could feel their dark almond eyes scrutinizing every inch of me. Slowly, they drifted in line behind me, as if I were a pied-piper. One, then two, then three and more, careful to remain at a curious distance, yet mirroring my every move. When I stopped, they stopped. When I moved on, so did they.

It was becoming a game.

Each time I looked into a shop window, took a picture, or even checked my map, they dared to wander in closer. Too, I noticed they were growing in number as well as noise. Soon I counted some forty children milling around me, giggling as they pointed to my blonde hair and height. In contrast to the diminutive people passing by, I was perceived as a "giant." Becoming bolder, they would brush up against me and touch my clothing.

At first I was amused, but after a few hours, what began as a novelty, was now becoming an annoyance. I was deeply into a situation that I was not quite sure how to handle.

Many of the youngsters had small siblings tied to their backs; others frolicked about, and some sucked on balloons filled with colored water, the Japanese version of Coca-Cola.

Hoping to discourage them, I hurried along, ignoring their presence, but the children only scurried faster to keep up with me. I entered shop after shop, hoping they would gradually lose interest in me, but they only waited patiently for me outside. Then, when I could no longer dally and had to re-enter the street, the parade would resume.

Being the center of all this attention, I was now attracting passersby and bystanders who were a normal part of the street scene. It was apparent that the youngsters were not going to let go of their object of curiosity for as long as I toured the maze.

Several hours into the charade, I no longer had the sense of adventure, rather, I felt smothered and on the verge of panic.

Then an idea struck me.

I went into a small department store, and in the universal language of smiles and fingers, I managed to communicate to the clerk that I wanted to purchase a large selection of toys. After agreeing upon the required yen, I returned to the street where I took each child by the hand and squeezed a toy between their little palms.

"I want to give this to you...now, please go home!" I pleaded.

Judging from the ragged appearance of many of the tykes, I could safely assume these were probably the first new toys they had ever received. One by one, they smiled and squealed in delight, then ran off in different directions.

When the last child darted off, I hurriedly departed, leaving in my wake the empty boxes. I had lost all sense of direction and had no idea how to find my way back to the hotel.

During the course of all the distraction and winding my way down the unfamiliar narrow streets, I was sure that I did not accurately mark the map I was making to retrace my route. Japanese signs were everywhere, but nothing was in English.

The mountains across the bay were my beacon. I remembered an earlier trip to Colorado and the navigational lesson one soon learns being in a city with mountains.

"My God, I wonder if I will find my way back?" It was getting late.

"Problem solved," I thought. I would find a cab...but there were no taxis in the narrow streets; only carts and bicycles. In stopping Nagasakians to ask directions, they merely shook their heads and offered a polite smile. Lost, I was left to wander aimlessly.

The sun was setting and soon it would be dark. My stomach ached and I felt light-headed. I realized that I had not eaten since breakfast, nor had I had anything to drink all day. The fact that my body was still in a post-hospital recovery process from encephalitis rendered the neglect to myself even more foolish. I was exhausted, disheveled, but the area soon began to look familiar. The hotel courtyard entrance was just ahead! I trudged up the cobblestone incline with a sigh of relief, thankful that the excursion didn't exceed my physical limits.

Just a little further and I would find the comfort of a shower and my room.

Then...

There they stood...three little girls holding the dolls I had given them earlier, waiting to "pounce" on me again! Even more exasperating, they knew the route back to the hotel!

"Please, please go away..." I motioned with my hand. I had no smile for them now. Angry, I brushed past and hurried to the door.

Then, one of the little girls caught the hem of my dress, trying to prevent me from entering the hotel. I raised my arm to brush her aside, but as I did, she grabbed my hand and forced a wilted flower into it.

I was stunned.

The little girl looked up at me, smiling, her eyes blinking merrily at her gift. The other little girls babbled in their tongue, and although I could not understand them, they communicated happiness and smiles.

The surprise of the moment waned and I began to understand, despite my exasperation, that they were attempting to thank me. They continued to point to the dolls I had given them.

Then, a moment of silence followed and I stooped down, now more patient, as the children came closer to me. One of them squeezed my hand with the flower still in it, repeating my earlier gesture in giving her a gift.

In the unencumbered language of non-verbal communication, I finally understood their message of love and friendship. It was I, after all, who was the intruder. I had not experienced their poverty and isolation or their threshold of curiosity in seeing someone so different...so strange.

Korea...Okinawa...Indochina...another memory emerged.

The war in Vietnam was also part of the experience. The French were engaged in a fierce battle in the valley at Dien Bien Phu in 1954. I recall the night someone came into the Kadena Wing Club where flight crews were gathered and leaned over the table to murmur to the pilots seated there that Captain James B. McGovern, who had been a legend in Indochina (just as he had been a legendary figure in World War II) had been killed that day, May 6, 1954. McGovern celebrated an international reputation as a "pilot's pilot" and was a favorite topic for conversations; everyone felt they knew him personally. A huge bearded man he was nicknamed "Earthquake McGoon," after the character in the Li'l Abner comic strip. McGovern took a direct hit as he flew his forty-fifth mission over the Dien Bien Phu Valley. It was the end of a living legend, and his demise brought the Indochina war closer to our island-world.

In early May, 1954, rumors of Indochina were put to rest when the Americans offered to airlift the most seriously wounded French soldiers from Dien Bien Phu, and treat them at military hospitals in the United States. The classified movement was referred to as "Operation Wounded Warrior." The airlift put down at Kadena Air Base on Okinawa before proceeding to Westover Field, Massachusetts.

During the refueling procedures, food, supplies and medicines were distributed, and treatment of the injured took place on the flight line. Some of the wounded hobbled off the transport for a breath of fresh air, while litters were lined up under the shade of the wings. The sight was overwhelming as medics swarmed over the wounded, giving relief as needed.

Occasionally a French soldier, still in dirty fatigues, covered his face with his forearm, and the distorted rhythm in the palpitations of his chest revealed the level of his emotions. The early morning stillness was broken by the wracking sobs of a man full of despair. The overall silence of the scene, with hundreds of figures milling about, indicated that there were no words adequate to communicate the compassion we felt for the defeated French troops. It was an unforgettable sight and a tragic conclusion to the French involvement in Vietnam. Who could predict that in twenty years, America would endure a similar humiliation in Vietnam.

Of the 16,544 men in the Dien Bien Phu Garrison, we were seeing some of the 8,221 casualties. It was later learned that some 7,000 French troops were left as prisoners on May 8th in Indochina and suffered the same fate in a death march as did the Americans at Bataan.

Suddenly, the memories of those days in the far east abruptly stopped. I was back in a snowstorm in Denver, hearing on the radio about the Vietnamese orphans. Why that news on that particular day struck such a chord with me is rather inexplicable. I don't believe things happen by accident—I'm more inclined to believe they happen by design. Had I left my office a short time earlier that day, or if the storm hadn't slowed traffic—or I hadn't been alone with my thoughts—the news of the orphans may have eluded me and I would have missed the moment in history altogether. Beyond that, I had definite feelings against Vietnam. There were just too many issues on the table surrounding the war which had a negative influence on life in America at that time. I felt no obligation to get involved. Like most Americans, I wished the war would just go away.

I was, after all, an Air Force wife and aware of the consequences of world conflicts, and that men were called to war. My husband, a retired colonel, was a combat pilot and a veteran with 27-years service who had seen three wars. I was grateful our children were too young for this one. But, like many Americans, I felt a fear of the extent to which it could escalate, namely, a confrontation with Russia.

Labeled "the politician's war," Vietnam had long been perceived as the wrong war at the wrong time. Not that the lack of interest had anything to do with patriotism. The adult generation of America had been raised on wars. World Wars I and II and Korea promised lasting peace—they were wars of aggression by the Axis and Communists, uniting the country. Further, the American people had total trust and confidence in their government during those conflicts. Everyone was involved. Everyone had something to lose.

But Vietnam was different. It was a kind of war that Americans had never before faced. There was no battlefront, no demarcation point to measure victory or defeat. Only casualties.

Too, corruption and graft ran rampant in the small Asian country. America was pouring out over a million dollars a day to hold back Communist domination over a simple piece of real estate that had neither rich oil deposits or any strategic military significance. The only wealth of the country was in its rubber plantations and rice fields of the Delta, which produced three crops each year—just enough to feed the three small countries of Vietnam, Laos and Cambodia.

In America, demonstrations against the involvement in Vietnam were intense. There was a consensus that protesters only contributed to prolonging the war by giving the enemy the faith that, with time, they would break the morale of the American people and win. Contributing to this were the "flower children" of the sixties who were adamant demonstrators, but based on generalizations and media impressions, most were just here to "have a good time." It was "the thing to do." They demonstrated in sign-carrying marches, conducted sit-ins, and even defied their government by burning draft cards in public bonfires. Some even burned flags. They took pride in being conscientious objectors.

The average American taxpayer could only grit his teeth. The Vietnam Veteran was ridiculed and felt betrayed by the demonstrations. It was his sacrifice, above all others, that preserved their freedom of expression. Ironically, much of the sentiment was sympathetic to the GIs... "bring our boys home!"

Also of great consequence, the Vietnam War emerged during a time when the nation as a whole was undergoing rapid social change. The average American was on a treadmill from day to day as new causes and demands surfaced to demonstrate and push for social reform. Big issues were ecology, feminism, population control and distrust in our government. And who could overlook the whole OPEC mess—the gasolines—Agnew and Nixon? Too busy solving the dilemma of how to keep their homes and families intact with all that was going on around them, people went on living with less candor for the problems of the world.

Violence was erupting during the early days of the American involvement. The assassinations of John F. Kennedy, Martin Luther King, and Robert F. Kennedy, traumatized the nation, and a new fear emerged that the terrorism erupting in European countries had found its way to America. Civil rights issues surfaced, and new laws against racial and sex discrimination were on the docket of legislatures around the nation. These were perceived as great movements for humanity, but they, too, were not without incidents of disruption and acts of violence.

Finally, morality—the one thing that preserves the institution of mankind—got a whitewash as changes in attitude were vastly deconstructing our society; what was once a shame was now considered normal. As a direct result, pornography flooded the market under the guise of "freedom of speech and expression," and abortions became an approach to birth control. A loss of trust permeated the country. Gone were the days when Americans left their doors unlocked, or when doing something right for their neighbor or standing up for their principles was respected. Gone, too, were the heroes for which young Americans could look up to as role models. Celebrities from every spectrum seemed to be involved with drugs, multiple marriages, or public scandal. Even music, the universal language that brings serenity to the soul, was revolutionized. Loud, senseless tunes with explicit lyrics, excited youth, while it raised the blood pressure of another generation. Change is inevitable, but not all change is good. Where would it end?

Evidence of the changes in American society came as a cultural shock when many of the American prisoners of war were released from Hanoi in 1973. Little did Captain Jeremiah A. Denton, Jr. realize, as he stepped from the plane, that he was coming home to a different country from the one he left nine years earlier.

In his account of captivity, *When Hell Was in Session*, he wrote:

"Slowly the new America unfolded me. It appeared cleaner and better groomed. There was obviously a greater sense of commonality of purpose and respect among members of different religions, and more respect between black and white people."

In the first weeks, unhappily, I began to note some dark corners in America. I saw evidences of the new permissiveness, group sex, massage parlors, X-rated movies, the drug culture that represented to me an alien element. I also noted a mood of national political disunity which has damaged the foundation of the most powerful but compassionate nation on earth.

Sadly, I believe that apathy and disunity at home led to the betrayal of millions of Southeast Asians. The war that was won by the heavy bombing of North Vietnam in December, 1972, was lost in the following months by a mood of disunity and by a weakness in the national character.

When I returned from Vietnam, I was shocked at the deterioration of our society. It quickly became obvious that the basic problem was a deterioration in our national attitude towards the family and family life. The personal values of spousehood and parenthood stand too far down the hierarchy of society's values relating to individual responsibilities, accomplishments and vocations."

Crime in America shot up...prisons were overflowing...and the land of the free was becoming the land of mace, alarm systems, and shrinks. To try to understand it was difficult, if not impossible. If the children of Vietnam were experiencing upheaval and turmoil as the result of a hot war, American kids were being emotionally damaged by the effects of divorce. They were caught in a "crossfire" of another magnitude. The breakdown in the social system gave way to a new kind of American—one who was less patriotic and too preoccupied with what was going on at home to pay attention to what was going on half a world away.

But somehow, as I drove home that evening, the news of the Vietnamese orphans took precedence over all the social issues and tempered any ill feelings I had about the war. To give added meaning to my conviction and concern for the orphans, I am also the mother of an adopted child. Therefore, I had a personal understanding of the needs of children who were relinquished and alone. Along with my memories and personal experiences, foremost, my human values compelled me to become involved.

The snow was falling heavily by the time I reached the comfort and security of my home, and my only thought was to call Cheryl Markson, Executive Director of Friends of the Children of Vietnam, to offer my help.

It was to be the beginning of a glorious yet complex experience that would affect my life for years to come.

I recalled the words of Edwin Markham...

"There is a destiny which makes us brothers,
None goes his way alone.
All that we send into the lives of others,
Comes back into our own."

CHAPTER X
RAINBOW

"Home is where, when you have to go there, they have to take you in."

– Robert Frost

Among United States agencies handling the adoption of South Vietnamese children were Friends of the Children of Vietnam (FCVN), Friends for All Children (FFAC), the Holt Adoption Program, Travelers Aid-International Social Service of America, Catholic Relief Services, Migration and Refugee Services, World Vision International, and the Pearl Buck Foundation. All of these agencies were overwhelmed with the magnitude of their mission; it was beyond anything anyone could have predicted. There was a feverish determination by each of these groups to evacuate as many of the orphans as possible. As long as the planes came, children would be placed aboard.

Then, abruptly, at the end of April, 1975, the planes stopped coming as the airfield at Tan Son Nhut was declared inoperable. All of the children who were ever going to get out of the country via the airlift already had. The rest would be left to face whatever destiny had in store for them and what was to be determined in the course of events.

The lucky ones, those fortunate enough to escape on the evacuation planes, either to America or to other countries, were in the process of beginning a new chapter in their lives. And though they were too young to understand the significance of leaving their homeland, they were departing from a heritage that was their birthright—one to which they might never return.

Plane loads of orphans arrived on the west coast of California, and processing kept pace with the incoming children. Operation Babylift was dependent upon volunteers to get the babies and children to their ultimate destination. Providing escorts for the thousands of children seeking passage to their new homes was an impossibility; therefore, use of airline passengers as escorts was the only available option. Passengers en route on both local and international flights suddenly found an infant or a child thrust into their arms for the journey. Airline personnel, the world over, went beyond limits to assure that the children were well-cared for during flights. Many a businessman discarded his briefcase to the floor and found himself a "surrogate mother" on flights where children were hurriedly placed aboard minutes before departure. Passengers found it a new experience; it was a typical rallying of Americans coming together for a crisis situation.

While the majority of the agencies children were processed directly to permanent homes upon their arrival in California, many of the groups bringing orphans to America had to designate temporary facilities as staging areas. Both FCVN and FFAC sent their overflow of children to Denver, Colorado.

The Mile High City structure, a temporary processing facility, was located at the intersection of 22nd and Downing Streets near the hub of downtown Denver. Newly constructed that spring, it was a two-story building scheduled to open in June as a long-term care unit, accommodating 120 psychiatric patients.

Even the new name—"Continental Care Center"—implied ambiance, when indeed it was lacking in luxurious surroundings. It was to be a basic extended care operation, offering none of the frills of other opulent facilities. As the newly appointed administrator, I knew it would require positive public relations to off-set the reputation of the previous structure that once stood on the site. Called "Old Downing," the former nursing home had been an eyesore of the Colorado Department of Health's Long Term Care Division. Officials of that institution heaved a sigh of relief when the depressed building was finally reduced to rubble. Still, it had served as a haven to thousands of homeless, sick people who found their way there through Denver General Hospital.

A bit of history, too, went with the demolition of the old building, as it was the last remains of the first Children's Hospital of Denver, which originated there more than half a century before in what was first a Victorian mansion. Chartered in 1910, it was a proud contributor to the annihilation of children's diseases and a forerunner in its field in the West. But growth demanded a larger facility, and a new hospital was constructed a block south of the 22nd Street corner.

Thereafter, the mansion was modified and additions were made over the next half century. It had served as a hospital, a TB sanitarium, a clinic, and a nursing home before it fell under the demolition ball in 1974.

Denver began to get excited. The Vietnam War was coming home to the Mile High City. Stewart Jacoby and Dave Minshall, two of Denver's most prominent TV reporters at the time, stuck close to what was becoming the biggest story to hit Colorado in years. Daily news releases created a momentum of excitement to the point that activity around the 22nd Street corner became a traffic jam even before the children arrived at the facility.

The preparations for the children's arrival were extensive and cost-ly. Daily TV appeals called for the multitude of equipment and sup-plies that were needed. Since the building was in its final stages of construction and not yet approved for occupancy, it had to be cleaned and prepared in every respect. Even protective sealing of the newly tiled floors to accommodate massive traffic was a priority. The neces-sary equipment for maintenance had not yet been acquired, so a dozen unsuccessful calls were placed to fellow administrators appealing for use of their machines. Ray Morris, an administrator who had some uphill battles himself, simply said, "Come on over...keep it as long as you need it."

To speed up the occupancy permit that sometimes takes weeks, Governor Richard Lamm's office responded to the request, and the permit was issued.

Coordinating the project was a massive undertaking. There was no federal agency designated for assistance. Solicitations for food, clothing, supplies and equipment were done on an individual basis. Imagine preparing for 600 unhappy, desperately heartbroken children who were now alone and without a future of their choosing? The mechanics of caring for so many children captured the hearts of Denverites. In all, more that 3,500 volunteers responded to staff the facility around the clock.

All was ready. Then everyone waited.

Ed Daly made his daring flight with the FCVN children and a cheer went up. Yet no children arrived in Denver. (They were con-tained at the Presidio in San Francisco.)

Then the C-5A Galaxy sent to rescue the FFAC children crashed. We assumed these children were all destined for the Denver facility.

Despite the ill-fated flight, President Ford ordered the evacuation flights to continue, and they did.

Still, no orphans arrived in the Mile High City. Volunteers began to wonder if all the preparations had been made in vain.

Several days passed without word of the orphans.

Then, unexpectedly, an early morning television bulletin announced the arrival of the orphans to Denver, but *not* to the Continental facility. There had been no previous indication that another center was soliciting the Babylift program since both FCVN and FFAC approved and accepted Continental's "in-kind" offer to house the orphans. It was a foregone conclusion that both groups would share the same facilities.

The last-minute shuffle behind the scenes remains a mystery...that despite the extensive preparations and verbal agreement, somehow, someone managed to sway the FFAC group to another building. It would surface, years later, that a church-affiliated organization intervened and made other arrangements; no one bothered to inform Continental of the change.

Little was known at the time of the organizational split between the two groups, yet it was evident that some of the old scars were still there and the old grudges were not put to rest.

When two dozen FFAC babies arrived in Denver at the Life Care Center, much of the medicines and supplies earmarked for Continental ended up there as well.

The Continental group felt both confused and misled, since weeks of effort, time and expense had been poured into the project with only a "handshake" agreement. It was beginning to look like a hoax. Media coverage surrounding Continental's involvement was updated to the public in daily segments. The coming of the orphans to Denver was an impossible secret to keep. The unexpected switch of the FFAC children to another facility, however, implied their desire for privacy and seclusion, thus an air of secrecy was suddenly injected into Operation Babylift. The change only stirred public curiosity.

To further complicate matters, FFAC decided not to allow the media access to the children. Ironically, the privacy they hoped for was violated when pictures of the babies appeared in the press. It was rumored the pictures were sold to the media—not by the FFAC, but by those providing sanctuary. Continental, however, felt it was in the best interest of the children to cooperate with the media. The basic philosophy was that these orphans deserved all the attention, understanding and consideration that was possible. They were "celebrities" of sorts, and what better way to make them feel welcome than for Denver to rejoice in their arrival. Too, open and honest information, would actually temper some of the rumors now surfacing regarding the airlift.

Media coverage, at first, was overwhelmingly positive, then the attitude abruptly changed...years later a coordinator would confess her fears: "We were thought of as heroes...God's gift to the forsaken. 'Aren't we just wonderful,' we thought. Even the military escorts who brought the children from the airport lauded us. Then it got old. So...they (the media) had to find a different angle to keep Babylift on the front page. When they came back, they had a different perspective...like we were hiding something. In a day's time, it changed. The new angle was that bad things were going on...we were concealing information. It made me skeptical...paranoid. Whenever the kids went out, I had a hard time dealing with it."

Within days of the orphans' arrival, not only was the FCVN office and Continental Care Center deluged with threatening letters and phone calls, but extreme critical comments emerged daily in the newspapers as well. It was inconceivable that anyone would have second thoughts regarding unfortunate victims of war caught in a crossfire of political upheaval and death. Further, it was suggested that the parents adopting the children were on a "guilt trip"—that they were acting out of culpability and selfishness.

Numerous articles provided statistics of minority and disadvantaged American children who were already available for adoption, thus accusing Babylift of flooding the adoption market with foreign children. In truth, Babylift was a many-faceted issue. The fact that thousands of lives were saved and an alternative solution was not forthcoming seemed irrelevant to its critics. Other than the efforts made by the volunteer support of the orphanages in Vietnam, before the fall of the country, there was little else done for the abandoned children. Only a fraction of the available children got out on the airlift. Thousands of Amerasians were conceived and abandoned during the Vietnam war and for that, all Americans, if not the soldiers themselves, had a moral obligation to help those children.

As more critics of Babylift surfaced, it became apparent that there existed a segment of society quite judgmental about the tragedy. The warning came in a telephone call: "Why are you getting involved in this? There are people in places of authority who have strong feelings about bringing these children here. This is going to damage your career; it will always be with you." When such criticism was directed to me, I found solace in my father's affirmation: "If you want to be known as a 'good guy' you have to behave like one!" The dice were on the table—there was no turning back. I was "in for a penny, in for a pound."

Then, that which we had prepared for during the past weeks, and hoped for, finally happened on April 9th. The children of war came to Denver. Unlike their arrival in California, they came not in a blaze of glaring lights and flashing cameras or milling crowds of the curious. Rather, they came to warm arms welcoming them in the dead of night into a cold climate which they had never before known.

Their nocturnal arrival was the end of a long journey filled with the confusion of escaping a war. They were finally safe. They had at last found a haven free from bullets, explosions and the terror they had only known all their young lives. Their faces, though soft in texture and youthful in appearance, had a veneer of maturity, undoubtedly the result of the pain and suffering they had endured.

Upon entering the lobby of the Continental Care Center early the following morning, a quick appraisal of the area revealed an assortment of discarded items. Clearly the children had arrived. I noticed a baby bottle lying atop a mountain of blankets...a child's sock, an untied sneaker...an abandoned doll looking worn but cherished.

"They're here! They've finally come!" a staff member said excitedly. The high pitch of the children's voices drifted down the open stairwell, cementing our sense of exhilaration. "These are the children who were on Daly's maverick flight out of Saigon!" she exclaimed.

Together we ascended the stairwell into a large upper lobby. We could see children everywhere, scurrying about uncontrolled. A few were laughing and frolicking as they explored their new surroundings, but most were tiny children, crying and showing their irritation and displeasure. It was easy to see they were tired, frightened or confused. Perhaps all three.

A small group was mesmerized by the blasting television set, probably the first they had ever seen (courtesy of Sears Roebuck & Co.). The magic of the animated cartoon and the message of pantomime transcended the language barrier, and giggles erupted through fingers cupping their mouths. Within a few days, one youngster would become overzealous in his attempt to rescue the TV hero and smash the screen. (Sears understood.)

Some older children were passive and looked out the windows, seemingly bewildered and intrigued by the tall buildings in downtown Denver.

The kindergarten tables, provided by the Denver school warehouse outlet, were surrounded by small tots squatting in various positions, both on and off chairs. Patient volunteers coaxed a mixture of rice and eggs into their small mouths, yet no one felt like eating. It was easy to tell everyone was homesick; the whimpers and cries of the littlest ones could easily have been soothed by a mother they would never see again.

The entire scene was bedlam. There were more than sixty children in all, each one in need of something...someone. A handful of adults, who could not speak the language, tried desperately to respond in various ways. For the moment, there seemed to be no sense of organization—just an attempt to do something—anything. The mass confusion was commonplace to the children who were all too familiar with the experiences of neglect and survival in Vietnam. There was no parent to discipline them. Some were out of control. Considering they were confused, afraid and in cultural shock, their behavior was understandable.

Each moment was a drama unfolding. Walking down the corridors, open doors revealed infants asleep or crying in their cribs. They tugged at the rails, sucked their thumbs, and one desperate toddler banged his head against the crib in frustration. Others were being soothe in the many rockers interspersed along the hallway, which often presented a navigational challenge.

Mattresses lined the floors of the rooms and displayed rumpled sheets. In one area, innovative older children had already assembled several mattresses to simulate a trampoline and took turns running and jumping onto them.

Toys that had been acquired and stored in a linen closet, awaiting the arrival of the orphans, were now scattered everywhere. Tricycles and red wagons raced through the hallways. All the volunteers were too busy to pay attention or were too sympathetic to detour any of the action. With every kind of toy and food to pacify the orphans, it was like Christmas.

Then, there were some children who weren't interested in any of it. They displayed an almost abnormal composure and sat quietly along the walls, seemingly engrossed in coloring books. That is, until the sound of clicking heels approached.

"American mother?" Their little faces lit up.

This same confusion was to be repeated hundreds of times during the next six weeks.

The following morning, a second group of airlift children arrived. The scene was repeated, but this time the noise and straining voices were even louder; they could be heard on the sidewalk outside.

The third and fourth days produced the same state of confusion. More volunteers appeared, but rather than temper the situation, it became more chaotic.

Nothing, simply nothing, could calm the atmosphere. What the children were longing for, the staff could not provide. They simply wanted their mothers, their *own* mothers—not these people with strange faces who could not speak their language. The bad behavior of children renders a stranger helpless. Something had to be done.

The piano in the corner was inconspicuous, though it beckoned like a magnet. Remembering the French influence in Vietnam, I sat down at the piano and made an amateurish attempt at playing "Frere Jacques," the French tune that was not only a primer for American elementary school children, but surely familiar to children the world over. It was a gamble that paid off.

For a few moments the music went unnoticed and was drowned out by the children's cries. Then I banged the keys harder and opened the top lid to expose the sound board. At first, there was little response. Then slowly, the background noises diminished and the sound of little voices permeated the room. Smiles erupted... "Frere Jacques, Frere Jacques, dormez vous..."

It came in a few weak strains...then within moments, a room full of children were singing loudly and joyfully.

Voilá!

The magic that overtook the room was miraculous. Dozens of little brown eyes were now dancing with happiness and they began milling around the piano. Occasionally, a little finger would reach out to touch a key. The sadness that enveloped the room only moments before was all but forgotten.

When the song ended, I turned facing the children and began to applaud, hoping they understood my gesture to mean "approval."

They gleefully began clapping themselves.

The ice was broken.

"Amen," I thought to myself.

A young girl of 15, who understood the magic of music, came to take my place at the piano and began to play Vietnamese songs. Within seconds, the youngsters scrambled to stand beside her and in unison every child in the room became alive.

The international language of music had not only diffused the earlier scene of bedlam, but transcended all barriers and became a communication to soothe pain. (A bonus came to me years later when Esther Hahn, a volunteer who had the awesome task of scheduling other volunteers for the program, produced a tape she had made of the children singing that morning.)

When the piano was eventually returned to Piano's Unlimited, a Denver contributor to the Babylift, it was in shambles. Curious youngsters had broken off keys and reached into its inner workings, snapping hammers and other parts. Pianos Unlimited didn't mind a bit. The instrument had done more for the morale of the children then anyone could have anticipated.

On occasion, the same 15-year-old Vietnamese girl who rescued me at the piano would play selections of Chopin and Bach on the old upright. Since members of the press were constantly interrogating volunteers as they left the facility, word of the young girl's talents drifted to the ears of a female reporter who was determined to lay truth to some of the allegations that many of the children were not truly orphans. The young girl who played classical music was immediately presumed to be a member of an aristocratic Vietnamese family and that quite possibly, she was the daughter of the Commanding General in Saigon. It was further alleged that many children of the rich were smuggled out of Vietnam with the orphans.

Some of the older children themselves injected subterfuge into the matter, telling translators at Continental that they were not orphans. "My father is a General. They pushed me on a plane to get out of there." Considering that these children survived on the streets of Saigon, it was a story they could easily concoct. Admittedly, the girl who was familiar with Chopin and Bach had to have been privileged to obtain such training in Vietnam, which indicated that there may have been, in part, some truth to the allegations. It was an inference that wouldn't die, and the matter escalated to the point that I discovered this same reporter rummaging through the trash container at the rear of the building. It shocked me, to say the least, to uncover the extent this individual would go to develop her story.

My attempt to admonish her behavior only encouraged a lucrative counter offer: "Barnes, if you will cooperate in providing me with information regarding the orphans, especially those whom I am convinced are children of the elite, I promise unlimited media coverage, with public relations promotion, when you open your facility."

The timing of Operation Babylift was perfect. Admittedly, when the opportunity fell into my lap, I was aware of the potential of positive public relations. Nursing home facilities had long been the target of bad press, resulting in a fear among the elderly and a hesitation of families to use the facilities as care providers. In truth, the majority of nursing homes are well-run and provide a valuable service to humanity. Considering the alternatives, what would we do without them? This reporter was resurrecting a nursing home administrator's dream—the opportunity to get the real story and the positive facts of long term care out to the public. But soliciting press coverage for my facility was the farthest thing from my mind in making the housing offer to FCVN. That was a decision of compassion, duty and moral obligation—nothing else intended. There was no hesitation, on my part, in declining the reporter's offer. I was furious and I let her know it.

Just when it appeared that the children billeted at the center were achieving a sense of calm and settling into a routine, a new group would arrive and the early morning hysteria would be repeated. The tears and wailing of the newcomers would set off a chain reaction of homesickness and the orphans would revert back to their initial feelings of abandonment.

Meanwhile, FCVN was processing adoptions as rapidly as possible. Home studies, reference checks and all other formalities were required. The procedure paralleled that of the adoption of an American child.

Each day the scene was repeated. Children were meticulously dressed, groomed and, along with a small satchel of their personal belongings, taken to the airport for destinations all over the world.

The treasures the children clung to were often small items they accumulated as they were passed along way-stations en route to Denver. A few had pictures of their natural mothers. More often, their prized possessions were crayons, pennies, screws, small toys, or even old hair ribbons. Some prided the small gifts given to them by a soldier, such as a cap or unit patch.

One particular youngster grasped a small green metal box that possessed the usual items, along with a tattered picture of a young Vietnamese woman, undoubtedly his mother. For some unknown reason, the box was left behind at the center, probably forgotten in the excitement as the child left for his new home. A year later, it resurfaced from a storage closet and was placed in the skillful hands of Pat McGuire, a reporter for the *Denver Post*. McGuire was able to trace the child from an FCVN identification number scrawled on the box. Luckily the family lived nearby in Boulder. The adopted mother had heard the child's story of the box and had lost any hope of its recovery. A picture of the child's mother (who had been killed) was the coveted treasure. The fact that the little box was not discarded in the cleaning process and returned to its owner was a small miracle.

Volunteers became attached to the children, and departures brought a flood of tears on both sides. Hearts were broken daily among the children themselves who clung to their companions, the last link they would have with their past. It was a separation that would last forever.

With the extended family concept the Vietnamese shared (that friends and neighbors often took a child into their home when the parents were dead), departures were sometimes grossly misunderstood by Americans. The children looked to each other as brothers and sisters, although there usually were no blood ties. Several children had been thrown together in the extended family situation and were thought by many of the volunteers to be actually "related." When they were adopted by separate parents, some volunteers assumed it was a permanent separation of blood-related kin.

As a result of this lack of cultural knowledge, gossip circulated which led everyone to believe that FCVN was, indeed, actually separating siblings.

Each dawn brought new separations. While some children came and departed within a few days, others remained for weeks. It was a pitiful scene as they watched their friends depart and waited for their turn to go to their new homes. The existence at Continental was becoming a bore to them. Without a doubt, some may have sensed nobody wanted them.

Good medical attention was lacking in Vietnam. The nuns were left to provide whatever relief and comfort they could offer to the suffering and undernourished, without medical knowledge and supplies. The health of the children, therefore, was the foremost consideration on the minds of the rescuing agencies.

Three physicians manned the Continental program and were outstanding in not only their medical fields but in their humanitarian desire to help the children of war.

Dr. Ted Ning, a Denver Urologist, and his colleague Dr. Richard Flanagan, a cardiologist, were both members of the FCVN Board. Both adopted orphans as well.

When it appeared that Babylift was "bottle-necked" on the west coast, Flanagan hopped a plane to San Francisco to personally cut through the red tape, expediting the children to the Denver center to be processed quickly to the homes awaiting them. He was shocked to discover that other agencies considered the children "up for grabs" and the FCVN children were actually being sent to other states.

With several flights arriving each day and eight different agencies involved, a state of confusion existed at the Presidio. Strangers, who were not familiar with the orphans, staffed the program. As children were fed, bathed or treated and moved to different areas, they were frequently mis-identified or not returned to the same location. Years later, the details of a kidnapping of eight FCVN babies unfolded. The infants were removed from their beds by strangers and their wrist bands discarded to the trash. Then, hurriedly, they were placed on a plane to Seattle. Through the quick intercession of the FBI, all babies were returned, unharmed. Undoubtedly, there were other incidents that went unreported.

Dr. Roger Cadol was the third physician who took up the daily visits to the children when the other two doctors had to return to their busy Denver practices.

Dr. Jack Wasinger, Dr. Richard Gander, and others offered dental treatment, which many orphans badly needed. In Vietnam, toothbrushes and dental hygiene was not available to the orphans, and most of the children had never before seen a dentist. But the children in need moved through the center so quickly that treatment was impossible. The dentists, on their own, proceeded to make a worthwhile contribution to the cause of the Vietnamese children by providing free dental care after the children were placed in homes.

It seemed that everyone wanted to help. When asked for donations, supplies or even their time, no one refused.

McDonalds sent over a thousand meals, consisting of hamburgers, apple pies, French fries and Cokes. A Denver coffee company kept the volunteers well supplied in beverages.

Three shifts of registered nurses staffed the program. Many Denver hospitals experienced a nursing shortage themselves, yet encouraged their nursing staffs to donate at least one shift a week to the airlift cause.

Children's Hospital, which once occupied the Continental site, was now a block down the street. They responded with supplies, equipment, and requests for emergency treatment for the very sick babies.

Likewise, Beth Israel Hospital also sent assistance. Two outstanding staff members, Estelle Radar and Chuck Campbell, responded spiritedly. Radar was In-service Director of the hospital and gave little thought to her status as she grabbed a mop. Campbell was head of the Dietary Department and rolled up his sleeves to staff and supply the kitchen. He cooked the first meal the children ate in America. Children were fed cautiously--scrambled eggs, rice, whole milk, light stews. Every effort was made to avoid a rich American diet in order to prevent diarrhea. One of Radar's staff members, Darlene Roberts, and her husband, Rick, a sales representative for Skufca & Shelton Real Estate, single-handedly went into the community asking for donations. They filled a room with new toys for the children.

Then, there was the mother of them all, the American Red Cross, who equipped the kitchen, stock-piled the pantry, provided blankets and sent hundreds of volunteers.

It was this kind of coming together that made Operation Babylift a success...and somehow it was a small healing of the horror of Vietnam.

Even simple things became news. Late one evening, as a Lowry Air Force Base bus shuttled an incoming group of orphans to Continental, a fan belt broke on an isolated stretch of the route from the airport. A young woman provided her panty-hose to substitute for the broken belt and the bus arrived no worse for the wear. The following morning the press hailed her a heroine.

The small babies seemed to disappear quickly as couples appeared daily to look at the infants who all seemed so beautiful.

One of the volunteers who had been at Thu Duc in Vietnam became a coordinator at Continental. She had also adopted a son, Luke, an Amerasian child while they were in Vietnam. She and her husband had reviewed the histories of many orphaned children as members of the FCVN team before they went to Vietnam. Luke's portfolio reappeared several times, and it seemed that the child, for some unknown reason, was not being chosen for adoption, perhaps because there were so many children from which to choose. When the couple saw Luke, it was love at first sight and they adopted him as their own.

Luke appeared daily at the center, along with his mother, and he blended right in with the children. The staff named him "Cool Hand Luke," lifting the name from the popular Paul Newman movie. Luke was about three years old, curly-headed and magnetic...the kind of child everyone wanted to pick up and hug, which is exactly what one couple did when they wandered about the facility trying to select a child. They carried Luke into the office, beaming.

"We want this little guy. This is our baby!"

Luke's mother hurriedly reached for him. "Sorry, this one you can't have. This is my son."

Through the generosity of merchants, supplies and clothing were plentiful. Storage closets were bulging with garments for both infants and children. The "boutique," a huge walk-in closet filled with frilly dresses, shoes, etc, was a little girl's dream. Happy giggles resonated through the halls as the "little ladies" entertained themselves by changing dresses several times each day. The boys, who preferred playing without shoes, were more interested in the bonanza of toys scattered about. Too, there was no telling how many times each day the same baby was bathed and dressed; each shift of doting volunteers felt compelled to repeat the ritual. But the babies enjoyed the attention, and the amassed mountains of laundry seemed a minor inconvenience.

Both the stairway and the elevator became a fascination to the older children who came from rural villages and had never before been in a two-story building. The elevator was constantly crowded and used for "joy-riding" until it was finally locked in place for safety.

The inevitable happened when one of the older boys discovered the fire alarm levers posted on the walls. When one was finally pulled, setting the fire alarms blaring, the children panicked. The shrill sound had terrorized them and they ran screaming to their rooms.

"VC, VC come! Viet Cong come...!"

Then the devaluation... "VC...no numba one...VC numba ten!"

The appearance of the Denver firemen in their black bunker gear outfits added a new dimension to the kid's confusion. It took some coaxing and convincing that they were not VC. Once the children made the connection between the fire alarm and the arrival of the big trucks outside, it became a game. Soon it became impossible to keep the children from pulling the levers, and the alarm system had to be shut down.

The activity transpiring at Continental became important to the residents of the minority neighborhood, and consequently, they became protective of the building.

Continental was located within the Capitol Hill area, a high-crime rate vicinity in Denver. A storefront across the street, well-known as a drug drop-off, even ceased its operation through the forceful intercession of Reverend Liggins, pastor of the local Baptist Church. However, incidents around the facility were minimized with volunteers coming and going at all hours of the day and night. There was never any threat to them. Guards, however, volunteered to monitor the entrances because of threats to the center. Someone who wanted a child could very well attempt to take one from the building.

In fact despite all the precautions, one such incident did occur. Sandy, a young woman who was a patient in a neighboring residential mental health center, had appeared at Continental wanting to help care for the babies. (I had known her as a patient in another facility, and she used that influence to gain access to becoming a volunteer.) Sandy seldom saw her own child who lived in a distant city. Her yearning to be a mother was reflected in what she did with her earnings, which was, to lavish gifts upon her daughter.

"Please, Barnes," her stuttering voice tugged, "Let me take care of the babies." Aware of her erratic behavior, I was concerned that might be a problem. She settled for sweeping and mopping floors, just for the chance to be near and occasionally hold the infants.

Since there was much housekeeping to do, she began her job enthusiastically, but after a while I noticed she was neglecting her work and spending more time playing with the children. In discussing this with her, she became angry and stormed from the building. The following day she appeared and began her work in a normal manner.

I sent word for her to come to my office after she finished her chores as I wanted to find some area of compromise. I intended to arrange for her to have more time to play with the children under supervision.

It may have been instinct, but I hurried out to catch her before she boarded her bus in front of the building. I sensed she would avoid my office, assuming she was going to be reprimanded again.

Instead of waiting at the bus stop as she usually did, Sandy headed down the street. I ran after her and saw she was carrying a parcel. Upon approaching her she suddenly stopped, a fearful expression frozen on her face. Without speaking she thrust a large plastic sack into my hands. I felt a movement inside and heard a soft whimper.

"Oh, my God," I thought, horrified. "This can't be what I think it is."

Opening the bag, a baby smiled up at me. Then came a shrill cry.

"I was going to bring her back, Barnes, honest..." Sandy slurred in her handicapped speech pattern. "I just wanted to hold her for a little while." Then she ran off.

I was concerned about getting the baby back into the building unnoticed and remembered an unattended entrance. I had surmised that Sandy slipped out of the basement exit, so I retraced her steps. With a passkey I let myself into the lower level leading to the laundry area. My ally would be Minnie Smith, a grandmother who responded to the call for help when Operation Babylift flashed across Denver's TV screens, and who manned the least glamorous job of all—milling through the mountains of laundry that piled up each day. I placed the infant in the laundry cart filled with clean linens, ready to be taken to the nursery area. An identification tag, noting the room and crib, was still intact on the baby's wrist. A short time later the infant was returned to its crib, unnoticed, and the incident went unreported for fear that an epidemic of panic would erupt. A fear always existed among the staff that a child would one day be found missing.

Numerous times children were caught swapping wrist bands. One child had six on his wrist when he landed in California. Since the children were not known, there was no way of judging if they were wearing the same identification originally placed on them in Saigon.

Of equal concern was that the processed adoption papers had to correspond with the child's I.D. bracelet. There was a possibility and concern that bands were swapped somewhere along the route. There just wasn't any way of knowing how big of a problem existed. The bands easily slipped off the small wrists. It may not have been relevant after all, since many of the children were abandoned and there was no trace of their true identities. It would have some consequence, however, if at a later time their natural mothers sought to retrieve their children. As was to happen later, some mothers did appear and claimed their children. There were incidents where the children did not recognize their parents.

Sometimes incidents occurred that took patience and forbearance in understanding the culture. One afternoon, I noticed a group of children peeking through the crack of a closed double door to the activity room. Upon entering I was shocked to find a small child tied to the wall rail. My first impression was that someone was playing a cruel joke on him. But as I began to untie him, a well-coiffured Vietnamese woman appeared, somewhat embarrassed, and cautioned me not to interfere.

"But the boy is bad," she insisted in perfect English. "This is how we teach bad children in Vietnam to behave."

"This is not Vietnam," I countermanded. "This will not happen in this building. If you do this again, I will ask you to leave."

Scooping the red-eyed child up in my arms, I took him down to my office. His name sounded like "Nuyet", and he became my little shadow from that day on. He would wait for me each morning and spend the day either following me around the building or sitting in front of my office door.

Over the weeks to come, we grew attached, and each day I would wonder if he would be gone the next. I did not want to see him leave and often thought about him into the night, wondering how I would approach my family about my feelings of wanting to adopt him.

I already had four young children, (three sons, and a daughter), which included a set of eleven-year-old twins. Four were an armful, and the reason I returned to the job market was to provide for their needs. Although I felt there was enough love in our house to take on one more, I didn't feel I had the right to bring another child into our family when so many couples were waiting for children.

I knew that Nuyet was attached to me, too, but I began to rationalize that he would have more advantages with a couple that longed for a son. It would be the right thing to let Nuyet be adopted by a smaller family. The day finally came when I did not see him. I knew in my heart he was gone and that it was the right choice for him. Still, it was difficult. And over the years, he was not forgotten.

Many others also formed deep attachments to the children and wrestled with the same feelings of adoption.

Several children gained a sense of security and felt protected by taking up positions at the door of Esther Hahn's office. Hahn, like me, had been an administrator and former nurse. She somehow found herself with the awesome task of staffing the program by making dozens of calls each day to make some sense of the schedule. At first, she was deluged with volunteers offering help for any schedule, day or night. But as the weeks passed, the offers dwindled. Her requests were often met with, "I have a PTA meeting...company coming," or any number of other reasons. It was a tedious job that committed her to long hours, seven days a week. She was often accompanied by her husband, Reverend Fred Hahn, who voluntarily performed a number of housekeeping tasks.

Esther had that serene professional appearance, and the children looked upon her like "Mother Superior." Some even thought she was a nun.

One particular youngster, who seemed never to be included in the groups of children playing and who always appeared to be off and alone by himself, waited patiently for Reverend Hahn's appearance each evening as he came to pick up his wife. Before Esther would leave, the two would proceed to the dining room where the minister would feed the youngster and then take him outside for a short walk. It was later learned that the youngster Reverend Hahn befriended was a Cambodian child, set apart from the others because of the centuries long animosity existing between the Vietnamese and the Cambodians. The Vietnamese considered them to be a lower class of people and as a rule did not associate with them. The children were openly repeating the prejudice taught to them.

Just as the Hahns were about to leave late one evening, they were asked to take a desperately sick child to Denver General Hospital. As they raced along the ten-minute route to the emergency room, the child stopped breathing several times, and Esther placed her mouth over his small face and blew life back into him. Of all her years of nursing, she remembered this incident, and her closeness to God, in those moments as she strived to keep the little life going.

Some of the nuns in Vietnam believed Americans wanted only small or young children for adoption and that older children might be sent back to the war-torn country. Therefore, ignorance and fear entered into the life of one child who was drilled by the nuns to keep silent about her true age. The young Vietnamese girl, considered to be about eight years old and small in stature, was placed with a Denver family who was thrilled to have her. But in the weeks following her placement into the home, the girl became withdrawn and would not respond to touch or kindness. The adoptive parents were to the point of returning her to the agency. When the matter reached a degree of frustration, the mother took her to a doctor and learned the reason for her behavior. The girl, after discovering her bloodstained undergarments, feared she was dying and refused to relay the incident to her adoptive mother. Uninformed of the normal physical change and her development into womanhood, she was too frightened to reveal her true age, which was fourteen. She was terrified she would be sent back to Vietnam for being "too old for adoption."

Because there were so many younger children and so much was always happening, the ratio of volunteers to older children was much smaller than to infants. There wasn't time to get to know or understand the problems of each child, and language was always a barrier. Consequently, many of the older children were left to fend for themselves. There was no one to listen to their feelings or to discuss what was happening or what was about to happen in their lives.

As the days wore on and the excitement of Babylift began to wane, reality took hold and there were doubting moments. Initially, there hadn't been time for conferences, training of volunteers, or to establish policies for the transitory program. Continuity was lacking. Upon the arrival of orphans each day, there was also a change in personnel. Nancy Hegel, an FCVN coordinator, did her best to juggle the flood of requests she faced each day, including those from Continental for help in maintenance. Just as we were making strides, she was transferred to the night shift and we had to begin again. Many children had adjustment problems; some slept during the day and played at night. Volunteers adapted, not knowing the language, and often guessing at a child's needs; interpreters were not always available. As wonderful as they were, most volunteers only wanted to handle babies. To ask one to perform a distasteful task was to risk losing them. As a consequence, much of the physical maintenance of the building was left to Continental staff members (who had been hired primarily to prepare for the licensing inspection in June).

The fact that the children were occupying the building did not alter the deadline Continental was facing in meeting the requirements established by the Colorado Department of Health. The initial opening was not without challenges. Employees to staff a 120 bed facility, including professional staff and department heads had to be interviewed and hired. Further, thousands of pieces of equipment and supplies were needed, and hundreds of policies and procedures needed to be written for each department. Along with scheduling both orientations and in-service, there were numerous Health Department Inspections and other criteria scheduled. The opening was a momentous task and only six short weeks away.

With so many children and babies to care for, and hundreds of volunteers coming and going each day, there was no doubt that Continental was a busy place. There were meals to prepare, baby bottles to wash, piles of laundry, phones ringing, supplies to replenish, and even meals to obtain for the volunteers themselves. Discernably, the abuse to the building was taking its toll. Newly hung drapes were torn and pulled down with the rods. Crayon scribblings were on the freshly painted walls, and toilets were constantly stuffed and overflowing everywhere. Bath tubs became swimming pools and mopping was an-on going effort to prevent accidents. Cleaning and trash pickup was awesome. The building was already over-budget in construction costs, and it was apparent that additional expenses would be required to refurbish after the children left. Each time a Board member checked in, I expected to be admonished. They didn't say a word. They were to be admired for the confidence they displayed and for taking a stand to help the children of the war.

There were numerous emergencies each day and night as a result of the turnover in volunteers. I heard each and every complaint, often in the middle of the night.

Late one night, a young man entered the kitchen and detected a faint odor of gas. One of the pilot lights on the stove had apparently gone out. Without rationalizing, he pulled the entire fire alarm system. Immediately notified, I hurried down to the building to find the kitchen looking like a white Christmas. A powder-fire-retardant covered the entire area.

Along with unfavorable stories now surfacing in the press, criticism of the orphans' care drifted back to the Colorado Department of Health. Irrespective of the fact that FCVN was a licensed adoption agency and Operation Babylift was a rescue mission, the state disregarded those issues and held me responsible for the conduct at Continental Care Center. As a result, everything was being scrutinized by the agency. Even I had not considered that Babylift could adversely affect the licensing process; the make-shift operation was one that needed both understanding and patience. I was getting a 'bum rap' and didn't know it. Because it was my building, it was presumed that I was in full authority and responsible for all matters of the Babylift program. Of course I was not. But it was one of those times when silence took over reasoning. I could sort it all out later, I thought. It was a naive assumption. (Even 25 years later, at an adoptee's reunion, a woman blatantly reprimanded me without prefacing her complaint. "My friend was a volunteer nurse at Continental and she said it was a mess! The Red Cross had to come and take over, it was that disorganized..." Taken aback, all I could reply was, "Excuse me?" It made me realize that 25 years was not long enough for an elephant memory...and especially one that got it wrong.) Nevertheless, early one morning, members of the state survey team appeared for an impromptu inspection of the premises. I was confronted with allegations that the children were receiving improper care.

A formula room was set up to meet a constant demand for bottles, and although highly-sterilized procedures were lacking (and deemed unnecessary since the bottles were washed in the commercial dishwasher under required temperature standards), the clean, neat setting did not lend itself to a hospital-like nursery. Considering where the children had previously lived, the expectations for an overly sterile environment seemed impractical.

What the health department responded to was a telephone complaint of "poor sanitation." What they saw obviously produced a cultural shock.

The loose casual environment and the sight of dozens of non-English speaking children involved in many different activities, may have awakened their conscience to the reality of Vietnam. Regardless of what they thought and what they objected to, the system was working and, even more importantly, was being done on a shoe-string budget. It could be more accurately termed "no budget." All things considered, the daily needs of the children were met.

Operation Babylift was something they hadn't bargained for and unlike anything they had experienced. There were no state regulations or written procedures that would apply. This was a time when only common sense should prevail.

When the inspectors re-grouped to compare notes of what they perceived as "deficiencies" in the facility, a toddler waddled up to the nurse surveyor and outstretched his arms, babbling, half-crying. It was obvious to everyone that the child instinctively wandered to the woman and simply wanted to be embraced. Instead of doing the "normal" thing such as giving him a hug, she stepped back and away from the him. Ever so carefully, with two fingers pinching his hand, she steered him away in the opposite direction. The two other inspectors couldn't help but look embarrassed. They both understood the child's need. Perhaps the nurse's insensitivity derived from not having children of her own, but that too was baffling considering she had had a successful career as an Army nurse. Not surprisingly, however, the discussion ended abruptly and the three inspectors departed. Nothing further came of the complaint.

But it was a brief victory. Retaliation was forthcoming during subsequent periodic Health Department inspections, in which my involvement in Babylift was viewed "unfavorably and, therefore, had consequences." Notably, throughout the six weeks of Operation Babylift's function at Continental, no city or state social service officials appeared in support of the mission. The politicians, too, were conspicuous in their absence. It was speculated that the sensationalism erupting in the press regarding the allegations that some of the children were not orphans by definition threw up a red flag. Continental was considered a "hot potato."

Much later, when the winds cleared, these same politicians, at taxpayers' expense, would travel half way around the world to view refugee camps in Cambodia. When history was unfolding right in their own back yard, they did not make the effort to concern themselves with the victims of war, or at the very least, offer assistance.

All the grand rhetoric about what America was going to do to save lives and to recognize its responsibility to the Amerasian children— was indeed falling by the wayside.

Boat people—those escaping from the Communist occupation of Vietnam—were now reaching the free world with stories that children were "taken" from them for the airlift. Refugee mothers were now setting their feet on American shores to reclaim their "stolen" children.

The fact that the adoption agencies had release papers, signed by the Vietnamese parents, didn't seem to matter. Further, in addition to photos, there was testimony to substantiate that parents of children, thrown over compound walls, were begged and counseled by the FCVN staff to reconsider their actions.

With various civil liberties organizations taking the initiative and pushing for the return of the children, Americans who had adopted the orphans were beginning to wonder if they would keep them. And, although the orphans had adjusted to their new surroundings, many Vietnamese nationals disregarded that fact and came to the States to reclaim them. After a separation of only six to twelve months, some of the orphans failed to recognize their "natural" mothers. Irrespective of the child's reaction, however, the biological parents were still awarded custody. Some children were returned to their Vietnamese parents screaming in protest. No thought was given to the possibility that perhaps some refugees were claiming children simply to fatten their welfare checks.

Neither the courts or the parents themselves offered compensation, to either the agencies or the families who adopted them, for food, clothing, medical care, housing, transportation or any of the other expenses that were incurred on behalf of the children. No one even thanked the rescuers.

At the end of April, when Saigon fell to the Communists, the number of orphans at Continental had dwindled to a few dozen. There would be no more children exiting from Vietnam. Over 600 children had passed through the facility during the preceding weeks and FCVN began to relax its grip on letting the volunteers take some of the children to outside settings. Unfortunately, some negative aspects were cause for concern.

By early May, most of the children at Continental were processed to their new homes. Several dozen orphans remained, and one can only imagine the sense of rejection they may have felt seeing their friends depart before them. The Continental environment provided only a small courtyard, a lounge and halls in which to play. Many requests were made to FCVN to take the children to parks, museums, pools, etc., but each invitation was met with rejection. Several incidents occurred that were cause for alarm, injecting a fear that a child would disappear. Coordinators, in their paranoia, had strong objections to taking the children on outings.

One such incident that gave credence to their fears was when a family known to the group requested to take a child home to dinner. A beautiful little girl, who was already placed and awaiting transportation arrangements to her new home, was selected to go for the treat. Later, the couple called FCVN to insist they wanted to adopt her. They had already spoken to the little girl and convinced her that she should live with them. The child was ecstatic and did not want to return to the facility. FCVN had a difficult time getting the child back. There were other incidents of people spontaneously showing up at the building wanting to adopt a child. One such couple *insisted* that they should have a baby; they had already purchased a crib and infant essentials.

When the Continental staff made a request to take the children to a school, there was some objection. Then, approval. It was with great anticipation that Principal Dean R. Pope and the students of Red Rocks Elementary School in Morrison, Colorado, planned for a visit from the orphans. It would be the Vietnamese children's first glimpse at an American classroom.

Pre-arranged, all six grades of the school made crafts or drawings to offer to the orphans as tokens of friendship. The most meaningful gesture came from the first graders. Each child had taken great pains to draw his own picture for the orphans, which were then assembled into a large accordion-like card. The drawings were typical of what first graders usually imagine. Painstakingly scrawled flowers, rainbows, pets, sunshine, families and bright skies with lots of "I LOVE YOU's" scrawled in a child's hand. The message in each picture was clear; the Vietnamese orphans were loved and welcomed with open arms. Printed on the cover of the booklet were bold large letters: "Welcome to America!" And on the back cover was the most endearing invitation of all... "Stay as long as you like!"

Later, when the station wagons were reloaded for the return trip to Denver, one of the orphaned boys was missing. A frantic search of the classrooms came up empty. Stewart Jacoby, a TV reporter covering the event, found the boy on the playground nonchalantly pitching ball with the American youngsters. There was no language barrier here. The atmosphere was very American...very "matter of fact." In the gift that only children have, each had accepted the other unconditionally.

On a sunny Saturday in mid-May, the few remaining children at Continental were readied for departure to their adoptive homes. They would be the last of the orphans to be placed under the six-weeks Operation Babylift program.

At noon, they were all gone. Operation Babylift was over.

I found myself suddenly alone in the building. It was a strange feeling—a sense of both euphoria and desertion. My first inclination was to hurry and leave...it was too quiet . To secure the building, I went upstairs to make one last round.

Toys were scattered everywhere. Rooms looked occupied, but no one was in them. The nursing station appeared normal, as if the staff had just stepped away for a moment. Charts were neatly stacked beside a silent telephone, the lights still ablaze.

The click of my heels was the only sound echoing through the halls. I descended to the lower level to bolt the basement door. It was then that I noticed the obvious silence of the washers and dryers for the first time. Rising to the main level once again, I stepped into the deserted lobby and locked the elevator into position.

It was an abrupt halt...the kind of calm that comes after a devastating storm. A let-down of sorts...like sitting in an empty stadium after an exciting game, or the solitude of being the last person to leave a church.

It was over.

The volunteer's sign-in roster was still atop the security desk, opened to the date, May 17, 1975. The last signature was "T.C. Ning." Instinctively, I picked up the pen to sign out, then realized there would be no more entries. I scrawled the word "Rainbow."

Now Operation Babylift was a part of history. Thousands of orphans were scattered around the world, miles from their heritage, but finally "home" to wherever home was to be for their lifetime.

Fate often brings people together in the most unusual places and circumstances, and when they part, something of each remains with the other. Though only a thread, it endures and sometimes strengthens. That holds true with Operation Babylift. Most assuredly, the children remember something of their days in the building at the corner of 22nd and Downing Streets in Denver. Maybe they recall a special person...the confusion and crying...or just that they found their very own peaceful corner, away from bombs and fear. Or perhaps they remember being some place warm and cozy...finally in loving arms and, for the first time in their lives, *safe*.

The 3,500 volunteers who staffed the Continental Care Center in Denver surely will never forget those terrified little faces and how they struggled to stay awake the first night, too frightened to sleep.

For them, there will always be a certain child to recall...the never-ending curiosity of wondering if somehow they made it. "Please, God..."

For the powers-to-be, those which determine the outcome of events, it appeared it was in the natural order of things for the acre of land at 22nd and Downing once home to the Children's Hospital, to become ordained once again...to hear the sound of little voices, to witness their pain...to be a haven from life's sorrows. The chances of such an occurrence happening twice within this century was indeed not without odds. It was a highly visible act of destiny.

I often wonder if, in the years to come, there will be another coming of children to that special place.

And I wish I could be there again.

CHAPTER XI
AFTERMATH

*"Older men declare war. But it is the youth that must fight and die.
And it is youth who must inherit the tribulations, the sorrow, and the
triumphs that are the aftermath of war."*

Herbert Clark Hoover

In the years following Operation Babylift, many of the orphans returned to Vietnam in search of their roots and to put to rest many of the demons associated with their heritage. At the same time, many of the agencies involved with rescuing the orphans remained in touch with them through newsletters and arranged reunions. In the words of an organizer: "The reunions were well-attended the first few years, and the kids all seemed to enjoy meeting each other. We tried to make the events interesting and informative in presenting Vietnamese history, culture and traditions. But, as the years progressed and the children grew, attendance dropped dramatically. It became apparent that the adoptees were no longer interested in their heritage and were completely Americanized."

All that has changed. The 25th anniversary of Operation Babylift, and perhaps the maturity of the adoptees have brought a resurgence of interest in that moment in history. Many of them now accept the fact that destiny played a role in their lives and that they are indeed a unique group of people. Babylift was an unprecedented historical event. Never before had a government sanctioned the evacuation of so many children to its shores, and the chances of it ever happening again are most unlikely. The children of Vietnam will forever be a part of history. The Vietnamese themselves refer to them as "The Golden Children"—the fortunate ones who were taken to a better life.

Three organized reunions were well-attended during the 25th anniversary year—one in Baltimore, Maryland, another in Vietnam, and a third in Estes Park, Colorado. I was fortunate to attend the Colorado reunion and was most impressed in hearing the adoptees' stories. Because I felt that they, themselves, could best express what the airlift meant to them and how it influenced and affected their lives,

I invited them to share their stories in this chapter of the book. Here, in their own words, are a few of their stories. They will touch your heart.

HUYEN FRIEDLANDER BRANNAN

Author's Note: Huyen Friedlander Brannan was four years old when her mother left her in an orphanage in Vietnam. Days later, Huyen boarded the last orphan evacuation plane out of Saigon, arriving at the Continental Care Center shortly thereafter.

Today, Huyen lies in California, is married, recently became a mother and is pursuing her goals and aspirations of working with adoptees and parents. In 1995 she returned to Vietnam and, through a fateful encounter with a priest in a local village, she was reunited with her birth mother and other relatives. Since then she has kept in contact with her birth family and has returned to Vietnam to visit them. She was unable to attend any of the reunions. However, I had the pleasure of being introduced to her through a typical "six degrees of separation" fashion...through a friend, who knows a friend, who has a friend.

Upon reading an early draft of "The War Cradle" and expressing her appreciation that it filled in many of the gaps of the events surrounding Babylift, she consented to an interview with a friend of mine, Steve LuKanic, who is writing a screenplay based on this book. Her story is symbolic of so many children who came on the airlift, and it validates what I have always felt...that Operation Babylift is an unforgettable moment in history, the impact of which is still being felt today.

HUYEN'S INTERVIEW
How do you pronounce your birth name?
They do it backwards, so the last name is first, then the middle name and first name. So my birth name is Le Thi Huyen (pronounced Lay Tee Hwin).

And your birth mother's name is Dieu? How is that pronounced?
It's different from on the birth certificate. Her name is actually Dem. Le Thi Dem (first name being Dem).

You were only four when you left Vietnam, but even at that young age, certain memories can stay with you. What memories do you have of your life in Vietnam before you went to the orphanage?
Probably the first two memories I used to always talk about when I was first here were one, that we had pigs in our kitchen. Which no one understood, but in Vietnam, their kitchens are outside—four posts with a slanted roof—and the pig stall is literally next door to the fire pit where they cook. So I wasn't crazy—the pigs were in the kitchen there. And I have a memory of a pig delivering piglets, and my grandmother—I'm not sure it was my grandmother, but in my memory it was an older woman—putting all the piglets in a basket. And then the other memory—it's not really specific—but I just always have this memory of sitting in the dirt in front of our house. Which was interesting, too, because when I first came (to the U.S.), I sat in the dirt. I just remember sunlight always coming down on me and sitting in front of a kind of stucco building. And people would say "But Vietnam's tropical, not dusty; you wouldn't be sitting in dirt." But it was just that American people here didn't understand because I wasn't in an urban area. Where I lived, their streets were dirt.

Other than a kitchen, do you remember the house inside? How many rooms?
They don't live in that particular house anymore, but I've walked by it and I've seen it, and it's really just a one-room structure. So I never remembered it as having anything on the walls—which doesn't mean that's the way it was—but in my memory, it was just very barren.

When you returned to Vietnam in 1995, you only had the name of your birth mom and the name of the village where you were born?

Is that right?
Yes.

And the name of the village was Hanoi Honai?
Yes, it's a refugee camp. In 1954, there was this mass exodus from Northern Vietnam to Southern Vietnam because the French—that's when they were kicked out of the North—and all of the people who'd been converted to Catholicism moved South. So my family, who are heavy-duty Catholics, immigrated to the South. Hanoi Honai roughly translates as "resettlement of Northerners."

When you went back in '95, where did you go? Because Hanoi Honai is not on the map, right?
Right. And that was the thing that took the longest in my search...that at the time I was born, there was one settlement. And now there are maybe four or five because it's expanded so much and the population is so dense. For example, the first one I went to was the wrong one because it was new, so I just kept backtracking until I found the original settlement.

So you have those two memories as a child...but you don't really remember anything about the village itself?
No...mainly because of the way I disassociated myself from Vietnam. I never remembered my birth mother's face. I used to tell people I had two mothers, both with long black hair, but that was all that I remembered about these two women. And that never made sense to people either, that I had two mothers. Then the day I found my grandfather and my aunt—the two people who approached the church first—I realized it was this aunt who had been in my memory. She was fourteen at the time when she used to take care of me...when my mother was working...so I really did have these two primary caregivers.

Of the adults, you really only remember your aunt, your mother...and possibly your grandmother?
Yes...it probably was my grandmother. And I really didn't have any memories of my grandfather either, but when I reunited with him I learned he was particularly attached to me because I was the first grandchild. My family told me all these stories of how he was basically like a father to me. Every time I see him he cries, and he's a very

emotional person anyway. But they tell me this story of how he would come home from work and I would run over to him and take off his shoes for him. So it was a very close relationship. In fact, when my birth mother took me to the orphanage, she didn't tell anyone what she was doing. When she came home that night, and I wasn't there...I'm not sure exactly what happened, but it sounded like she definitely suffered verbal abuse, at the least. She was yelled at and ostracized, and I don't know if she was physically abused, but she definitely committed a major sin by doing that. Because they function so much as a family, and for her to make an independent decision like that without consulting anyone—she was punished.

Roughly how many other kids or people were actually living in the house at the time?
Quite a few. My birth mother was the oldest of nine and she would have been 24 or 25 at the time of me actually leaving. So including me, there were at least twelve people living in the house.

So you said they were staunch Catholics...but you don't remember anything about that?
Well, I did have this memory that I always thought was a dream—it was one of those things you're not sure is real or imagined—of people marching at night, holding candles. So when I was there on one of my trips, I told them about my memory and asked if they knew what it was about. And they said that on Christmas Eve and other religious holidays, everyone in the village would light these candles and march to Mass. And since I wasn't brought up Catholic here (in the U.S.), I never understood that or what that was about. It could have been a political protest for all I knew.

You were born in Vietnam when the country was in the midst of a full-fledged war. Do you have any perceptions of that...or being afraid, or a sense of fear within the family?
No...but I did have this one memory, that never made sense to me either, of a man with a bandage over his eye. He was probably one of my uncles or someone who was nearby us who may have been injured or something. But I never fully understood who or what that was about.

With so many people living in the house, do you remember the sleeping conditions?
No. But since I've been back, I know families basically all sleep together—there are maybe one or two mattresses in a house—so there are at least five people sleeping on a mattress. That's still how they do it when I visit there—I have all my siblings and my birth mother sleeping with me! That's just cultural.

So there were children in the house younger than your 14-year-old aunt?
Yes. My uncle—who I guess was my playmate. He's very attached to me.

And what is his name?
Tien.

And what was your aunt's name - the fourteen-year-old?
Her name is Hien (Hee-in).

What happened the day you went to the orphanage? What do you remember?
I remember going with my birth mother to this woman's house—she was Caucasian with long blonde hair, maybe pigtails—and she definitely had another child with her who may have been Caucasian. The four of us took a pedicab—I remember being in the pedicab—to the orphanage. There were these big iron gates, which is typical of the Catholic churches in Vietnam; they're all surrounded by gates. And I didn't know what it was, but there were all these other kids and—for some reason this sticks out in my mind—there were all these plastic Fisher Price-type toys, the kind that make noises with bells. And I just remember being totally caught up with toys. Probably, I'd never been around that kind of thing. And at some point, my birth mother and the woman said they were going to come back that night with dinner, and they left. The other child and I were still there. Then it got dark out, and the Caucasian woman came back and got her child—and I remember calling after her, and she just completely ignored me. She walked out without ever looking back. Of course, I was frightened—it was dark out. The other children had lined up because a nun had come out—I don't know if this was their routine—but basically it was time

to go inside. And I just remember saying to her, and this would have been in Vietnamese, that my mother hadn't come to get me. And I remember her saying "We have a place for you." And that's when we went inside. Of course, years later, when I met my birth mother, she told me the last thing she said to me (at the orphanage) was that she was going to come back and bring me dinner. So she has that memory, too. And she told me she hid behind a tree all day and watched me. She says, "I saw you and you cried and cried." And it's strange, because when she says that now, she kind of giggles about it. But I think it's probably just that she's uncomfortable taking about it. But she was there, and she was watching the whole time. Of course, I didn't have a clue.

Did she tell you what she said to her family that night she went home without you?
She told them she had taken me to the orphanage and I was going to America.

Did you realize that night that she wasn't coming back at all?
No, I still didn't know what was going on. I remember going inside the orphanage and sleeping in a crib. I always described it like being in a cage. And I don't know if it was days later—it was probably just a matter of days, because that was the end of April—but my next memory is getting on the airplane.

Do you remember making friends with any of the other kids at the orphanage?
I have no recollection of it at all. I mean, I imagine I probably was pretty withdrawn. And I just have no memory of anyone.

When your mom took you there, she didn't bring any clothes for you or anything, right? What you had on your back was it?
Yes.

It must have been so hard...many of the kids were given crayons and coloring books at the orphanage...and for a lot of them, it was all so foreign.
It probably depends on your age. I was just four. To an older kid, it might make more sense. To me, it was like that whole Charlie

Brown/teacher thing, where you just hear mumbling noises. I didn't know English.

And no one really made an effort to provide any special care, knowing there was a language barrier...
Right. And I think I fell into a weird age group—and this is more of a Denver memory—but there were infants who needed to be held and older kids who interacted and played with each other. I just remember kind of wandering around the facility, not feeling like I had any place to go.

You were probably at the age where you still needed to be held, but the nurses were busy with the infants, and they assumed you were old enough to play with the other kids, but you weren't.
Right.

What do you remember of the airplane trip to the United States?
My initial memory is that there weren't seats—that I was sitting on the floor. And I remember getting sick—I threw up. And this is kind of an overriding memory from that point on, too—being sick and approaching an adult and not getting comforted, or a seat, or whatever you would do now if a kid approached you. There were probably just too many kids, and they (the adults) were too caught up in what they were doing. And even when I was in Colorado—and I'm sure there was a language barrier, too—but not being able to communicate or connect or get people to really respond..to me.

What do you remember after the flight?
My next memory—I don't know if it was San Francisco or the Philippines, or Guam—but I remember getting a health check. I remember nuns escorting us somewhere, and I remember getting my temperature taken. And this was confirmed, too, when I met Cherie (Clark). On one of the bases they had set up this hangar full of tubs and they were doing a mass washing of the kids.

I wonder if that was at the Presidio in San Francisco?
I have a memory of that—all those metal tubs. And really, that was the last memory before Denver. And I don't remember how long I was in Denver. I think the whole time frame was probably two weeks.

264

What do you remember about the Continental Care Center in Denver?
I remember we were sleeping on mattresses on the floor there and that it was pretty spartan there also. And the main memory is walking into a closet, which felt like an enormous room. It was a walk-in closet, but it just seemed like one of those weird dreams you have where there are just racks and racks of clothing, and everything is sparkling and beautiful. And I remember getting to pick out a dress and then a pair of shoes...and I think I had a cardigan sweater, too. I still have the dress. My dad bronzed the shoes and gave them to my grandfather. The shoes were a whole funny story, too, because the social workers had told my adoptive father that I had never owned a pair of shoes or had shoes in Vietnam, and that I probably wouldn't like wearing shoes. And after the first day I spent with my adoptive family, they couldn't get me to take off my shoes! I was just obsessed with these red shoes. And it's funny, because you can see in the bronzed shoes that they're completely cracked, their thread is coming out of the shoe, and to me they must have just looked like the ruby slippers.

And where is the dress now?
My mom has it at home. It didn't really fit me, either, which is funny because there are pictures of me and you can see my training pants falling out underneath! But it's a little blue chiffon dress with some pink flowers embroidered on the bodice.

Do you remember at all the day you met your adoptive parents?
Yes...and they didn't actually come to the facility. Lori Gallagher—she was a volunteer flight attendant—escorted me from Denver to Sacramento, and I remember her giving me this plastic doll. I don't remember what happened with her after that point because that's when I met my family.

How did all this seem to you? I mean, at this point, you still didn't really know what was going on...
No. No one had ever explained anything to me.

It's mind-boggling...everything was so alien...you were moved from one place to the other. You didn't speak English, and no one

was talking to you in Vietnamese. Do you remember at what point any of this started to make sense?

No. In fact, I got to the airport...and my adoptive dad is a 6'4, curly-haired Jewish man, and my adoptive mom is 6'1, blonde, blue-eyed. My sister, who's only eight months older than me, has always been and still is a foot taller than me, so she was five, but she was HUGE compared to me! So I just remember getting off the plane and her coming over and swinging me around! And I didn't know English at the time, but I remember my mom saying "Carrie, put her down!" It was all very overwhelming. They were very excited and there was a lot of energy, and of course, I had no idea what was going on. Then we went home, and I remember we had dinner at the table. And then we had a bath—and we have a tape recording of me and my sister in the bathtub and I'm speaking in Vietnamese. I had it translated and I'm saying, "I'm going to wash my mother's hair." So I'm pretending to wash my mother's hair. And the next memory is that night, too—they were trying to have me sleep with my sister, because they were told that the family (in Vietnam) all sleeps together. But when it came time to go to bed, I tried to make a break for it! I tried to run to the front door and get out of the house—all very traumatic—and I think they were surprised. I just think that was the point at which I was really scared and didn't know what was going on.

You still probably hadn't comprehended that your (birth) mom had left you and you didn't know who these people were.

Right. And even in the bathtub translation, you hear me saying (to my adoptive sister) "Oh, your dad is coming in the room." So I knew these parents were her parents, but I certainly didn't say, "Oh, this is our dad." And I think I just blocked out a lot, because I really can't remember making the transition from that to speaking English a month later. They said I was pretty quiet for about a month, and this was early May. And by the time I started pre-school in August, I was more verbal than my sister. I made a major turnaround—I completely stopped speaking Vietnamese.

Which brings us to your return trip to Vietnam in '95. Regarding your birth mom, is her English broken, or does she speak very well?

No, it's broken...and it's sort of stereotypical, almost a caricature of

English. I mean, she's fascinating to listen to—her voice, etc. But it's like a caricature...and her expressions are still in that time-warp of "GI-speak." For example, if something's really good, it's "Number one." If she's de-valuating herself, she'll say, "Oh, I'm number ten." My grandfather told her she was "number ten" when she came back from the orphanage that night.

Describe your trip back to Vietnam and how you met your family?
Basically, I went on this trip with my (adoptive) aunt. We arrived in Saigon. The next day I met this woman who was a friend of my adoptive mother, who had been putting ads in the newspaper for me trying to find my birth mother, but none of it had amounted to anything. And then I had approached her about continuing the search—maybe putting something on the TV—because I didn't know how long the search would take. So after I met with her, my aunt and I decided to take a cab ride and try to find the orphanage, which we never did, but we ended up on this street that had the same name as the orphanage, and we went to the number (it seemed like it would be where the orphanage was) but there was this business there. And we met this guy who happened to speak English—which is unusual; his English was so good—and he said, "Oh, it's no problem to find your birth mother." He thought it would be really easy, and he was willing to help. He just wanted me to call him if I wanted his help. So, technically, my second day in Vietnam, I found a car—you have to hire a car...you can't drive yourself. The government rents out cars.

So they don't have typical rental car places?
No. I don't know if it's different now, but at that time you weren't allowed to drive. And I don't think you'd want to drive, because it's so crazy how they drive there. So I hired a driver—and I called him (the guy we'd met). His name was Triet. And I said, "We're going to go look for the town where I was born. Do you want to go with us." And he said "Sure," which is typically Vietnamese—to not really have a rigid work schedule; it's like "Oh, this exciting thing is happening, I'll go." So we went and picked him up—and this was in the morning.

Where were you and your aunt staying?
My dad had a Vietnamese intern at his work, Tuyen—a Vietnamese

woman who had moved back from Vietnam, which a lot of people in my generation have done, and she wanted to work there for a couple of years and get to know Vietnam again. She had an apartment in Saigon, so she invited us to stay with her. She's also the one who helped us hire a car.

Okay, so you picked the guy up in the morning...
...and we drove looking for Hanoi Honai. We probably hit about three different police stations before lunch, which was scary, because I had pictured this stereo-typical Communist police station, but they really weren't that bad. In fact, some of them were quite friendly. I remember one guy offered us tea while they were talking to us, and his hand was mangled—he was missing a few fingers. Clearly, he'd either been in an accident or he'd been in the war, so we just knew a lot of the people we were interacting with had once been on the South or North sides—it's just not clear anymore who was fighting who. Anyway, after lunch—and they take a very long lunch break—we went to the last police station, probably our fifth or sixth in all. They kept redirecting us to try to find Honai.

So at every police station you were inquiring how to find Honai?
And giving the name of my mom on my birth certificate...Le Thi Dieu. So the last police station said, "We don't know this woman, but according to your birth certificate her church is on that corner over there."

That's amazing.
And by the way, there's a hospital across from the police station, and Triet said to me, "If you were born in a hospital, that's the hospital you would have been born in." We knew we were in the right neighborhood, and it did turn out to be the hospital I was born in. So we went over to the church, and there were a couple of more glitches—the priest wasn't there, so we went to a different church—and then we went back to this church. And we met the priest and I showed him my birth certificate.

What was he like? What do you remember about him?
He was very elegant. Most of the priests are trilingual—they speak French, Vietnamese and English. I think his name was Father

Dominique. The priests just seem so sophisticated over there. So anyway, there are three signatures on my birth certificate, and he recognized one of them. And within five minutes, he brought that man to me and said, "This is one of the witnesses to your birth. His daughter delivered you."

So what did he do, leave the church to go and get this man?
One of the people at the church went and got him. And then...we were visiting with this man for just a matter of minutes—and I was confused about what was going on—and that's when my grandfather and aunt arrived at the church. Someone had gone to get them. And by this time it was probably six o'clock at night and it was dark out, so we'd spent all day doing this. And technically, this was our second day in Vietnam.

Were you jet-lagged?!
I think I was just in shock. Plus, everybody had been feeding me these paranoia stories about being careful of all the hoaxes. Amerasians are often referred to as "The Golden Children" because they're the ticket out of Vietnam. At one time they were mistreated and abused, discriminated against, not allowed education—which were all the things my birth mother feared, although she especially feared physical harm coming to me—but when the Orderly Departure Program got started in 1980, then in 1989, Vietnamese started seeking out Amerasian children to adopt in Vietnam so they could get passage over to America. So it's kind of another way in which Amerasians have been exploited. So, in my mind, I had to worry whether or not these people were playing a hoax on me—I mean, I wouldn't have a clue. But looking back, clearly they wouldn't have had time to do that.

Do your birth aunt and grandfather speak any English?
No.

So you were using the translator all the time?
Yes. And when my aunt walked up, she was holding this small picture of a child...and it was me. She said it was me at two years (and I had left at age three). But she was the only one who had a picture of me. She had carried it around with her all these years.

When they first walked into the church, what happened?
They were crying. And I was in shock. I was probably holding back a little bit because I wasn't sure exactly what was going on, and it just seemed unbelievable to me. And we were really tired at that point in the day, and we needed to get to Saigon, which was a good hour's drive back. So my meeting with them actually didn't last that long—just long enough to find out that my birth mother had five other kids and she lived about a half hour away and that they wanted to organize a reunion on Sunday. This was Friday.

So they left and you went back to Saigon. And then you had to prepare for the reunion with your mother?
Right, on Sunday. I was just thinking about the reunion, and I hadn't brought anything nice on the trip because I really didn't think I was going to find her. So I had to look for a perfect dress that conveyed that I was healthy! You know...I wanted her to know I'd had a good life. So that's what we did. And also, because we were washing with well water, even in the nice apartment in the city, I went to a hair salon to have my hair washed! Saturday was all about preparing for the reunion.

Then on Sunday, you took the cab back to Hanoi Honai?
Yes. And we actually had a video guy, too. Through that intern who had worked with my dad, she helped find a videographer. That's how we got it all on video. And it's really well done, considering we had one day to find this guy.

Where did you go...to their house?
We went back to the church actually...and just waited, because no one was there when we got there. And then someone drove my birth mother up on a scooter, and she ran up to me and just threw her arms around me and was sobbing and was trying to get on her knees to beg for my forgiveness because she thought I was angry with her for having sent me away.

And what were you saying to her through the translator?
I was just trying to pull her up so she wouldn't be on her knees and saying, "No, no..." Basically I kept saying to her all day, "Things worked out...things worked out as they were supposed to"...that I've

had a good life and that she'd done the right thing. Of course, the first thing she wanted to communicate was how she'd been afraid—how she'd heard all these stories about the Viet Cong dismembering and killing children who were mixed race and that she was really fearing for my safety and for my life. And she certainly didn't have any support from my birth father, in terms of getting us both out.

Regarding your birth dad, this is the one area I know is a big mystery. Although I know you've started to search for him and have made attempts to find him through the Internet, what did your birth mom tell you about him?
Basically, they dated for a year and, according to her, they were madly in love But they were young—I think she was twenty when she got pregnant, and he was twenty. He had no rank—he was just an enlisted person.

And she doesn't remember his name at all?
No. They call him "the boyfriend."

Did he speak Vietnamese?
A little bit.

So they really didn't have a whole lot of language going on...
No. It just sounds like they were having a good time! But she has such a vivacious personality...just imagine two young kids.

And she met him at the base?
Yes. She was working in the cafeteria at this base at Long Binh, which is right near Honai. And basically, she didn't remember his name, but he was her age, which was twenty...twenty-one...and he had my coloring. He sounds like he was a person of color. The villagers told me that he was Mexican and that he was tall—which is weird to me since I'm only five feet tall. And she described him...he had a pot belly, he had a mustache...but very beautiful! She's always saying how beautiful he was. And his parents had been killed in a car accident and he had one sister. He was Catholic—and she wanted me to marry a Catholic because my father's Catholic, she's Catholic, I'm Catholic. I'm supposed to marry a Catholic.

Is Greg (Greg Brannan, Huyen's husband) Catholic?
No! And she doesn't know this!

So your birth father knew about you?
Yes. She tells the story about how he used to rub her belly when she was pregnant with me. And he was with her up until seven months, and that's when his tour ended. But he picked my name because he liked the meaning of my name.

Which is?
"Beautiful eyes." And he didn't know I was a girl. I don't know what they would have named me if I was a boy. But he had picked the name. And he sent money—he sent support to her.

For how long?
It sounded like years—like they maintained contact for years, up until the war ended. The whole timeline is that I went to the orphanage within a couple weeks of Saigon falling.

But he was long gone by then...but still communicating with her by mail?
Right

So he obviously had her address...
Right. But she burned all his letters and photographs.

When did she do that?
When the war officially ended in '75. And who knows if he tried to contact her after that point. And I'm not totally clear on this, but he may have helped set her up with the Red Cross or Salvation Army to get me food and clothing.

Then his contact with her ended before you went to the orphanage?
Yes.

So we know he spoke a little Vietnamese, your mom spoke a little bit of English, they communicated back and forth via letters...he sent her money. He knew about you. And then contact stopped with him roughly around the time that you went to the orphan-

age?
And I don't think he knows what happened to me. For all he knows, I'm still living there (in Vietnam).

And what about your birth mother's family...did they approve of him?
They liked him. They talk about how he used to bring candy to the kids and that he was a very nice person. And he had a car, which is weird to me—maybe he was a driver. Although what they've described is that he worked with Morse code...because that's one of the things I have tracked down—is that he worked in a very small unit, maybe 50 people total at this facility. It was a communications facility at the base. So, at any given time, there would only be 50 employees...so if I were ever able to get a roster of the employees who worked there during 1970, then his name would be on it. But gaining access to our military records is so slow. One of the guys I met on the Internet requested that roster a year and a half ago and still hasn't received it.

So you said he left Vietnam when his tour was over, when your mom was in her seventh month of her pregnancy?
And that was actually his second tour. He was there for awhile, left, and then came back.

She was so close to having you. That must have been so disappointing for your mom to see him leave.
Yeah, it was. It's just really sad to me, because she's gone on—she's had five more kids. But it's so clear that this was the love of her life, and she's kind of stuck back there. And she was really invested in me finding him. She still seems to have this fantasy of what it would be like if I were to find him.

Are you still really interested in meeting him?
Yes and no. I mean, I'd like more history—I'd like a name, a photograph. I'm so overwhelmed by everything with my Vietnamese family...it's just had a lot of implications in terms of supporting them financially, when I can. And if he was kind of down and out also...I don't know. Right now, that just feels like taking on too much.

And how often do you contact them (your birth family) or write to

them?

I send them money between every four and six weeks. And we go back and forth on the writing. Probably every other month.

She must be so happy that you're having the baby now!

Yes! Her next daughter...the next oldest—I think she's twenty—is also pregnant. She may have had the baby by now, but we've been pregnant at the exact same time.

And you've met all your step brothers and sisters?

Yes.

How has your adoptive family reacted to you finding your birth family?

They been really supportive. I'd say it's been good. The one area where it's been difficult has been with my adoptive mother, just in terms of what it means with our relationship, but we're working through that.

When you returned to Vietnam in '95, what was your first impression? How would you describe what it's like today?

For me, getting off the plane and being there was more like just a feeling of coming home. And I don't know if this is an idealized memory, but it was just perfect. I don' know how to describe it exactly. But it rained the first afternoon we got there, and it was like being in a tropical music video or something! We brought ponchos, because it rains a few minutes every day. But it's crowded and noisy, and there are a million motor scooters everywhere. And at the same time, the architecture is so beautiful, at least in the area where we were staying, and there were a lot of mature tree-lined streets. It had a very French influence to it.

So what are your specific feelings about Operation Babylift? Was it a good thing? Was it necessary? Do you feel cheated in any way?

There's no clear-cut answer to that. It's hard to explain what I would want to convey to you. If you look at my early memories, there is all this chaos about leaving at age four. And now the chaos has been put to rest; there's healing and peace. I mean, on one hand, I lost my language, my culture...my roots. Maybe it would have been okay if I'd been a rice farmer and not had the benefit of an upper class upbringing. Not that I would have it differently, because this is how my life turned out. But this probably wouldn't have been my choice. Ironically, if I'd stayed (in Vietnam), through the Orderly Departure Program, I would have been allowed to come to the U.S. with my birth mother. I don't know. There's a different pace in Vietnam. Their culture is just so rich...the family traditions and their lifestyle. There's a loss there."

STACY THUY MEREDITH

My name is Stacy Thuy Meredith, and this is my story.

My mother's name was Ngo Thi Diep. She was a 19-year-old Vietnamese girl from the City of Can Tho. She left Can Tho without the permission of her parents and went to Saigon to work as a clerk in a bar. During her stay in Saigon, she met an American soldier with whom she had a personal relationship and even lived with for a short time. The American soldier (my father), apparently left her and returned to the States during her pregnancy. I don't know if he really went back to the States or was even aware that she was pregnant, or that he left because she was pregnant and didn't want the fatherly responsibility. On July 22, 1972, she had a daughter, naming me Ngo Thi Ngoc Thuy. I was born in a hospital in Saigon, at 284 Cong Quynh.

Maybe because of family honor, or fear of the family disowning her, she hired a woman to help raise me in a remote province so her family would not know about me. When I was 25 months old, she decided that she could no longer take care of me. On August 23, 1974, she brought me to the Holt Nutrition Center. Shortly after I was put with a foster family. My foster mother was married to an MP Officer and had five children of their own. I lived with them until I was put on Northwest Airlines Flight 6 out of Saigon, arriving in Anchorage, Alaska, on March 6, 1975 at 6:30 a.m. My new parents (Larry and Jeanne McLaughlin), and new brothers (Shawn and Scott) were there awaiting my arrival. They had chosen the name Stacy Thuy McLaughlin, keeping my Vietnamese first name as my new middle name. I was almost three years old when I came to America.

I would like to say it was happily ever after from then on, but I can not. My childhood was a struggle of survival, and it wasn't until my adulthood that life and my adoption became a blessing.

My adoptive father was an Air Force pilot and flew in the Vietnam War. My adoptive mother had two biological boys and decided to adopt a girl after two miscarriages. Maybe my father's intentions were good, and he really wanted to adopt a daughter. Sometimes I wonder if he struggled from post-war memories and it caused him to resent me. His reasons I will never know, but the scars he left me with will never go away.

As a child, I struggled with severe nightmares which would cause me to scream, sweat and even sleepwalk on occasion. My mom described my scream to be so horrific that it would sound like someone was physically attacking me. When I was awake, I would even get upset if I heard the sounds of a siren from a fire truck or even the sound of a tea pot whistling. She said I would become hysterical, then run and hide under the kitchen table or my bed. The nightmares continued until my young teenage years when I began seeing a psychologist who helped interpret my dreams. He said my dreams were so detailed, and I knew so much information, that many of them were probably actual things I had experienced as a baby prior to arriving at the orphanage. They began to subside after working through my fears. I struggled with the prejudices of looking different from my family. People would come up and make remarks such as, "Is that really your child, too?" I struggled living in an all-white community wherever we moved; little kids would come up to me with their eyes pushed back, chanting slang remarks at me. (The weird thing is, my eyes are round like a Caucasian.) I was under the assumption as a child that my biological mother gave me up because she didn't love me. At home, through my entire childhood, I was physically beaten by my father and brothers and repeatedly told I was "the Devil" and no one wanted me. I felt that there was something terribly wrong with me; no one loved me or wanted me. I felt it was my fault and wished I'd never been born. At age eight, I tried to kill myself with a knife.

As a teenager, things got progressively worse. Once my school discovered the abuse, that began a vicious cycle of me being placed in and out of foster homes, making my father more abusive with each return home. I avoided reality through drugs, loud music, skipping school and running away from home. I was placed in and out of hospitals for suicidal thoughts and attempts. At age 17, I took a bottle of antidepressants (about 100 pills). The doctors said I shouldn't have survived. I hated God and really had lost all faith that there was a God, or at least a God that I should love and be grateful to. If he did have a plan for me, it sure was hard to understand his plan and even appreciate it. He put me through HELL to get to where I am, and I am not thankful for that. I hated him even more for keeping me alive and not letting me end the pain. It took many years for me to believe again and return to the church. I believe now that God had a future planned for me and wasn't going to let me go just yet. I am thankful for that, but I am still not thankful for the childhood I was given. When I was 18, my father tried to strangle me; a friend walked up to the house just at that moment and carried me to safety. I immediately dropped out of high school, got my GED, moved out of the house and found work to support myself.

On January 18, 1991, I met my future husband. The very first night I met him, I knew in my heart he was the one. This was the turning point of my life; this is what God had waiting for me. Unfortunately, I was addicted to cocaine at the time. I wasn't about to lose the first good thing that had happened to me in my life. I admitted myself into rehab a few months later. He stood by me every step of the way; we married two years later.

Today we have two wonderful children which we are devoted to raise with all the love and structure I never had. I am a full time mom and wife, and I do day care in my home to help. My husband is an incredible husband, which makes my girlfriends envious. He is a devoted father who is never too tired to play and spend time with his children. We've been together for nine years and life is the greatest thing that happened to me. To think I struggled for so many years wondering why I was even alive. I felt so alone and my life seemed meaningless; to want to die and feel no one would even miss me. Now, each day I am so grateful that God knew there was so much still for me to experience.....to live! I look at the family I have now with my husband and realize I am where I am suppose to be. There is no sense of not belonging; I would not have this if not for being adopted. If I had to go through all of that to get here, it was worth it. I would not want to go through it again, but I think that the obstacles and challenges in my childhood may have helped me become a more strong-willed person and appreciate just how wonderful life can be.

To help with some closure in my life, my oldest brother, Shawn, apologized about ten years ago for the way he treated me when we were children. Since then, we have a closer relationship and my children adore him.

Another closure came when my mother came to me a couple years ago and apologized for not being the "Mother" I needed her to be. She said she regretted turning away when she knew what was happening to me, but felt she was too weak of a person to do anything. I feel sorry for my mother, but I give her so much respect coming to me to say those things. Our relationship has grown so close and is finally the relationship I have always wanted it to be.

In January, 2000 I received a letter in the mail from Holt International. It was an invitation to a reunion for the first generation of Vietnamese adoptees prior to the fall of Saigon on April 30th, 1975. At first I made the decision not to go for financial reasons. We had worked so hard to get out of debt the year before and had just paid everything off, but didn't have any extra money. I didn't want to set us back again for my selfish reasons. My mother said that I couldn't miss this and I'd regret it forever if I didn't go. Between her and my brothers, our trip for two to Baltimore was paid for and we were on our way!

As April came closer and we prepared for our trip, my journey down a new path lay ahead. I was finally going to meet others "like me" for the first time. I wondered if they had gone through similar experiences growing up as a child, or if they were all going to have happy stories with happy endings. I wondered if we would have a connection with each other, even though we'd never really met, or if it was going to be awkward and distant. A couple days before our trip, I began to experience a huge range of emotions that I had not felt in a long time. Whenever I had talked about my past in the previous years, it had brought me to tears. This, too, was having the same affect, maybe because I felt this was the only way I would get to connect with my Vietnamese heritage. I have now learned this is not so.

The reunion was an incredible experience for me as well as for my husband. He was able to share a part of me that was so deep and personal that he had never done before. We met so many wonderful people, adoptees and others who had first-hand experiences with adoptees and our journey to the States. The connection with the other adoptees was so intense. It was like we had found lost siblings from years past and were reunited once again. It was a time for many to give thanks for adoption and a few to still question whether the adoption experience was a good thing. It was a chance to share our similar experiences of childhood uncertainties and success stories. It was a weekend of making special long-lasting friendships that will last a lifetime. All of it went well for me, though I had trouble speaking with the parents who attended and asked me questions about my adoption. I had a mom come up to me and chat. She just kept saying that I should be thankful for my adoption and that my parents did the best they could. If my father beating me for 16 years and my mom turning her back instead of protecting me and acting as if nothing was happening to me is the best they could do, then that is a distorted definition of "best". I believe in God, and I have come to terms with him. I have gone on with my life and have a wonderful one at that, but the baggage is still there, the wounds are still there, and always will be. I decided not to talk with other parents about my adoption because they didn't want to hear the truth about how many "lives after adoption" really were. They wanted to hear the happy stories. The reunion also gave us the opportunity to hear success stories of adoptees who traveled back to our motherland and found their biological families. This helped me to decide that it was time to search for my biological mother and journey back to Vietnam.

Recently I began the search for my biological mother. I am still in the very beginning stages of the search, it's a lot of paperwork. The reason for my search is not to "replace" my mother...I already have one. It's not to find a sense of belonging; I have that, too. I've decided to search for her for myself and for my family. I want to learn about the "motherland" I came from. I want my children and husband to learn, too, about the place on the other side of the world where a little frightened and lost child came from. A place where the people look different, speak different and have a way of life unfamiliar to us. I want to meet my mother to thank her for trying her best and giving me up when she felt she couldn't give me what I needed.

To my mother who gave me life...thank you. I hope someday we can be reunited. To my mother who adopted me...thank you for your love and support over the last few years. Thank you for apologizing for my childhood. That was an incredible step for you and for our relationship. You are my one true mom and no one can take that from you...I love you.

My journey has only just begun.

TUY BUCKNER

I am not a writer...I am more inclined to be vocal. This is a brief version of my story:

I was born Nguyen Quoc Tuy. My mother placed me with the nuns at the Sadec orphanage in 1971 when I was a year old. Inasmuch as I was a sick baby and my mother's health was poor, she was unable to care for both my sister and myself. Rationalizing that I would have medical attention at the orphanage, she intended for me to get better and vowed to reclaim me within three years or so; hopefully, her own health and economic conditions would improve as well. My father was a Philippine national who came to Vietnam to work under the Marcos Committee of Responsibility and was employed by the U.S. government. He left Vietnam in 1970.

Early on at Sadec, it was discovered that I had polio. One of the nuns, Sister Desiree, sent me to Saigon to the FFAC nursery at Allambie in the hopes that I would receive the medical care I needed. My future in Vietnam was bleak and there was little to offer in reha-bilitation. Somehow the fact that my mother intended to reclaim me was lost in the transition, and like so many children there needing spe-cial attention, it was decided that it was in my best interest to be adopt-ed by a family in America. On September 2, 1974, I arrived in Berkeley, California, as the adopted son of the Buckner Family. I was thought to be three years old and the new addition to an already large family. The Buckners were Caucasian, with two children of their own and four adoptees—two from India, one from Vietnam and an African-American girl from Oakland.

Although disabled, I grew up in a normal American family and felt that my disability caused more problems than any racial or cultural issue. I blended into American life and attended UCLA, studying graphic design.

A search for my roots and returning to Vietnam was never a prior-ity in my life, but an opportunity presented itself in 1991 when my mother became active in the American Trade Embargo against Vietnam. I spent three short weeks there, with little opportunity to search for my roots. A brief trip to Sadec was to no avail.

Another opportunity to visit Vietnam for three months arose in 1993, during which time I traveled extensively around the country. Again, I returned to Sadec in search of some answers to the first years of my life. Admittedly, I was one of the many adoptees who went there with no great expectations and truly didn't expect to find my mother. I tried to get to Sadec earlier in the tour, but the bridge was out and the area inaccessible. With just a few days remaining before I was to return to the United States, I was able to reach Sister Desiree at Can Tho who was discouraged that there were no records to help learn of my family's whereabouts. I was determined to put to rest any "longing" for those early years and wanted to make peace with myself...to know that at least I tried, and to put the unresolved issues concerning my birth behind me. I was anxious for a sense of closure—to even a failed attempt in the search for my birth family.

In a gesture of appreciation for the care the nuns had provided to me as a baby, I wanted to make a donation to them. They, in turn, wanted to host a banquet in my honor as an expression of how happy they were that I was there, The response to my visit was overwhelming; everyone wanted to talk with me. I became the center of curiosity as well. I was "the golden child...one sent to a better life now returning home." (It was the consensus of the people themselves when so many children left Vietnam during and at war's end.) In the politeness and cordiality of the occasion, one nun went into the church and returned with an old record book. One of the entries was my birth name, Nguyen Quoc Tuy, indicating that I was one year old when I was admitted to the orphanage. When I was sent to Allambie, the date placed on my birth certificate was the day I entered Sadec. The discrepancy came as a surprise...I was actually one year older then I had been led to believe.

Since there was always a shortage of employees at the orphanage, it was a common practice for older children to help with the toddlers. And, as fate would have it, on the day that I was at the church, a Vietnamese woman, Nguyen Thi Phiem, appeared for a visit. Phiem was in the area to visit a relative at the hospital and on such occasions she would stop by the convent to visit the nuns. She examined the entry in the record book and recognized my name as one of the children she had cared for so long ago. "Your mother is here...working in the fields," she said. "I know your family. I will be back in one or two hours...I will find your mother and bring her here." It was an amazing coincidence. I could not believe my luck.

Although I was somewhat skeptical and didn't allow my hopes to soar, I agreed that I would wait for her return. In the past, I had received many warnings about false starts in the search for families in Vietnam, and I had been cautioned that many people were anxious to claim adoptees as their children in the hopes that it would better their status. News spread throughout the village with great speed...that a "golden child" had returned and his mother was coming to greet him.

The drama unfolding was surreal. People crowded all around outside the building, looking at me, pointing, talking. I was their main focus of attention. A few approached me and tried to teach me to greet my mother in Vietnamese. "Practice this," they insisted. "Your son has been gone for twenty-years, and has come home to meet his mother."

After awhile the crowd fell silent and there was some commotion in the back. You could see how it progressed through the group...someone was slowly, cautiously, making their way through the throngs of bystanders. Slowly, the crowd parted to let the person pass. It was a drama unfolding as I was seated on a bench, when suddenly a little woman stood before me. She just popped out of the crowd. Others urged me to speak...to say what I was coached to say..."after twenty years your son has come home..." I was stunned. I mumbled something...trying...I think I said something about a buffalo. It was select memory.

Without warning, the woman mumbled something and at the same time pulled my head down. I had long black flowing hair that reached down my back. Gently, she parted my hair and moved her fingers around my head...looking for something. After a few moments, she stood tall, slapped me on my hand, and declared to the crowd, "This is my son!" Everyone understood what she said, except me. There was joy in the air and shouting...then someone translated her words for me and explained that my mother was looking for the scar she had left on my scalp twenty years earlier, before relinquishing me to the orphanage. It had been her sister's idea to mark my head in such a way that if I were to ever return to Sadec, she would know that I was truly her son. And that is just what my mother did.

The elements of the reunion were diminished by the fact that I was returning to the States within a few days. I had mixed emotions. It had all happened so fast, so unexpectedly. I had a completely different vision of what finding my mother would be like. I would be well-dressed...look handsome. She too would be beautifully dressed...perhaps in a bright brocade ao-dai, the traditional trousers-dress with a mandarin collar...there would be a pond...lotus blossoms...semiromantic illusion...and she would look different than the woman before me. It is the fantasy of every adoptee...the grandeur of meeting their mother...how it will happen. The dream...come true.

But reality and truth kicked in when my mother produced a picture of me as a baby. There was no doubt that it was me. I, too, was convinced. While some prefer and insist on DNA, I needed no further proof. This was my mother, and I was home at last.

I soon learned that I have six half brothers and sisters and one full sister. I learned my parent's names and was told who my father was. Since time was of the essence and I was leaving for America soon, I convinced by birth mother to accompany me to Saigon for those last days, giving us an opportunity to make up for so much lost time.

I wanted to mark this reunion, 1993, as a point in time, so in a parting gesture, I cut my hair and gave it to her in a private moment between us. It was a symbol of returning...to replace the sadness of not having her son all those years...with the new joy that we will now have a future bond. We have found each other...there is instinctive love, and we will always be together even though there may be an ocean between us.

In 1994, I went to the Philippines in search of my birth father. I was surprised to find that there is an established office to assist in the search for missing persons. Within two weeks of providing the information my mother had given me, my father was notified and came to Manila. He had no idea that a son had been born to him in Vietnam; at their parting, my mother herself did not realize she was expecting me. My father was waiting as I stepped outside of the building and welcomed me as his youngest son.

There is a desire in all of us to have a sense of where we come from and who our ancestors are. That I was able to find those answers is truly a remarkable act of destiny. I have been to Vietnam seven times and twice to the Philippines. There is an acceptance and a serenity in having found both of my birth parents, although none of this has diminished the destiny that I have found here in America...my family, my friends and my life. I am a better person for having made the journey to the past and feel that I share a bond with all other orphans who left their homeland. We are all brothers. It's not what happens to you in life...it's what you *do* with what happens to you that matters.

TUAN-RISHARD F. SCHNEIDER

My name is Tuan-Rishard F. Schneider. I was adopted by Frank and Mary Ann Schneider in Minneapolis, Minnesota. I arrived March 6, 1975. I have a younger sister who is also adopted but from Korea.

I have had a great life from the outside looking in. But if you were to see me from the inside out, you'd see hate, anger, frustration, denial, low self esteem, racism, prejudice, shame, and betrayal.

For the longest time growing up I hated being different-looking from my friends. I hated the way others teased me, even though I had white parents like everyone else.

Growing up, I kept my anger inside, and when I got older, martial arts helped me. Although when push turned to shove, I retaliated and fought everyone who challenged me. I regret losing a friend in a fight and I wish I could have been there to help him; I have now stopped the violence and have studied the art and philosophy of peace. Also through sports, I was able to channel my anger through organized aggression with soccer, hockey, and rugby.

Now as an adult of 26 years, I coach high school rugby, soccer, and when time permits, aikido (a form of martial arts). I have two jobs. One as a design consultant for an interior company, which is moving me to San Diego in the fall, and as a International Trade and Sales Consultant for a soccer company. For part-time work, I also model and do commercials.

Being Asian, I have learned to use my once thought-of "disadvantages" to my advantage, using my minority status to get scholarships and more ethnic jobs in commercials and print ads.

As of now I am single and I am very fond of another adoptee from Vietnam. (I'll keep her name private since she and I kind of want it that way.) But if time, patience, and dedication work out, who knows?

I can't say I have a sad story, but I can say I have had a very privileged life here in America. My family has traveled around the world with me to Europe, Asia, Russia, and the Middle East. Both with my family and on soccer teams, I was fortunate to be enriched with other cultures and races, which lead my college background to international public relations and marketing. With minors in philosophy, psychology, and sociology, I used my studies with coaching and my other talents in helping organize the first North American Adoptees Vietnamese Organization, as both the international and national public relations and media liaisons for both www.adotpedvietnamese.org (international) and www.vietnamadoptees.com (national).

Ever since the Baltimore reunion this year, I am proud of my people, who I am, who I missed, and who I seek to find.

JARED REHBERG

Where do you start when your own beginning is a mystery? Let's start with the truth, hoping we end up with love. I can feel angels standing by. It is an honor to write to someone who took place in the most important time in my life, the beginning. There are so many self-less, hard-working men and women who took time out of their personal lives to make sure I could write this passage today.

I was adopted in York, Pennsylvania, in 1975 by two beautiful souls. I was given the opportunities to live a life most children would dream of. They shared their cultures, values and beliefs in an open-minded house. They always supported the never-ending search for the truth.

This story almost sounds too good to be true...because it is. I spent many years battling ADHD, learning disabilities, mild depression, and abandonment issues. I was just one of many growing up American. We woke every morning in a world that sometimes didn't welcome us or even give us a chance or the respect we deserved just because of the color of our skin. Some fought back while others took the pain. I still dream of seeing my birth parents to thank them for life, a clean slate. I'm a 25-year creation rising to the call. Vietnam's surviving orphans have grown up with so much to offer. Some will forget a few facts, so we might have to remind them:

1. We didn't ask to come here, so don't tell us to go home. But if you want me to go back that badly, give me the money...I would love to visit my homeland.

2. I speak English first, so don't change your speech...don't insult me. Give me a chance like everyone else, and we could have a great conversation. You might even like me.

3. We have the power to change the future. We, as adoptees, have made it this far growing up in a world different from us. Lost and confused sometimes, surrounded by love, we taught people around us one by one that the secret to peace is yet to be discovered. It may be found in small steps and an open mind, fair treatment of others, and time. From one soul to another, be good to all your sisters and brothers... make life enjoyable for everyone this time around.

KIMBERLY BRINKER

My name is Kimberly Brinker from Denver, Colorado. I came over in April, 1975, and I was adopted into the Brinker family. My parents picked me up April 16, 1975, at the New York City airport. I lived in Warren, Pennsylvania, with three older brothers. I moved to Denver after the 20th reunion five years ago.

I had the pleasure to go back to Vietnam this past April. I went with forty others, and among them was Mary Nelle Gage who gave me my orphan name "Hermia" when I was in New Haven in Saigon. It was an honor to travel with such a great group of people. I got to meet childcare workers who took care of me so long ago. I visited the two orphanages I stayed in when I was an infant. The first was in Soc Trang, the other in New Haven. The feeling that overcame me was just an overwhelming sense of joy. Whoever thought that 25 years later we would be standing there face to face with people who cared for us when we were infants? And to top it off, we were able to say "thank you".

We went out to the C-5 plane crash sight and gave the ones we lost a proper good-bye. Lord knows that was long over due. What an honor to be standing out there, only imagining what happened 25 years ago. I had the pleasure to meet Susan McDonald at the 25th reunion. She showed me my name in the record book that she has kept for so many years. Once again, I was so overwhelmed and felt so blessed. She explained that I should have been on that C-5 flight, but because I was too weak to make the long flight, Susan decided to keep me behind a little longer. Wow! That was some powerful information to soak in. I do truly believe we all have an angel watching over us.

I have so many people to thank, from my birth mother for giving me a better life, to all the childcare workers, hospitals, doctors, my family, and most of all, the Lord. Thank you all...and no matter what path I take, I will never forget the people who got me down that path.

I must say I am well blessed!

JOSHUA J. WOERTHWEIN

Prologue

From what I know, I was born as Chiem Ngoc Minh (it means "brilliant jade") at the Tu Du Maternity Hospital in Sai Gon, Vietnam, at 04:40 on 30 July 1974. My mother, Chiem Ngoc Diep, decided to put me up for adoption; I resided at the maternity hospital for a few days and then was moved to the Holt Reception Center/Nursery for a short period of time (Holt International Children's Services was the agency that handled my adoption). Then I lived in foster care (with Ba Hong) for a few months before being picked up by U.S. Military Police and put on a Pan Am 747 out of Vietnam. I left Vietnam from the Ton Son Nhut Airport when I was just eight months old and landed at the JFK International Airport on 06 April 1975. My new parents, Mr. and Mrs. Kenneth F. Woerthwein, were waiting there with open arms. My adoptive parents named me "Joshua" because it's the biblical name that means, "God's deliverance." They told me they picked it because they went through so much to "get me" and that it was a miracle that I made it here to begin with.

On 31 July 1997, I—now Joshua Joseph Woerthwein—watched a segment on "48 Hours" about a group of Vietnamese adoptees who returned to Vietnam to revisit the orphanages, hospitals, and child-care facilities where they were as children before they came to the United States. The most touching part of the story was when a young woman, whose name I cannot remember, visited the site of the U.S. Air Force C5A that crashed a short distance from the Ton Son Nhut Airport, a crash that she had survived 21 years ago.

After watching the episode, I cried for hours. It never occurred to me how close I was to that incident, and to that young woman. I was on the second plane out of Vietnam in "Operation Babylift" in 1975, the same plane which the young woman who had survived the C5A crash was put. I grew up feeling guilty about that, and still feel a little guilty about that...like why was I spared? Why did so much information accompany me when so little came with other people? Why, why, why? When you start to ask questions like that about your life, not only do you start feeling sorry for yourself, but you start hating yourself for being alive, and that's no good, since I should be honoring my birth mother, who had enough sense and love in her to want me to live somewhere where I could have a better life...

A few days before that, I had gotten a flyer in the mail from Global Spectrum ("Vietnam Travel Specialists") concerning the "Revisit Vietnam Tour '97." I really didn't think anything of it, namely because I did not have the money to afford the trip. After some discussion with my parents, who agreed to lend me the money, I called up Global Spectrum and spoke with Ms. Thuy Do. I had to get my passport application expedited and scrambled to get the necessary information I needed for my revisit to Vietnam, but by the time the scheduled departure came, I was more than ready to go.

I arrived at the JFK International Airport from the BWI Airport around 18:30 on Saturday, 06 September 1997. The first person I met from the "Re-Visit Vietnam Tour '97" was Jen. She and Evelyn's dad, Lee, came into the departure terminal at Gate 14, and I approached them when I saw them talking with Sister Mary Nelle Gage. Evelyn and Tia rounded out the last of the group. After we all got acquainted, we talked with Erik Nelson, a freelance journalist who contributes to *Newsday, The Long Island Voice, The Washington Post,* and the *Baltimore City Paper.* He asked us some questions, and the photographer with him took a few shots of us, individually and as a group. After all the questions and photos, we finally boarded the plane around 21:30.

At least 23 hours later, we finally touched down at the Tan Son Nhut Airport in Ho Chi Minh City (HCMC), around 09:30 on Monday, 08 September, 1997. Seeing the country from the air for the first time and landing at the airport from which I had departed brought tears to my eyes. Weary from the flight, we all stumbled off the plane into an airport bus that took us to the terminal. After a few moments with customs and the passport/visa people (the Vietnamese officials did not stamp our passports, because we—the four adoptees—were born in Vietnam; at least, that's the reason I was given for them not stamping the passports), we collected our bags and met our tour guide, Tran Dinh Song (Song), outside. We had to wait longer than expected to leave the airport because Lee's bags never showed up. His bags eventually showed up about a week later, thanks to some detective work by Song; the bags were lost at JFK and never even made the flight when we did.

Song and the driver loaded our baggage into the minibus and drove us to our hotel, the Bong Sen Hotel (117-119-121-123 Dong Khoi Street, District 1), in what seemed like the heart of HCMC. After a refreshing shower (there's nothing like sitting in your own funk for 23 hours on a plane...pretty picture, eh?) and a brief rest, we all met in the lobby for lunch. I loathe to admit it, but I can't remember the name of the first restaurant I ate at in Vietnam. One memorable thing about the food in Vietnam is that it was all fantastic.

After lunch, we visited the Presidential Palace (Dinh Thong Nhat Palace, also known as Unification Palace), the Old Post Office (Buu Dien Trung Tam), and the Notre Dame Cathedral (Nha tho Duc Ba, the Saint-Marie Cathedral). We went back to the hotel for a little bit before dinner. We were driven to a restaurant that was also a private residence on an island on the Sai Gon River. Whoever's house it was (I think the name of the residence/restaurant was "Lang Binh An," and the owner is Tuyet Lan), it was amazing. There were three or four private dining areas, all with their own walkways, bars, even billiard tables, right along the river. After dinner, we drove back to the hotel and got some much needed sleep.

Tuesday morning, we went to the Phu My Orphanage (which is still active), where Evelyn had resided; New Haven (which is now a private home, owned by a doctor), where Jen had resided; Thu Duc (which is now an apartment complex), where Tia had resided; and the Holt Reception Center (it was a nursery, but now it's a restaurant), where I had resided.

Near the Holt Reception Center, Song said he knew of a woman who may or may not know some information about the old Reception Center. We stopped by to see this woman, whom Song had already spoken to a few days earlier. She directed us to see her mother, a much older woman. The elderly mother allowed us to come into her home. The house she and her family resided in was far below the poverty line standards for America, but Song said her home was about average for the Vietnamese. I pulled out a picture for the elderly woman to look at, and before I could say a word, she pointed to the woman in the picture holding me and blurted out, "Ba Hong." "Ba Hong" is the name of my foster mother, and the only evidence I have that she exists is a picture of her holding me as a baby.

Through Song's translation, she said the last time she saw my foster mother was in 1976, after the government had "changed." At first, I was skeptical. I thought that the elderly woman had been put up to it, to say that she knew who my foster mother was. I thought Song had showed her the picture of my foster mother and me before we had gotten there, and told her the name, too. As it turns out, the first time Song had seen the picture of my foster mother and me was in the elderly woman's home. So I'm going to believe that she was telling the truth.

After the chance meeting with the elderly woman, Song took us to Holt's old office building (431A Hoang Van Thu Street, Tan Binh District). After Holt left in 1975, the building was used as a police station; the military used it as a post until 1989. The Travel/Tourist Service took control of the building after that and still does business out of there to this day.

We also visited To Am, Allambie, and Hy Vong (other orphanages from which more Vietnamese adoptees had come) on Tuesday. In all honesty, visiting the orphanages was depressing, seeing so many babies and young adults (and some adults)—some physically or mentally handicapped (or both), some in perfect health—and not being able to do anything about the conditions in which they're living. We had lunch with some Vietnamese caretakers who worked for Friends For All Children (FFAC). One of the women from FFAC is the widow of an attorney who did the paperwork for most of us Vietnamese adoptees. After seeing the orphanages, we stopped by the old U.S. Embassy.

Wednesday morning, we met the FFAC women for breakfast and went to the maternity hospital where I was born (Benh Vien Phu San Tu Du—the Tu Du Maternity Hospital, 284 Cong Quynh Street, District 1). Sister Mary Vincent (she signed a few birth records of mine) was still there, doing the same job in the same office. She took me to the ward in which I was born way back on 30 July 1974. We couldn't go back to see the actual rooms because of sanitary reasons, but I got to see the halls of my birth. It is still hard to describe what I was feeling, mainly because I was never expecting to find anything, but even more so because nothing like my meeting with someone so close to my past had ever happened to me before. I can say without a doubt that it was the most spiritually moving moment in my life. I hugged Sister Mary Vincent and cried for what seemed to be an eternity. It felt so good to be held in her arms (even though I'm a good 25cm taller than she is); I felt like never leaving her embrace.

After the emotional goodbye and small donation (as it turns out, childbirth at the Tu Du Maternity Hospital costs about $50, which covers the cost of labor and a room for three days; meals and linen service are provided by the family), we visited the An Dong market in the Chinese district of Cholon. After lunch, Song took us to the Cong Ty Lamson, a lacquerware company in HCMC. The work that was done there—the time and effort that was put into each piece—was mind-blowing. Actually, the rest of that day was a blur for me; my mind was (and still is) spinning from meeting Sister Mary Vincent.

Thursday morning, we awoke early to take a 3-4 hour drive to the Mekong Delta. We got onto the tour boat at the Cai Be Floating Market in the Vinh Long province. We cruised along the river and through some tributaries before stopping at Nguyen Thanh Giao's bonsai farm for lunch. The food that was served to us was exquisite: spring rolls, deep-fried elephant ear fish, and numerous other delicacies. The owner gave the adventurous ones in our group a taste of some of his homemade sake. Before I knew where I was drinking from, I had already swallowed half a glass of the most potent sake I've ever tasted. Nguyen Thanh Giao showed me a jar from which the sake had come from; a dead anaconda was coiled around the inside of the jar, helping out the fermentation process. Nguyen Thanh Giao also let us "play" with his two pet anacondas (one 6m long, the other 4m long...magnificent creatures).

After lunch, our Mekong tour guide, Mr. Hy (I'm not sure if I've spelled that right; he worked for the Cuulong Tourist Agency in Vinh Long), pointed the boat in the direction of a brick-making factory. We then cruised back to a plantation, and after a brief snack provided by the owner, Mr. Tam Ho, we took the boat to Muoi Day's House-on-Stilts. There, Sister Mary, Jen, and I took a dip in the Mekong River (that was an experience) and then we all had a pleasant dinner.

We awoke early Friday morning and left for Vinh Long (the "capitol" of the Mekong region), Jen's native province. After checking into the Ninh Kieu Hotel in Can Tho, we visited Jen's orphanage. It was depressing, because all that was left of her orphanage was an empty lot filled with rubble. The government was erecting some new buildings in the general area. We visited the Providence Orphanage after that, Evelyn's orphanage. We met Sister Eugeny, who had cared for her. The Providence Orphanage is still active and serves as a day care center and school, too. The government supposedly runs the orphanage, but in actuality it's run by the order of nuns who cared for Evelyn as an infant under the watchful eye of the government. The government man in charge with whom we spoke seemed to be pretty clueless about the goings-on at the orphanage.

Saturday morning we drove back to HCMC and had the day to ourselves. I had some time to think about what had happened so far on the trip, and I felt nothing but guilt. I came back with much more information than most Vietnamese adoptees could ever hope to have, allowing me to find out more about my roots than the other trip members (and last year's trip members). And I had actually found someone (Sister Mary Vincent) and something (the maternity hospital) that were close to me; I got to see where I was born. And so far, no one else found anything, except empty shells of buildings, or nothing at all. Yes, Evelyn had found the Sister who had cared for her, but I could tell that something was up. A few nights before, during dinner, Sister Mary Nelle had said that Jen may have something that I didn't (we were discussing the types and amounts of information that had come over with us during Operation Babylift). She said that Jen had medical records of the first few months of her life in Vietnam. Without thinking I said, "But I do, too. I have all that stuff. Records, x-rays, immunization charts, everything." Evelyn said, "Sheeze, don't rub it in." I didn't mean to be hurtful when I said that. But after mulling over what she said, and seeing Jen's reaction, I can see how they thought I was trying to be.

But then I thought, "I had nothing to do with any of this...it was all out of my control, so why should I feel guilty?" And why do I still feel guilty? Rationality and logic say that I shouldn't feel guilty, just for that reason alone. But I still feel guilty. Sister Mary Nelle wanted us to share what we felt and what the meeting with our "roots" meant to us. I don't know if I'll ever be able to articulate what was going through my head when I saw my birthplace, when I saw Sister Mary Vincent, when I cried and cried. It felt good inside for the first time in a long, long time, but a cloud of guilt and self-hate surfaced to hang over my head.

Jen, Tia, Ev, and I ate dinner at the Lemon Grass (04 Nguyen Thiep Street, District 1) Saturday night; when I say that the Lemon Grass was one of the best restaurants we ate at (Thank You, Song!), I think I can speak for the rest of us. We went back to Cong Ty Lamson to get some more lacquerware and then turned in for the night.

Sunday morning, we caught an early flight to Danang, Song's hometown. After checking into Khach San Thanh Lich (Elegant Hotel, 22A Bach Dang Street), we drove to the Sacred Heart

Orphanage where Tia had spent some time before going to the Thu Duc orphanage in Saigon. We met the Sister who had cared for her; one of the other Sisters had copied, by hand, the names, birthdates, and departure dates of over 1600 children who were at Sacred Heart before handing the original records over to the Vietnamese government in 1975/1976. Even more amazing was that Song found Tia's Vietnamese name in the book. (Song told me that seeing Tia's name in the book was the happiest moment of the trip for him—that his heart skipped a beat). After lunch, we went to Marble Mountain and then took a swim at China Beach (which was absolutely gorgeous).

Monday morning, we took a 45 minute car ride to Hoi An. We checked into Hoi An Hotel (06 Tran Hung Dao Street) and met for lunch at a floating restaurant. After lunch, I visited the Japanese covered bridge and the Old House of Phung Hung, a 200+ year-old private house, which is now lived in by the family's 8th generation.

We left the tranquil town of Hoi An Tuesday morning for Hue—the old capital of Vietnam—via the Hai Van Pass. After lunch and checking in at the Thanh Lich Hotel (another elegant hotel), we took a Dragon-boat cruise up the Perfume River to the Thien Mu Pagoda. Jen, Sister Mary, Lee, and Song visited the Citadel, a former royal compound of the Nguyen Dynasty. The next day, we toured Tu Duc's Tomb. We had the rest of the afternoon to ourselves, so Evelyn and I took a cyclo to the market in Hue. Our flight to Hanoi was delayed on Thursday, so Thursday morning/afternoon we hung out around the hotel (the highlight there was when some local men challenged me to an arm wrestling contest after seeing my karate shirt).

We didn't arrive in Hanoi until around 18:30 Thursday. We checked into the Saigon Hotel (80 Ly Thuong Kiet Street), grabbed a quick bite to eat at Cha Ca La Vong (107 Nguyen Truong To Street), a restaurant that is famous "home and abroad" (all they served was fish, veggies, and vermicelli noodles), and went to the Thang Long Water Puppet Theatre (57 Dinh Tien Hoang Street). Friday we toured the outside of Ho Chi Minh's Mausoleum (the inside was closed for renovations), his House on Stilts, and his Museum. After that, we visited the One Pillar Pagoda (Song told us that when people think of Vietnam, they break the country down into three parts: Northern, Central, and Southern. They equate the One Pillar Pagoda with Northern Vietnam, Hue with Central Vietnam, and the Mekong Delta with Southern Vietnam) and the Temple of Literature, where

Vietnam's oldest university is. Then we met with Pete Peterson, the U.S. Ambassador in Hanoi. Unfortunately, Song could not get in because he had not gotten permission from his government in time (gotta love bureaucracy). That night, we dined at the Indochine (16 Nam Ngu Street, Hoan Kiem District), one of Hanoi's finest restaurants.

Saturday morning, we awoke and left the hotel for the airport. We said goodbye to Song at the airport, and flew out of Vietnam at 10:00, departing from Hanoi for Hong Kong, and eventually, America. I said goodbye to Lee in Vancouver, British Columbia, to Tia and Sister Mary in NYC, and to Evelyn and Jen in Washington, D.C.

Epilogue

It was hard, going back to the place of my birth, and being seen as an outsider. Not only did I not know the language—my language—or the culture—my culture—my physical attributes told everyone that I didn't even "look" like I was born in Vietnam. It has always been assumed that my biological father was an American soldier, and that may be why my skin is a little lighter, my size is a little taller (I'm about average height by American standards). And when I told people in Vietnam that I was born in Saigon, I got looks of doubt and bewilderment. Jen, who was told she looks Korean or Chinese, and Tia, whose biological father was black, had even harder times convincing people they were born in Vietnam, because their physical attributes said otherwise.

Aside from the emotional strain and heart-strings being pulled on, every other aspect of the trip was fantastic. For me, this was the end of the beginning of a new chapter in my life. I am not going to say that this trip changed me, for better or for worse. The trip back did diminish my feelings of inadequacy and self-hate in that I got to see and experience what it must have been like—even though it's displaced 23 years—to have to make the decision of putting your own child, your own flesh and blood, up for adoption.

Thanks to the trip, I appreciate more what I have; to know how fortunate I am; to know how lucky and loved I am by my biological mother, by my adoptive parents, and by all the people in between who have never even met me but did what they could anyway in order to save the life of another human being. This trip has also made me think about what I could have been if I had not been adopted (not that I haven't thought about that before; now the feelings are just intensified). A lot of my internal conflicts have been resolved, many questions I had now answered. But the feelings of guilt remain, lingering, leaving a bad taste in my mouth.

Thoughts, comments, and questions can be e-mailed to me at: jawshoouh@earthlink.net

Information on adoptees may be obtained from:
www.adotpedvietnamese.org (international) or
www.vietnamadoptees.com (national)

EPILOGUE

"We will discuss you till you are nothing but words."

– Christopher Fry

We are not yet through with Vietnam. Even these many years after the end of the war, the mere mention of the small country's name still evokes strong feelings. It is remembered as the wrong war at the wrong time.

The majority of soldiers who returned tried to carry on with their lives in a normal fashion. Yet Vietnam would remain the event of their generation; to this day, some can still recall every detail of their involvement. For others, the war will never be over. Their physical and emotional scars will endure for a lifetime.

After the fall of Vietnam in April, 1975, the victors wasted no time renaming Saigon "Ho Chi Minh City." There was iron-clad discipline as the new government nationalized large businesses and decreed an end to American-like activities. As for the fate of the orphanages, after the fall of Saigon, buildings were requisitioned by the new government, evicting the nuns and the children. Monies placed in banks by the departing agencies to sustain the orphanages in the months ahead was also confiscated. Nor was there a concern for the orphans. The Communist attitude was: "These are the children of our enemy...the men who fought against us...why should we care?" The predicted blood-bath that was feared never happened, nor did the end of the war bring peace. Shortly after, the Vietnamese invasion of Cambodia contributed to widespread starvation, leaving over one million dead and draining the Vietnamese economy further. The predicted domino-effect—that the loss of Vietnam would topple all other countries in Southeast Asia–didn't happen either.

The Communists won the land in Indochina, but not the hearts of the people. Hundreds of thousands fled the small country and became known as the "boat people," departing on anything that would float.

These attempts to escape more often met with tragedy and death, yet despite the risks involved, their exodus was testimony that they were convinced anything would be better than a life under Communist domination.

The flow of refugees from Vietnam set a new crisis in motion, and new concerns emerged regarding Operation Babylift. Mothers who had abandoned their children to the orphanages in Vietnam in the hopes that they would be taken to America were now searching and reclaiming their sons and daughters from adoptive homes in the West.

At war's end, it was estimated that over 1.5 million orphans and children in Vietnam had lost one or both parents. Over 300,000 were abandoned.

It is almost impossible to articulate the emotional dimension of the abandonment of children in Vietnam since most of the children were relinquished at birth. (Birth control or abortions were not readily available options in the poverty-stricken country). Moreover, a parent could not be forced to care for a child if they did not want to, and a child could be disposed of with total impunity. Since birth certificates were not commonplace, there was no possibility of tracing the parents of either newborns or small children left at orphanages. Despite this sociological fact, a controversy surrounding Operation Babylift erupted with the emergence of these natural parents, including charges that it was not a rescue mission, but a "babyheist." Critics, too, asked why foreign children were being adopted when America had so many "unadoptable" children begging for homes. Initially, the issue of concern was for the Amerasian children; surfacing was an awareness to provide some accountability for their existence. But the flood of non-Amerasian orphans could not be overlooked since those numbers also swelled to uncontrollable proportions.

On a national level, not all Americans were receptive or enthused with the influx of Vietnamese orphans or boat people to the United States (estimated at over 700,000). Groups of residents in communities around the country gathered to complain about the refugees. A Gallup poll revealed that an astonishing 54% of Americans thought that the dispossessed should be resettled somewhere else. There was a predominant fear that the new immigrants would quickly join the welfare rolls and compete with out-of-work Americans for scarce jobs. Congressional liberals who had long been vocal in the anti-war movement were also unenthusiastic about the Vietnamese refugees. Senator

George McGovern declared: "I think the Vietnamese are better off in Vietnam, including the orphans." He was joined by countless other individuals and agencies who regarded the airlift the same way.

Following the war's end, a class action lawsuit against the adoption agencies that functioned in Vietnam hit the courts. Civil liberty groups demanded the return of these children to their natural parents, who were now flooding refugee camps and searching for the children they relinquished earlier. Under the guise of being orphans, kids were smuggled on the airlift by influential families who hoped to later rejoin and claim their children in the U.S. Others had signed adoption releases, but in their hearts, they never intended to give them up at all. Adding to the complicated entanglement, court testimony confirmed earlier suspicions of agencies falsifying orphans' documents. It was revealed that a live baby was often substituted for one who had died and who had already been processed for adoption. The court imposed no judgement and looked to the subterfuge as a humanitarian gesture rather than a criminal act. As a result of the legal intervention, many children were voluntarily returned to their parents while others hesitated, taking into consideration the future of the child. At the center of this controversy were the children themselves. Some neither recognized their natural parents nor wanted to return to them; they were taken from judges chambers screaming for their American mothers. Hearts were broken on both sides of the courtroom until the matter settled to dust with the passing of time; the children grew up and the issue resolved itself.

None of the adoption agencies involved in the airlift were ever compensated by either the natural parents or the civil liberty groups for their role in the rescue, the medical and living expenses, or the transportation of the children to the United States.

Lockheed Aircraft Corporation and the U.S. government agreed to settlements of court claims brought on behalf of the orphans in the C5-A Galaxy crash. Seventy-eight injured orphans received $19.7 million, forty-five adopted orphans received $17.8 million, and families of seventy-six orphans who died in the crash received $10 million. Equal amounts were awarded to all prospective parents. Some suffered terribly at the loss of their child, especially since they had already established a strong bond through gifts, pictures, and staying in touch by mail. Others, who had just received the name of a child they were to adopt, accepted equal amounts of the award and later bragged about the financial windfall and how it allowed them to enjoy luxuries they could not previously afford. Only a few recipients donated a modest amount of the award money to the foundation established by FFAC for orphans in other countries. Few even bothered to thank the agency for their eleven-year effort in pursuing a settlement. Most never responded to FFAC'S appeal "that this money belonged to children in great distress and should not be regarded simply as a piece of private good luck to be spent on pleasures."

The financial gain to individuals who had merely placed application for an orphan lent an air of cupidity to the tragedy.

Operation Babylift wasn't all roses. There was negative fallout in several countries involving both adoptive parents and volunteers. Incidents of child abuse later surfaced, with children themselves making direct accusations. Social Services around the country were alerted to parents who were unable to cope with foreign children. And over the years, misplaced bravado and volunteer efforts were often blown out of proportion...indicative that some lost sight of doing it for the children and ended up doing it for themselves.

Continental Care Center, the building that made a home for 600 war orphans in Denver, opened in June, 1975, on schedule, despite last-minute efforts by health officials to padlock it for "contamination." The accusation disintegrated when results of multi-culture tests proved negative. Coat-tailing the state's charge was a threat of litigation from a volunteer who claimed she contracted salmonella from the center. It was an indication of things to come. The stigma of Operation Babylift emerged time and again during health department surveys and created both personal and administrative conflicts for many years. The reaction from peers was also a "mixed bag" and varied in political attitudes.

Continental justified all the attention it received and went on to become one of the more successful facilities in its field. An innovative program expanding the roles of non-professionals was developed and produced phenomenal results in returning psychiatric/geriatric clients back to the community despite insurmountable odds. Research teams were impressed to the point they declared the COUNSELOR/AIDE CONCEPT program important enough to be documented and identified. Then the report was filed in the bottom drawer of a state agency. The old guard didn't agree. "Taking on city hall" remains to be one of those "inequities" of a free society. It just isn't done single-handedly, unless you're a John Wayne...or an Ed Daly.

The generous couples who provided the children the opportunity to make a good life are to be admired and emulated. During the years following Operation Babylift, many of the orphans and their new parents visited the center. Perhaps it was an attempt to retrace the past, particularly since Continental represented the first memory of America for many of them. It is in all of us...to go back and look for the remains of what is gone. It's a warm place... "going home" again.

And it wasn't just children who found the need to return. Each spring, around April, one of the physicians who had been deeply involved at Continental would appear at the facility unannounced. Engulfed in private thoughts, he would saunter the halls of the second floor and then leave just as inconspicuously.

Many of the Babylift volunteers in Vietnam never returned to the same plateau in their lives again. Some suffered from post-traumatic stress, had recurring nightmares, or feared going out at night. Others developed detachment disorders and were physically exhausted. All suffered some degree of emotional pain.

Cherie Clark went to India to open "The Mission of Hope" and dedicated herself to sheltering unwanted babies of that country. She currently lives in Hanoi and founded the International Mission of Hope-Vietnam, building clinics and orphanages and facilitating adoptions of children of that country. She recently wrote a book, *After Sorrow Comes Joy*, an account of her early years in Vietnam.

Sue Walters continued with FCVN for several years after the war. She currently is on the staff of Boulder Social Services in Colorado.

Ross Meador took on a new challenge as he graduated from law school in Berkeley, California, and later returned to Asia, working for an international law firm in Seoul, Korea. He currently resides in Berkeley with his wife and two daughters.

Friends of the Children of Vietnam still functions as an adoption agency in Denver under the banner "Friends of Children of Various Nations." Rosemary Taylor and Wende Grant also continue to rescue children with their Asian foundation, FFAC Thailand. They co-authored *Orphans of War,* a detailed diary of their work with the orphans of Vietnam.

Sister Mary Nelle Gage, who was a solid rock for FFAC, currently resides in Colorado. She remains a valuable resource for the orphans in arranging reunions and trips to Vietnam for those in search of their roots.

Dr. Ted Gleichman distinguished himself as a Denver Specialist in internal medicine and lung disease and in 1987, he won both the Minoru Yasui Award and the A.H. Robbins Award. Plagued with health problems after his tour in Vietnam, Gleichman continued in his medical practice until he passed away in 1988. His last wishes reflected his concern for humanity; he donated his body to medical research. As founder of the Friends of the Children of Vietnam, he started a movement to indeed "empty the ocean' of despair. FCVN did, after all, play a key role in initiating the Babylift evacuation.

Ed Daly's gallantry captured the imagination of the people of the free world. Poor health forced Daly into retirement but friends said his spirit remained undaunted to the end. "He was still Ed Daly," said a friend who knew him for 30 years. "Still the impulsive, driven, foolhardy, stubborn—and sometimes very gentle—man who seemed to fit in somewhere between Wyatt Earp and J.P. Morgan. He was an original." Daly passed away in 1984, after a lingering illness. His pilots, Healy and Keating, continued in the airline industry in California and affirm, "It's too bad you never really got to know Daly...he was one of a kind!" Daly was not without his critics. He held the majority of stock in World Airways, which profited handsomely from the Southeast Asia cargo runs. (The stock, too, shot up after Babylift). Nor did Daly's generosity to aid the orphans cease after 1975. He frequently provided airline passes to other orphans and families in transit. Daly was a much-often misunderstood man, yet never to the degree as during his involvement in Vietnam. An evening news commentator aggressively summarized World Airways involvement in Babylift: "That any of these orphans got out is a credit to Edward J. Daly's bulldog-like tenacity."

Mike LeClair, the marine who found a different window to human suffering in Vietnam, works with a Denver television network.

Doctors Ted Ning, Richard Flanagan, and Roger Cadol are in private practice in Denver and continue with their involvement in easing the suffering of the less fortunate. As a part of a United Nations fact-finding tour returning to Vietnam in 1988, Ted and Connie Ning found conditions there "horrendous" and initiated Friendship Bridge, a humanitarian effort to bring much needed-medical supplies and equipment to the war-ravaged country.

Several of the agencies that functioned in Vietnam still place foreign children for adoption as well as provide support to orphanages in depressed countries. There is a need to document and analyze the relationship between these agencies and their mission and to explore what did and didn't work in Vietnam. An attempt to research the millions of documents on file that exist in Washington would be an ambitious effort in itself.

The thousands of volunteers all over America who made the commitment to Babylift reaffirmed the worth of human life. They, along with thousands around the world, gave their time, money and themselves to the mission. Then, quietly and without fanfare, they returned to their own space. Sadly missing—at least for those of us at the Continental Care Center—was a formal word of appreciation from any of the agencies involved. Were a pencil put to the cost of Operation Babylift and the involvement of thousands of volunteers, it is doubtful that a dollar figure could be realized.

Esther Hahn and Minnie Smith never missed a day at Continental throughout the six-week crisis. Combined, they gave over a thousand hours of their coveted senior years. A selfless contribution by any standard.

Sign-in sheets at Continental–containing more than 3500 volunteer's signatures–were preserved, and it was my intent to include that roster at the end of this book. But in the interest of those who expressed the desire to keep it a private matter, I honored their wishes. Many of the individuals interviewed for this account requested anonymity. It is as if they have imposed some kind of silence upon their deed. How I wished they would allow me to reveal their names for the historical record. I would like to think of this attempt as a tribute to each and every individual who participated, large or small, in the Babylift story. Equally confusing was the research. Much of the data is the subjective expression of those interviewed and differs in dates, statistics, and certainly points of view, and while every effort has been made to assure accuracy, no responsibility can be assumed by the author for misrepresentation or error. I used my best judgement in many instances to present an over-all picture of the events as they happened. This is, after all, for the adoptees and not a citation of achievement as to who did the best job. Mistakes were plentiful and there were enough to go around.

The Continental building has since changed names and ownership

several times. Efforts to get a commemorative plaque on its corner-
stone have not been successful–sad, considering a pioneer effort to
save children happened there twice in the same century. Philbert
Martinez, a Continental employee who worked for me after Babylift,
embedded my name in the concrete sidewalk, a gesture that both surprised and pleased me. After all these years, it's nice to know it's still
there.

As for myself, after the children left Continental, I continued as a
healthcare administrator for several more years, and while the work
was rewarding, nothing changed in a system severely lacking in
progress and attitudes, and my career was often complicated by old
"politics" that kept resurfacing. For example, when my name was submitted, with endorsement, for three official positions, my candidacy
was rejected. "It's the 'Babylift' thing," a well-respected peer cautioned. "When you're active in a controversial cause and outspoken,
you will always draw criticism. It's the nature of the beast...there's
nothing you do that doesn't have a price attached to it."

Discouraged with the lack of change in policy, along with hag-
gling 45,000 regulations, I left Continental in November, 1977.
Within a few years, after I completely divorced myself from the
healthcare system, I encountered an unrelenting state surveyor in a
mall. He was enthusiastic in his greeting: "Hi Barnes. You look
great... where are you now?"

"Where you can't get me!" I replied...and kept on walking. My
own response was a final insult to those years of dedication that came
up short...as I can only remember them being filled with conflict, rivalry and discredit.

I looked for another challenge and found it after meeting Dr.
Clifford Bennett. He convinced me that the story of Operation
Babylift needed to be told and insisted that I write about the human
experience rather than compile pages of statistics. To date, hundreds
of books have been written about the Vietnam War, and there will
undoubtedly be countless more. In contrast, only a few personal experiences address the subject of Babylift, which is all but extinct in the
historical record. Operation Babylift was an important part of the war,
and the loss of so many young lives may, perhaps, even be its greatest
tragedy. Assuring that it does not happen again can only come in documentation and taking a stand for children in war. There is no place
for privacy here. Some experiences run deep and pain is not always

easy to share, but the selflessness of Babylift is not yet over. The job is not complete until others give an accounting of the experience. The winners in the written word are the orphans.

The other side needs a voice also. The Vietnamese people suffered the loss of thousands of children. In an effort to document that point of view, I applied for an entrance visa into Vietnam in 1984, and surprisingly, I received preliminary approval from Hanoi. Ross Meador, Stewart Jacoby, Mike LeClair and my son, Rob, were all prepared to accompany me back into the country that was all but closed at the time to westerners. Within the same time frame, several major television networks submitted similar requests to film documentaries depicting the conditions in Vietnam ten years after the war.

Competing with the big media structure was like trying to take on Goliath. I am no David. My modest request was placed on the bottom of the pile in Hanoi. It was dead in the water.

In the process, however, I did get to meet Tran Trong Khanh, Press Secretary to the Permanent Mission of the Socialist Republic of Vietnam to the United Nations in his New York office. It was a meeting filled with intrigue as well as, I believe, a sincere effort to exchange concerns about the children of war. A three-hour chat, conducted beneath a dominating picture of Ho Chi Minh and the NVA flag, demonstrated another characteristic of a free society. It could only happen in America. Our discussion revealed that the new government of Vietnam viewed Operation Babylift as a humanitarian gesture; further consensus was, without a doubt, it saved many lives.

I came away from the meeting with the distinct impression that Khanh's government was somewhat grateful that the airlift happened, even though Hanoi did not have the veracity to publicly state as much. But for those who know the Vietnamese character or motive, they are very much a fiercely independent people, therefore, without comment.

At the conclusion of our meeting, we retraced my earlier access through locked doors with peepholes, past clicking machines and elevators to different levels. It was pretty clandestine.

Khanh carried my suitcase to the deserted street below and placed me safely in a cab, but not before bussing me on the cheek and thanking me for coming. I was impressed with his warmth and sincerity. Too, I couldn't help notice another Vietnamese who was discreet in his stance a few feet away, keeping us under surveillance. I later learned that Khanh was restricted to a twenty-five mile radius of the Mission.

In the weeks to come, Khanh and I exchanged notes and phone calls in which some discussion centered around the missing MIAs. His country, too, had well over 300,000 men missing in action. I felt an obligation to relay the substance of our conversations to a Washington agency, along with some exchange regarding a resolution. I received only a "stock file" response: "The matter was being handled efficiently." The MIA issue still remains unresolved.

The mixed reviews regarding the "Return to Vietnam" documentaries by the networks disappointed both Khanh and myself. We both believed that a coming together on behalf of children would have been a gesture toward unification and could conceivably have initiated a common ground. Sometimes sincere, simple solutions, by ordinary people, can accomplish more than all the strategists can imagine. But it wasn't meant to be.

For years, I wrote off *almost* getting into Vietnam in 1984 as one of the big events I missed in life, but those who know me well know that the drive and the convictions were always there. (Miss one...gain one. In 1995 an unprecedented honor was bestowed as a result of my tour of duty on Okinawa in my youth. The Air Force invited me back to Kadena for the unveiling of a plaque honoring the girls who served there during those early years. It is the only known monument dedicated to American civilian women on foreign soil.)

Twenty-five years after the end of the war, Vietnam is not much better off. Foreign investment is flat, the economy is stalled, and the country is impoverished. A third of the children in Ho Chi Minh City can't afford to go to school. City resources are being severely strained by an alarming population explosion of 70,000 more mouths to feed each year. The villages and hamlets are not much better.

Poverty, polio, tuberculosis and a multitude of diseases continue to ravage the country. The Communists do not seem to have a plan for a better Vietnam. Still remembered is the American-style prosperity during the sixties and seventies. Sans war, it may have been the best of times after all.

From time to time, the lives of the orphans and refugees continue to draw interest. Many have achieved outstanding recognition and have mastered complicated subjects and became engineers, doctors, teachers and achieved academic prominence. Several have graduated from military academies with honors. A national spelling bee champion was a refugee who, until a few years ago, could speak no English.

There were some who were not as lucky. Many never adapted to their new environment and continued to be psychologically irretrievable victims of war and, to this day, are permanent clients of the social service system. A few committed suicide. Many continue to return to Vietnam in search of their heritage,....and all still ask, "Why?"

Most Vietnamese refugees made the transition into American life, and heads no longer turn with curiosity. Yet, one can't help but wonder if they weigh a sense of loss or displacement in a country so geographically different than the one of their birth. There is a longing for roots in all of us. To date, a multitude of subjects regarding Vietnam periodically appear in the news, though they are now on a lesser page. The Agent Orange syndrome resurfaces, there is a never-ending quest for the MIAs, the U.S. trade embargo has its supporters, and on occasion a Vietnamese family reunion is seen in a tearful photo. It's all there to remind us there was once a war.

Hundreds of Veterans and ex-POWs are returning to Vietnam with the hope of resolving some demons and to find peace within. Most recently, in a humanitarian effort to curtail further tragedy, some veterans returned to Vietnam to clear a mine field they had placed years earlier. There is some healing. And although the Vietnam Veterans mentioned earlier in the book are making it somehow, their eyes often get misty when they talk about the war. It is apparent that they cherish the camaraderie they experienced in that faraway place. Some never found it again, not even in marriage.

Occasionally, the issue of the Amerasian resurfaces in the media to tug at the hearts of Americans who left children there. In Vietnam–a land that considers racial purity imperative–the mixed-blood kids are often treated with discrimination and destined for a lifetime of half-wondering why they exist and who they are. Many of the orphans who were integrated into American life have the same desire to search for their roots, as does any adoptee, but are realistic in the fact that they officially were non-existent until the adoption agencies gave them an identity and birth certificates. They are the innocent victims of the tragedy of Vietnam. There is no foreseeable solution to their dilemma other than, perhaps, time.

In October, 1982, Congress eventually passed legislation allowing Amerasian children to enter the United States under the sponsorship of their natural fathers. Too few benefited from the law and their reunions were both awkward and heartbreaking; hurried or inept explanations were made to American families who were not aware of their existence.

The unclaimed children are destined to spend a lifetime wondering who their fathers were. Many are reminded of the drama they are living–that they were born because of a war.

Books often come into existence to fill a need for awareness and more importantly, to provide answers. *The War Cradle* is an attempt to open the door on a subject that to date has had minimal exposure...only a paragraph here, a slight mention elsewhere, and only a sentence in the history books...more often, not at all. It is hardly enough to have the lasting impact it deserves. Hopefully, these pages will fill in the gaps and provide the much-sought-after window to the past previously denied the victims of the tragedy and moreover convince the agencies involved to open their files to adoptees in search of their roots. What happened to the children of Vietnam will be forgotten unless the injustice is reverberated and the lessons learned. Sacrifice is wasted if nobody notices. It may be too late already in light of more recent tragedies involving the children of Bosnia, Romania, Somalia and other countries where chaos overtakes reasoning. Undeniably, history is repeating itself before our very eyes. No corner of the world was spared from the wars, holocaust, and tragedies that occurred too often during the past century. The survivors of those events, above all others, have an obligation to denounce, act, and put a halt to the repetition of such injustices to others. Memorials are futile if their patrons allow a repeat of those horrors to *any* nations or peoples.

What we are witnessing in the abandonment, destruction and starvation of children in numerous parts of the world today indicates that the job of rescuing the young may never be over. Efforts to save children by international foundations is but a trickle of what is needed. Much more needs to be done, and quickly. Long overdue is the need for an agency with clout, under the auspices of a strong United Nations, to set up a place..."a war cradle"...a shelter of sorts, to support, protectively and intimately, within the children's own environment, until (in the language of kids) "the bullies" have settled their squabbles and life becomes tolerable again.

The hour is late..."If not *us*, then who? If not *now*, then when?"

The true wealth of any country is its children. They are its very future, a new garden just sprouting to replace the old. To stomp on the new growth or to send them away forever is within itself an act of destruction. We have been good at that for centuries. The potential we are destroying is our very own; the Mozarts, the Churchills, the Michaelangelos of the future, lost forever.

The war in Vietnam, the war we couldn't win, has become the war we cannot forget. The scars of the people of this nation are not yet healed from this era in our history. Witness to this is the outpouring of grief at the Vietnam Veteran's Memorial in Washington, D.C. The names inscribed on the Wall represent the tomorrows that will never come for over 58,000 men and women killed in Vietnam. The Veterans have their place to mourn. There should be a memorial for the children, too.

There is a greater lesson we can learn here. In the words of Bengali poet, Rabindranath Tagore, "With the birth of each child comes the message that God has not yet tired of man..."

Herein lies a new hope.

Our own.

BIBLIOGRAPHY

In addition to the author's personal involvement, listed are the interviews and sources of material used to develop this book. There is no citation for speeches and quotes; these can easily be found in widely accessible news accounts and other contemporary publications.

INTERVIEWS

Dr. Ted Gleichman, Denver, Co. 1984.
Ross Meador, Ramona, Ca. 1983.
Sue Walters, Denver, Co. 1984.
Esther Hahn, Denver, Co. 1984.
Bill Brown, Denver, Co 1984.
LeSanne Buchanan, Denver, Co. 1985.
Anthony Quintana, Denver, Co. 1985.
Dr. James Ralph, Denver, Co. 1985
Mike LeClaire, Denver, Co. 1985.
Ron Dell, Denver, Co. 1985.
Minnie Smith, Denver, Co. 1984.
Tran Trong Khanh, Vietnam Mission, New York. 1984-85.
Ken Healy, Oakland, Ca. (Telephone Interview) 1985.
Continental Care Center Volunteers, Operation Babylift, 1975-85.
Mike Barter, Denver, Co. 1984.
James Fall, Marion, Indiana at Colorado Springs, 1993.
Dr. Ted Ning

FILES

Friends of the Children of Vietnam - Orphanage reports, memos, letters, rosters, photographs and files of record, 1984.

Continental Care Center, Operation Babylift files of record and events recalled by the author and staff.

SELECTED READINGS

Isaacs, Arnold R. *"Without Honor."* Baltimore, Maryland: The Johns Hopkins University Press, 1983.

Bonds, Ray. *"The Vietnam War."* New York: Crown Publishers 1979

Boston Publishing Company. *"The Vietnam Experience."* Boston, Mass: 1981

Fincher, E. B. *"The Vietnam War."* New York: Franklin Watts, 1980.

Fall, Bernard B. *"Hell In A Very Small Place."* New York: J. B. Lippincott, 1967.

Gasser, Ronald J., M.D. *"365 Days."* New York: George Braziller, 1971.

Robbins, Christopher. *"Air America."* New York: B. P. Putnam's Sons, 1979.

Parrish, John A., M.D. *"12, 20 & 5."* New York: E. P. Dutton, Co., 1972.

Higgins, Marguerite. *"Our Vietnam Nightmare."* New York: Harper & Row, 1965.

Bartecchi, Carl E., M.D. *"Soc Trang."* Boulder, Colorado: Rocky Mtn. Writer's Guild, 1980.

Hensler, Paul. *"Don't Cry It's Only Thunder."* Garden City, N.Y.: Doubleday, 1984.

Smith, George E. *"Two Years With the Vietcong."* Berkeley, CA: Ramparts Press. 1971.

Jones, James. *"Viet Journal."* New York: Delacorte Press, 1973.

Marshall, S. L. A. *"Ambush & Bird."* Garden City, N.Y.: Nelson Doubleday Inc. 1969.

Burchette, Wilfred. *"Vietnam Will Win!"* New York: A Guardian Book, 1970.

Gershen, Martin. *"The True Story of Mylai."* New Rochelle, N. Y.: Arlington House. 1971.

Caputo, Philip. *"A Rumor of War."* New York: Holt, Rinehard & Winston, 1977.

Miller, Carolyn Paine. *"Captured."* Chappaqua, N.Y.: Christian

Herald Books, 1977.

Fall, Bernard. *"The Two Viet-Nams."* New York. Frederick A. Praeger, 1963.

Dooley, Tom. *"Deliver Us From Evil." "The Edge of Tomorrow." "The Night They Burned the Mountain."* New York: Farr, Straus & Cudahy, 1956.

Turpin, Dr. James W. *"Vietnam Doctor."* New York: McGraw-Hill, 1966.

Allen, George N. *"Ri."* Englewood Cliffs, N.J.: Prentice-Hall Inc. 1978.

Herr, Michael. *"Dispatches."* New York: Alfred A. Knopf, 1968.

Sheehan, Susan. *"Ten Vietnamese."* New York: Alfred A. Knopf. 1971.

Lowrie, Donald A. *"The Hunted Children."* New York: W. W . Norton & Co., Inc. 1963.

Hope, Bob. *"Five Women I Love."* Garden City N. Y.: Doubleday & Co., 1966.

Harvey, Frank. *"Air War-Vietnam."* New York: Bantam Books, 1967.

Baker, Mark. *"Nam."* New York: William Morrow, 1981.

Dareff, Hal. *"The Story of Vietnam."* New York: Parents' Magazine Press, 1966.

Maclear, Michael. *"The Ten Thousand Day War."* New York: Avon Books, 1982.

Anderson, Charles, R. *"The Grunts."* New York: Berkeley Books, 1976.

Strobridge, Robert. Taylor, Rosemary. *"Turn My Eyes Away."* Boulder, Colorado: Friends For All Children, 1976.

Hess, Dean. *"Battle Hymn."* New York: McGraw Hill, 1956.

Denton, Senator Jeremiah A., Jr. *"When Hell Was In Session."* Mobile, Alabama: Traditional Press, 1982.

Taylor, Rosemary. *"Orphans of War."* London, England: Collins, 1988.

Davis, Burke. *"Sherman's March."* New York: Random House, 1980.

Arnett, Peter. *"Live From The Battlefield."* New York: Simon & Schuster, 1994.

Buchannon, Keith. *"The Southeast Asian World."* New York: Taplinger, 1967.

Gettleman, Marvin E. *"Vietnam."* New York: Fawcett Publications, 1965.

Groen, Jay and David. *"Huey."* New York: Ballentine. 1984.

Durden, Charles. *"No Bugles, No Drums."* New York: Charter Books, 1976.

Sadler, Barry. *"Phu Nham."* New York: Tom Doherty Assoc. Books, 1984.

Mason, Robert. *"Chickenhawk."* New York: Penguin Books, 1983.

Donovan, David. *"Once a Warrior King."* New York: Ballentine Books, 1985.

Palmer, Dave Richard. *"Summons of the Trumpet."* New York: Ballentine, 1978.

Walsh, Patricia L. *"Forever Sad the Hearts."* New York: Avon, 1982.

Pollock, J. C. *"Mission, M. I. A."* New York: Crown Publishers, 1982.

Karnow, Stanley. *Vietnam: A History*. The Viking Press, New York 1983.

Van Deventer, Lynda. *"Home Before Morning."* New York: Warner Books, 1983.

Moore, Robin. *"The Green Berets."* New York: Crown Publishers, 1965.

Fall, Bernard. *"The Vietnam Reader."* New York: Random House, 1965.

Schemer, Benjamin F. *"The Raid."* New York: Harper & Row, 1976.

Nguyen Tien Hung and Jerrold L. Schecter. *"The Palace File."* New York: Harper & Row, 1986.

Karlson, Eric. *"Fall to Grace."* Boulder, Colorado: Mariposa Press, 1999

Lofton, B.S, Fox, T.C. *"Children of Vietnam"* N.Y.; Atheneum, 1972

Clark, Cherie. *"After Sorrow Comes Joy."* Denver, Colorado:

Lawrence and Thomas, 2000

NEWSPAPERS & PERIODICALS

The Los Angeles Times. March/April/May 1975
The National Observer. March/April/May 1975
The Denver Post. 1974 - 2000
The Rocky Mountain News. March - December 1975 - 2000
Stars & Stripes. March/April/May/June 1975
Los Angeles Herald Examiner. March/April/May 1975
San Diego Evening Tribune. 1975 - 1976
UPI San Francisco Examiner. 1975
The Press Democrat. 1975
The Associated Press. March/April/May/June 1975
Time Magazine. March - August 1975 - 2000
Newsweek Magazine. March - September 1975 - 2000
Highlights, World Airways, Oakland, California. 1956 - 1975
The Denver Post Empire Magazine. 1968
U.S. Agency For International Development-Operation Babylift Report. April-June 1875. *Document PD,AAQ-604.*

FROM THE AUTHOR

To the adoptees:

You alone were the motivation for writing this book. I hope that I have fulfilled your expectations in providing a better understanding of the events, circumstances, and especially the people involved in the Airlift.

Life is never what it seems to be for any of us. Every human being, regardless of his station in life, searches for answers as to who he is, why he is here. It is in all of us…to attempt to understand the work of the Creator. Often times enlightenment comes in strange ways.

In 1912, a woman in Poland scooped up her children and went to America alone. She did not know the language, had no particular skills, but in her reasoning, anything was better than the arranged marriage of her culture. Her life was filled with struggle; she was widowed twice yet raised seven children to be responsible adults. That woman was my grandmother.

In 1995, with an old tattered letter, I visited Poland and found my grandmother's family. They had endured the horrors of two world wars, poverty, communism and much hardship, yet I was overwhelmed by those stalwart people, the beauty of the country and my heritage.

Every day of my life I have said a silent "thank you" to my grandmother for coming to this land…her determination to survive was her gift to her future generations. This is a common story, yet it ties every American to a debt of gratitude to the ancestor who set foot on these shores, for whatever reason and under whatever circumstances, by choice or fate.

In time this story will take on significance for you. You have a most special place in history. Fate intervened and placed you on that same path. How you travel that road will determine your contribution to humanity.

Without a doubt, there is much love in this world…you need only to reach out to others, to be of some value…even if only in simple ways, to benefit from the love and generosity that is within your grasp.

Although you may never hear that voice in the future…that murmur of "thank you"…you can rest assured that you *have* found your warm fire… and you *are* home.

Shirley Barnes